FIRST
DOWN
AND A
BILLION

FIRST DOWN AND A BILLION

THE FUNNY BUSINESS OF PRO FOOTBALL

Gene Klein and David Fisher

WILLIAM MORROW AND COMPANY, INC.
New York

Library of Congress Cataloging-in-Publication Data

Klein, Gene.
  First down and a billion.

  1. Klein, Gene.   2. Football—United States—Team
owners.   3. San Diego Chargers (Football team)
I. Fisher, David, 1946–   .   II. Title.
GV939.K45A3   1987   796.332′092′4   [B]   86-23787
ISBN 0-688-06894-4

Printed in the United States of America

First Edition

1 2 3 4 5 6 7 8 9 10

BOOK DESIGN BY PANDORA SPELIOS

For Joyce, whose love, understanding, and kindness
make our every day together a jewel

Acknowledgments

The author would like to gratefully acknowledge the contributions of the following people: Harland Svare, Tommy Prothro, Frank Rothman, Jack Donlan, Sarge Karch, Jim Miller, Dennis Curran, Val Pinchbeck, Jr., Mike Gigante, Vera Iremonder, Jerry Schneider, Susan Wood, A. J. DeYoung, Bruce Barkel, Gloria Hayes, Roger Reutenik, Wayne and Shari Lukas, Jeff and Linda Lukas, Janet Cunningham, Mable Redic, Freddie Aguirre, Lou and Bea Klein, Bob and Marge Ramsdell (he knows why), Dr. Richard "Feets" Gilbert, Jerry Sherman, Robert Baker, Dr. Robert Koblin, Dr. Joseph Bonanno, Henry Morrison, Irving and Sylvia Fisher, and Stephanie Lee.

I would like to especially thank Oscar Dystel, without whose expertise and enthusiasm this book could never have been done.

And, with love, my son, Michael, and my daughter, Randee, and my grandchildren, Benjamin and Stacee King, and Adam Klein.

FIRST
DOWN
AND A
BILLION

1

Early in 1964, I was offered the opportunity to purchase all American music publishing rights for a young British rock-'n'-roll band named The Beatles. The offer was part of a larger deal I'd made to broadcast three Beatles concerts over a 250-theater closed-circuit system. The asking price was reasonable. I consulted an expert for advice, my teenage son, Michael. He shook his head. "They're just a fad," he assured me. I spent a little more time investigating the numbers, then turned down the offer. That decision cost me several hundred million dollars.

During three decades in business I parlayed four used cars on a dirt lot in the San Fernando Valley into a $1.1 billion conglomerate. As president and chief executive officer of the National General Corporation, I was responsible for the operation of banks, savings and loan institutions, the twelfth largest insurance company in America, large-scale housing developments and urban high-rise construction, two publishing houses, 250 movie theaters and a movie-production and distribution company, a portable office-building manufacturer, one of the first successful cable-television systems, even a candied fruit company and a fast-food chain.

I did make some bad decisions. Our movie-production company lost more than $20 million. I bought Minnie Pearl Chicken, a fast-food chain. At the party celebrating the purchase I ate my first piece of Minnie Pearl chicken. I got heartburn. The company turned out to be a $31 million turkey. On another occasion a bank called in a $120 million loan, forcing me to sell some National General subsidiaries. But not buying the publishing rights to The Beatles music was just about the worst mistake I ever made in business—just about. There was one thing I did that was worse— once I bought a pro-football team.

My name is Gene Klein. I'm sixty-five years old and each month I get a Social Security check for $711 to prove it. I've had two serious heart attacks and, even without that $711, I have more money than I will ever be able to spend. So I can say anything I want to. For almost twenty years I owned and ran a National Football League team, the San Diego Chargers. When I bought the Chargers I believed I could apply to professional sports the same principles of good business management that had enabled me to succeed in the corporate world.

I'm not ashamed to admit that. There was also a time when I believed in Santa Claus, the Easter Bunny, and the Tooth Fairy.

I think at some point in their lives most men dream about owning a professional sports franchise. I certainly did. I thought that a pro-football team was just about the best toy anyone could ever have. I learned. Oh, how I learned. Some toys just keep on giving—a pro-football team keeps on taking. Possibly the two happiest days of my life were the day I bought a controlling interest in the Chargers and the day I sold a controlling interest in the Chargers.

When I bought the team in 1966 the Chargers were still members of the American Football League. There were only fifteen teams in the rival National Football League. There was no such thing as a Super Bowl. Drugs were things like aspirin, or prescriptions purchased at the drugstore, or things used by hippies. The best players in pro football were making $100,000 a year and New York Jets owner Sonny Werblin made rookie quarterback Joe Namath the highest-paid player in history when he gave him a multiyear, $427,000 contract. NBC television was paying each AFL team $750,000 a season for broadcast rights, while CBS was paying each NFL team slightly more than $2 million. Radio rights sold for about $30,000 a year per team. The total annual income of an established NFL team was approximately $4 million. I had set the value of a pro-football franchise at $10 million when I purchased the Chargers.

I sold the team nineteen years later. By that time there were twenty-eight teams in the merged National Football League. The Super Bowl had become the most popular single event in sports, attracting the largest viewing audience in sports history. The use of illegal drugs, primarily cocaine and marijuana, was perhaps the major problem in sports. *Monday Night Football*, the most successful prime-time show on television, had been created by the NFL's Broadcast Committee—me, Cleveland Browns owner Art Modell, and Commissioner Pete Rozelle. We had also sold broadcast rights to the three networks for a combined total of $2.1 billion, with each team receiving slightly more than $16 million per season. Radio rights for Chargers games had been sold for as much as $1.5 million a year. The salary of the average pro-football player was more than $200,000, and some stars were receiving more than $1 million a season. A strong players' union had been formed and had called two strikes, had won a monumental victory in the courtroom when the player draft was ruled illegal, and had then negotiated it away at the bargaining table. For the first time in history, an NFL owner had unilaterally decided to move his team, then sued twenty-six of his partners for $75 million in damages. Two new pro-football leagues had been formed to challenge the NFL as the AFL once had. The annual total income of an NFL team was between $25 million and $30 million—and some teams were so badly run they still managed to lose millions of dollars.

Other than that, it was an uneventful nineteen years.

There are two ways an individual can acquire enough money to be able to afford a National Football League franchise—either be born extremely wealthy, or marry into money, or be smart enough to make your own fortune. The kindest thing that can be said about several of my partners in the NFL is that they were smart enough to be born rich.

I wasn't. I grew up in a small house on Matthews Avenue in the Bronx, New York. When the Depression hit, my father could not afford the mortgage payments on our house. The bank manager understood and asked my father to just continue paying the interest on the mortgage. After six months, my father could not afford the mortgage interest payments. The bank manager understood and asked my father to just continue paying taxes on the property. After six more months, my father could not afford the tax payments. The bank manager understood and asked my father to just continue living in the house to ensure that vandals didn't destroy it. In the Depression, that was known as being middle class.

Obviously, I never dreamed I'd be able to buy a football team one day. My dreams were more realistic—I wanted to be able to afford a ticket for a football game one day.

My father manufactured ladies' coats. The first real job I ever had was pushing racks of his merchandise to buyers' showrooms on Seventh Avenue. I was attending night school at NYU, studying electrical engineering because I thought there was a bright future in electrical engineering, and working days trying to make enough money to be able to afford day school. One problem with working in the garment district is that you are always selling a season in advance. So in the middle of summer I was pushing racks of heavy winter coats down Seventh Avenue.

At the end of my first week my father paid me $4. I couldn't believe it. Four dollars? For the kind of work I was doing? I was a son, not a slave—not officially at least. "I can't work for this kind of money," I told him. "I'm worth a lot more than that." He agreed, and promised he would raise my salary.

At the end of the following week he paid me $4.40. "You got to be kidding," I screamed at him. "Forty cents?"

"What are you talking?" he responded. "This is only your second week and already you've gotten a ten percent raise."

That ended my career in the rag business. My father then called a friend of his who owned a book bindery on Varick Street and convinced him that, as a college student at the famous New York University, I was well qualified to load heavy boxes of books onto trailers. "He'll pay you real money," my father said.

Six dollars a week, cash. Not a lot of money, but what there was of it was real. When I got my first pay envelope I was naturally very gratified. "What the hell is this? Six dollars? Forget it, I quit."

"You're nuts," my father yelled when he found out. "Whattaya mean, you quit? Any job you take you gotta start at the bottom."

"The bottom?" I yelled right back. "This isn't the bottom, this is China." My next job was selling encyclopedias, The Wonderland of Knowledge, door to door. I've had numerous jobs in my life—I've sold used cars, I've run a pro-football team, I've made movies, I've raised and raced thoroughbred race horses—so I can speak with some authority: Selling encyclopedias door to door during a worldwide depression is the most difficult of all jobs not requiring heavy lifting.

As I quickly learned, any job available during the Depression was available for good reason. In this case the reason was that most people, given a choice between a nice set of encyclopedias and starvation, will choose to spend their money for food.

The Wonderland of Knowledge was a fifteen-volume set published by the *New York Post*. Each volume cost $1.98 with the proper number of coupons from the paper. The salesman received a commission on each volume sold. It did not take me long to realize that, "Hello, my name is Gene Klein, would you like to buy a set of encyclopedias?" was not an effective selling technique. It rarely got me beyond the peephole, in fact. So I developed my own sales method. I wore my suit and carried a black clipboard. I'd ring the doorbell and as soon as someone peered through the peephole I'd hold up the clipboard and mumble as officially as possible, "Murmvey."

"Murmvey?" Invariably, they would open the door to hear me more clearly.

"Survey department," I'd announce. "I'm conducting an official survey. May I come in for a moment?" I was wearing a suit, I didn't look like I was carrying a gun, I'd usually get invited into the house. Once I got inside, every question I asked gave me information that made it easier to close the sale. I'd tailor my sales pitch to their answers. "How many children do you have?" If they had children, the books were for children. If they didn't have children, the books were for adults. Nieces? Nephews? The books made a wonderful present.

By the end of my second week I was the top salesman in the company. During a bad week I was earning $275, in a good week $400. That was ten times what my father was making. I went from a bum as a truck loader to a genius in about three weeks.

I discovered that I really enjoyed selling, and that I was good at it. I liked the challenge, I loved the results. What I lacked in experience I made up in persistence. If I thought someone was trying to avoid me, for example, I'd return to their house over and over until they were forced to open the door. Once, I remember, I went back to a clapboard house in Brooklyn five consecutive days. I knew there was someone inside trying to duck me. On the fifth day, I just lay on that buzzer. And finally, from inside, someone shouted, "What is the matter with you? Can't you see there ain't nobody home here?"

Eventually, I earned enough money to enroll as a day student at NYU, but the education I got selling door to door turned out to be much more valuable than anything I learned in the classroom.

On December 8, 1941, the day after the Japanese had attacked Pearl Harbor, I was sitting in class. It was impossible to concentrate on wiring, so I got up and started to go to the bathroom. "Klein," the professor snapped, "just where do you think you're going?"

I think at some point in their lives, everybody gives a smart answer he or she eventually regrets. Since I didn't want to tell the entire class that I had to go to the bathroom, I said, "Where do you think I'm going? I'm going to join the United States Army Air Corps."

People started applauding. Before I could take another step, three of my classmates jumped up and shouted proudly that they were going to enlist with me. Turned out to be the damnedest way of getting out of homework I've ever heard of.

I decided to become a pilot. I'd never been in an airplane in my life, but I didn't see why that would prevent me from flying one. Unfortunately, at six feet, five inches tall, I was three inches over the Air Corps height limit. It was some silly regulation that had something to do with fitting into cockpits. But the Air Corps was desperate. When I was measured, I simply bent my knees. The examining doctor realized that either I was bending my knees or I had the worst posture of any man he'd ever seen. "You really want in, don't you?"

I nodded, and thereby became the tallest six-foot-two flight student in the Army Air Corps.

They assigned me to flight school in Dothan, Alabama. It took me awhile to get used to Alabama; I had grown up being wary of any place you couldn't get to on the subway. Alabama, the members of my flight-school class discovered almost immediately, was a dry state. No liquor. We solved that problem as soon as we were certified for solo flight—we took turns flying a trainer to Georgia, landing in the street, and returning with enough booze to satisfy everyone. Everyone except the MPs, that is. I got caught returning to the base with my unauthorized cargo. They washed me out of the school.

Everyone kicked out of flight school received a three-day pass, probably so they could fly to Georgia to get drunk. I went home to the Bronx and stayed there a week. Time goes so much faster in New York that a week there seems like three Alabama days, but this really was a full week. I was listed AWOL, Absent Without Leave.

Upon my return to Dothan, the base commander summoned me to his office. I assumed he was going to issue my discharge papers. "I've been examining your records," he began, "and with your mathematical and engineering background, I believe you'd make an excellent navigator. I recommend you consider staying in the Air Corps."

"Thank you, sir," I replied, "but I don't want to be a navigator. I've decided to sign up with the Signal Corps."

He paused. "Uh, let me put it another way, Cadet Klein. Either you volunteer for navigators' school or I'm going to court-martial you for being AWOL."

"Colonel," I replied without hesitation, "I've always dreamed of being a navigator."

Being able to name every stop on the IRT was hardly sufficient background for a navigator. But once I found the school, the course was not difficult. I spent World War II ferrying brand new B-17's, B-25's, and B-26's all over the world as a navigator in the Air Transport Command or, as we in the ATC called ourselves, the Army of Terrified Civilians.

I knew why most of them were terrified too; they were flying with me. My job was to figure out where we were and how to get where we wanted to go. We had only the most rudimentary radar in those days, so we plotted our position and course by the stars. It was not easy. Those bombers bounced all over the sky, making it extremely difficult to take accurate readings with a sextant. Basically, what we would do was plot the position of three stars that formed a triangle, then pray we'd correctly identified the stars and the plane was in the middle of the triangle. Often we were right. Every navigator made mistakes, of course, so the key to being considered a good navigator was being able to convince the crew that the plane was precisely where it was supposed to be. On occasion, that proved to be difficult.

Once, for example, I plotted a course for Europe and, unfortunately, made a 180-degree error. That course would have gotten us to Central America. Another night, a formation of ten or fifteen planes was flying from Goose Bay, Labrador, to Prestwick, Scotland. Well, I wouldn't exactly call it a formation; call it a bunch. To the members of the ATC, a formation meant not crashing into each other. This turned out to be the worst flight I ever had. The weather was terrible, and we were buried in clouds all the way to Europe. I couldn't see the stars, so when we reached the British coastline, we honed in on an aircraft beacon in Scotland. I will never forget the thrill of dropping out of the clouds and discovering we were about three thousand feet above German-occupied France.

Even I couldn't convince the crew that that was where we were supposed to be.

Unbeknownst to us, the Germans had overpowered the Prestwick beacon and lured us into range of their antiaircraft batteries. Then the ack-ack opened up on us. I was petrified. Anyone who claims he was not petrified when being shot at is a liar. As the pilot took sharp evasive measures to try to climb out of range of the German guns, I kept thinking that all I really wanted to do that day at NYU was go to the bathroom.

We managed to climb into the relative safety of thick cloud cover. The next problem was that we didn't know where we were, and we were running out of fuel. We headed in the general direction of Scotland. As our engines started sputtering, our pilot spotted a training field. Its runway was too short for a B-17 to land safely, but it's very difficult to fly without engines. We went in hard.

The plane was ripped open as we skidded to a halt. As soon as we stopped moving, I leaped out. A sliver of German shrapnel was sticking out of my forehead, my face was covered with blood.

A group of people came running toward the plane. I sure hoped they were Scottish. "Where are we?" I shouted.

"Srrr," an older man replied in a beautiful Scottish brogue, "you'rrrre on the Mull of Kintyre."

"Where the hell is the Mull of Kintyre?" I asked. A navigator to the end.

Years later I would truly appreciate this experience. When the Chargers were in the midst of an eleven-game losing streak, or the first major drug scandal in professional sports tore apart the organization, or my star quarterback decided to sit out most of a season, or I was sued for $160 million by Al Davis of the Raiders for conspiring against him, I was able to look back on this flight and remind myself that things could be worse, things had been worse.

Toward the end of the war everybody started hustling to line up some type of civilian employment. One of my friends, the quartermaster of an airfield in Arizona, went into the military-surplus business. The only mistake he made was that the military had not yet realized the items he was selling were surplus. He was selling uniforms, jeeps, rations—everything he could get his hands on—he even sold the runway landing lights from the base. What finally got him into trouble was the staff car. One day he just took a camouflaged staff car and drove it home. For his sake, it should have been camouflaged as a Ford or Chevy. Even the Army could spot a camouflaged staff car in a civilian driveway, and he ended up in the stockade.

I didn't know what I wanted to do. I didn't see much future in flying for a navigator with a questionable sense of direction. I was discharged from the Air Force with $2,000 in my pocket, a wife, and an infant daughter. Selling encyclopedias was definitely out. At one point during my five years in the service I had been stationed in Wilmington, Delaware. My folks still lived in New York City. As it turned out, their neighbor across the street owned a used-car lot on Jerome Avenue. When I was home one weekend I went to his place and bought a 1939 Buick for $700. I drove to Delaware and put an ad in the post newspaper: ARMY OFFICER TRANSFERRED OVERSEAS. MUST SACRIFICE 1939 BUICK. The first person who showed up offered me $900.

Whoa! Hold on here a minute, coach. Even without a college degree I could figure out that that represented a $200 profit. Suddenly I was in the car business.

As often as I could I'd go to New York and buy a used car. It didn't matter what kind of car—I didn't know the difference anyway. I sold ten cars that way and I don't think I held on to any of them longer than a week.

During the war I'd also been stationed in Long Beach, California. The California weather had been gorgeous and the houses were considerably farther apart than in the Bronx. So when I was discharged, my wife and I put our daughter, Randee, in the backseat of our 1940 Chrysler, took the $2,000 I'd made selling cars, and drove to California.

The first thing any New Yorker realizes when he gets to the city of Los Angeles is that there is no city of Los Angeles. To me, a city is skyscrapers and subways. L.A. was sprawled over a vast area, and it had no tall buildings and no subway system. That meant that people had to travel long distances to get from one place to another, and there was no public transportation on which to do it. I went into the used-car business.

I rented a dirt lot in the San Fernando Valley, bought three beat-up used cars, shined them up, added a few dollars to the price I'd paid for them, and opened "Quality Motors." I opened at 10:00 in the morning. At 10:15 my first customer came in and bought a 1935 Buick. At 1:00 I sold the 1939 Studebaker. At 4:00 I sold the 1938 Ford. At 4:30 a customer made an offer for my 1940 Chrysler. "I can't sell it to you today," I told him, "it's the only way I've got to get home."

I closed the lot the next day and bought every car I could afford. Selling used cars in California in 1946 was easier than giving away cold water at an oasis. As fast as I put them on the lot, they were driven away—although some of them shouldn't have been driven that fast. I really didn't know how much a car was worth, and I overpaid for a lot of them. But the market was rising so fast that even when I had paid too much, all I had to do was hold on to the car for a few weeks and the market would cover my mistake.

Selling encyclopedias taught me persistence; selling used cars taught me patience, how to work with employees (or, for quite some time, employee), the fine art of negotiating, and perhaps most important, how to close a deal. Decades later, when I was negotiating the largest contract in television history, or when I found myself sitting across a stretch desk from some high-powered overeducated agent who believed he could outsmart and outgut me in negotiating a contract for the player he represented, the lessons I learned selling Chevys proved invaluable.

Those customers were tough. In Los Angeles a car was a necessity, but a good paint job was a luxury. Customers would ask me if I guaranteed my cars. Absolutely, I told them, I guarantee that they're not stolen. That was all I guaranteed. If a man complained about a car he'd bought from me I would ask him if he wanted his money back—I always asked, but I never actually offered to give it back. Most people just wanted their cars fixed. "So don't complain," I'd say. If a customer was foolish enough to demand his money back from a used-car dealer, I'd tell him, "Fine, just leave your car here and I'll try to sell it for you."

I had to deal with every conceivable situation on that lot. One day a man came in and asked if he could take a car and show it to his wife. Sure. An hour passed; he didn't return. Three hours passed. Two days. Finally, I called the police to report the car stolen. Officially, they informed me, I had no case—I'd given the man permission to take the car. Two weeks later I received a postcard with a picture of pretty girls in bathing suits on the front. "I'm in Miami," the man had written, "I drove the car here to show my wife. Sorry, she doesn't like it."

After a while I got a little smarter. Customers were always offering deals instead of cash. One afternoon a man came in and offered to trade me a percentage in an oil well for a car. It didn't occur to me to ask why a man who owned an oil well would need to buy a used car, so I drove to the town of Chatsworth with him. Sure enough, there was a deep hole in the ground. He lowered a tin can on a string into the hole, and when he pulled up the can it was overflowing with oil. I took a close look at that oil and was extremely impressed—this had to be one of the few wells in the world producing already-refined oil.

I ran the lot by myself for almost a year. I was there seven days a week, often from ten in the morning until ten at night, selling, buying, waxing the cars, hosing down the dirt, even trying to make basic repairs. I had a 1936 Pontiac with a broken steering knuckle. I bought a replacement part at the junkyard, took out the shaft, and installed the replacement knuckle. Then I took the car out for a test drive. It worked perfectly until I made a left turn at the first corner. I turned the wheel left; the car turned right. The next day I hired my very first employee, Ted the mechanic.

Ted was really a handyman. He'd fix cars, help me sell, clean up the place, and I'd send him out with the tow bar to pick up cars. I learned from Ted that an essential aspect of running a business, any business, is hiring capable people you can trust and giving them the opportunity and incentive to succeed. I learned how important that was when I caught Ted stealing from me. He was filling out sales reports for less money than he was actually charging the customer. Ted was not only my first employee, he was also the first employee I ever fired.

The used-car business in California became extremely competitive. Every dealer was selling basically the same product at about the same price, so I needed a gimmick to draw attention to my corner. I started advertising that my cars were "Cheaper by the pound than hamburger." Rather than putting a driveaway price on their windshields, I'd sell my cars for 44 cents a pound, 55 cents a pound, 66 cents a pound, which was, in fact, cheaper than chopped meat. That promotional gimmick attracted national publicity and a lot of customers.

I pushed a lot of used cars, literally, unfortunately, as well as figuratively, and by 1950 I'd changed the name of the place to "Gene Klein Motors" and was ready to expand. I bought a Kaiser-Frazer dealership in Burbank.

Admittedly, Kaisers were not Cadillacs. They weren't even De-Sotos. I didn't care. I knew that the more people I attracted to my showroom, the more used cars I was going to sell. Offering new cars as well as used cars was simply a means of increasing showroom traffic. At that time television was just beginning to become an important advertising medium, and some of my larger competitors were doing commercials. In fact, "Mad Man" Muntz, a major used-car dealer in Los Angeles, was one of America's very first television stars. I'd never knowingly given a competitor an advantage, so I decided to start advertising on television.

I bought four hours of time each Sunday morning for $600.

We'd show two movies while the other stations were doing religious programming. Our commercials were all live; my brother
Lou and I would just wheel up a car in front of our single camera
and I'd make a pitch. In the early days of television every person
on the screen was considered a celebrity—but it was necessary to
create an image that would make you stand out. Muntz was the
frantic "Mad Man," for instance. "Honest John" would never lie
to you. And for some reason, I decided to be a cowboy. Why I
decided to be a cowboy I cannot, in all honesty, remember, but
for four hours every Sunday morning I was "Cowboy Gene." I'd
stand in front of a car, wearing a cowboy shirt, boots, sometimes a
hat, rest my foot on the ol' fake wooden corral fence, and ad-lib.
"Howdy again, pardners, Gene Klein here for Gene Klein's Kaiser-Frazer dealership in Burbank, where we've got hundreds of
used cars for y'all to come on down and take a look at . . ." Then
we'd go back to the movie and Lou and I would push one car out
of the way and roll another car in front of our camera, "Howdy
there, pardners, lookee what we got right here for y'all for only
seven hundred and fifty dollars. This beautiful 1947 Chevy can be
yours . . ."

My ratings might not have been as good as God's, but on the
other hand we sold a lot more used cars than He did. I was selling
Kaisers and I was selling used cars, making substantial money for
the first time in my life. I had reached the point at which I had to
make a decision—be satisfied with my comfortable operation,
growing conservatively, or risk everything and attempt a major
expansion. You either do it or you don't. No one can make that
decision for you, and no business school can teach you how to
make it. You are either a born entrepreneur or you're not. And if
you are, the challenge is irresistible. If I hadn't known it before, I
learned it then—I was an entrepreneur.

I went to the local bank and applied for a $1 million loan. This
was 1952, when $1 million was just about the value of an NFL
franchise. My net worth at the time was about $40,000. I didn't
have any collateral; I did have a lot of guts and determination. I
intended to use the money to order 330 new Kaisers. "I'm afraid
there's going to be a shortage," I told the bank manager.

Now, there never had been a shortage of Kaiser-Frazers, and
anyone who had ever owned one could predict quite accurately

that there never was going to be a shortage of them. So why I thought there might be, I don't know.

The bank manager examined my application. I was selling a lot of used cars, the Kaisers would serve as collateral—who knows, maybe he had seen me on TV—the manager okayed the loan. Back in the Bronx I would have been considered a tremendous success: I was only twenty-eight years old and already $1 million in debt.

I ordered 330 new Kaiser-Frazers. One month later the Korean War began and the government instituted strict credit regulations. Anyone buying a new car, for example, had to put down one third of the purchase price in cash and pay off the remainder in fifteen months. In 1952, nobody buying a Kaiser had $1,000 cash to put down. I had to rent space on lots and corners all over Los Angeles just to store the cars I couldn't sell. And the longer it took to sell one, the more difficult it became to sell the next one, because cars sitting in the California sunshine deteriorated. The paint faded, vandals scratched them, air leaked out of the tires. Whenever we sold a car we'd pull another one off the street, put it in the garage, and clean it up.

The bank loan came due in six months. At that time I received a due bill for $890,000. I opened the envelope, looked at the notice, and did the only thing possible under the circumstances— put the bill back in the envelope, wrote "opened by mistake" on the outside, and mailed it back to the bank.

Steam poured out of my telephone the next morning. The bank manager was screaming so loudly I could hear him before I answered the phone. "You get your ass down here, Klein," he said.

The moment I walked into the bank he started yelling and didn't stop for a half hour. I didn't say a word. When he finished I reached into my pocket, pulled out my keys, tossed them on the desk, and started to walk out of his office.

"Just where do you think you're going?" he screamed.

"Hey," I said, "you own the agency, my friend. You go try and sell those friggin' blankety-blanks. I can't, not with a thousand dollars down and fifteen months to pay."

The manager realized I was serious. I had no choice—where was I going to get $890,000? I certainly couldn't borrow it; this bank had ruined my credit rating by loaning me a million dollars

I couldn't pay back. "Now just calm down, Gene," he said in a slightly hysterical voice, "let's see if we can figure a way out of this."

I sat down again. "I'll tell you exactly how we can get out of this," I said firmly. "All you have to do is loan me another quarter-million."

He didn't respond immediately. He just stared at me. Finally, he said somewhat incredulously, "Excuse me?"

"Give me another quarter-million. I can go out and buy used cars. I know I can sell them. Whatever profit I make on a used car, I can afford to sell a new one for that much of a loss. Give me one year and I'll get you out of it."

In for a penny, in for $1.25 million. The bank loaned me the additional money. I stocked the lot with used cars. Every time I sold one of those used cars for a profit, I could afford to sell a Kaiser for an equal loss. So when a potential new-car customer came in, I was able to give him much more than his trade-in was worth to ensure he'd have enough cash to make the down payment.

About eight months later I got a phone call from a gentleman who had moved to California from Minneapolis and was interested in buying an auto dealership. I still had about twenty Kaisers left. I told this gentleman that I might be interested in selling for the right price; what I neglected to tell him was that the right price was anything he wanted to pay. I had had it up to here, and I'm six feet, five inches tall. I just wanted out. He came in and we started negotiating. He was a tough negotiator, but I had a huge advantage; I knew no matter what the price was, he was going to own that place. He was going to own every last hubcap. We agreed to a price that covered the last of my bank debt. I handed that check to the bank manager and said, happily, "We're even, my friend."

He was happier than I was. "Mr. Klein," he said gratefully, "anytime you need anything, please come to see me."

"Well," I said, sitting down, "there is one thing. I need enough money to open another place." I wasn't crazy, not certifiably crazy; I knew I could sell cars. My agency had failed because the government had strangled credit.

Due to my newly established credit rating I was back in business in a few weeks. I began by selling only used cars, then got a Nash dealership. Kaiser, Nash, it didn't matter to me: The real value of a new car was that it attracted customers to my showroom and helped move used cars. I didn't even bother keeping more than one or two Nashes on the showroom floor. In fact, one afternoon the regional sales manager for the company came into the place and got very upset when he saw Fords and Chevys on the floor. "Get them out of here right now and put some Nashes on the floor," he warned, "or I'll cancel your dealership."

I told him where he could put his cars. That place was not the floor of my showroom.

I had to find another kind of new car to sell. A dealer-distributor on Vine Street in downtown L.A. was pushing a bizarre-looking German import called a Volkswagen. To me, the Volkswagen looked like one of those irradiated insects from a Japanese monster film. I'd seen linebackers that were bigger. I lifted the hood to look at the engine. That surprised me. It didn't have one. "It's in the back," the dealer explained. The engine looked like it had been lifted off a lawnmower—I understood why they tried to hide it in the trunk. None of those things bothered me, however; if it had four tires and would go downhill, I knew I could sell it.

I told the distributor I wanted to open a Volkswagen agency in the Valley. I think he was worried that there weren't enough potential customers in Southern California for two Volkswagen dealers, so he turned me down. "Okay," I said, "how many of these you got in stock?"

"Eleven."

"I'll take all of them." Thus I became the first VW dealer in the San Fernando Valley. My three salesmen laughed when the first VW came in. They suggested it was really one of those circus cars from which thirty clowns emerge. I told them we were going to sell them. They suggested I was one of those clowns.

Customers seemed to like the car, though. The thing that concerned most of them was whether we could adequately service it. I remember assuring one of the first customers, "Of course we can service it. I've got a mechanic who trained in Germany for two years. He can take these things apart and put 'em back together blindfolded. His name's Van Houser." The customer bought it—the car, that is. In fact, the closest Van Houser had been to Germany was eating a frankfurter.

The customer puttered toward the exit. The car stalled. He restarted it and bounced another thirty feet or so. Then stalled again. I walked over to his car, very, very slowly, trying to figure out what to do. The best defense, I've always believed, is a great offense. I leaned over and smiled. "You sure you know how to drive?"

He suggested my German-trained mechanic adjust the carburetor. Van Houser went over to the car—and opened the hood. "Where the frig'd they put the friggin' engine?" he asked.

I smiled sheepishly at the customer. "German sense of humor," I claimed.

The immediate success of the Volkswagen made it obvious that Americans were willing, even anxious, to drive European imports. I started selling every make I could get: MGs, Austin-Healeys, Morrises, Lancias, Jaguars. For the first time, I was selling more new cars than used cars. I opened a second agency.

One afternoon a friend of mine, Leo Hirsch, called to tell me that during a recent trip to Sweden he'd driven a really ugly car with a ridiculous name, a Volvo. Volvo? That was the silliest name for a car I'd heard since . . . Volkswagen. The manufacturer had shipped one to California and Leo wanted to know if I thought it could sell in America. I looked it over. The engine was where an engine was supposed to be. I suggested a few minor modifications and said that if it could be priced at $1,995 he could probably sell a few. If people would buy a Volkswagen, with its lawnmower motor in the trunk, I knew they would buy almost anything. Leo and I decided to form a partnership to import Volvos.

Our first task was convincing the Swedish government that the car would not embarrass the entire nation of Sweden. We appeared before a parliamentary committee and assured them Americans would like the car. "How many do you think can sell?" I was asked.

"Ten or fifteen a month, easy," I told them.

They were very impressed. "That many?"

Leo and I left Sweden with exclusive distribution rights for fifteen western states and an agreement that we would not have to pay for the cars we ordered until they cleared American customs. That meant we wouldn't have to make large advance payments.

I have to be honest. That was one ugly car. It looked like the Volkswagen's ugly older sibling. Leo and I realized that no one was going to buy a Volvo for its styling, so we had to promote another aspect of the car. We invented a slogan and slapped it on the back of every car coming in: A product of superb Swedish engineering. I challenge anyone to name two other products of superb Swedish engineering, besides blond models. Sweden was not known for its engineering, but people seemed to be aware that it was close to Germany, and Germany *was* known for its superb engineering.

The important thing about a slogan is that it sound intelligent. It doesn't have to make sense—it just has to sound as if it makes sense. Fortunately, the Volvo really was a superbly engineered automobile. In one year we sold fifteen thousand of them, proving that a great slogan will sell cars—as long as it is stuck on the back of a fine automobile priced at $1,995.

Our real profit came from the distribution deal. Every car coming to a dealer in the western United States had to be ordered through us, and we demanded full payment upon ordering. We didn't have to pay for the cars until they cleared customs. There is a word used in business for this kind of situation: *terrific*.

Two years later, 1957, Swedish multimillionaire industrialist Axel Wennergren, who was having difficulty converting Swedish currency, kronor, to dollars, contacted us. Since we were spending dollars in Sweden, and he needed dollars, he wanted to work out some sort of deal. "I got a good idea," I told him, "why don't you buy the distributorship?" He asked us to name our price.

How much was the exclusive right to import and distribute Volvos to the western United States worth? How much is anything worth? Exactly what someone is willing to pay for it. Setting a price for a product, a Volvo, a ticket to a Chargers game, is a difficult thing to do. As a businessman, I began by analyzing all the data: what I was selling, what the market for my product was, what my potential long-range profit was, what the current market value was, how badly my customer needed my product—and then I picked the most outrageous figure I could think of. If you have to start somewhere, start in the high-rent district. "Four million dollars," I said.

"That's ridiculous," Axel replied. "I'll give you two million."

Now I had some idea of how valuable the distributorship was to him. We settled for $2.5 million.

I was a millionaire. I did what I assumed millionaires were supposed to do: I retired. For ten consecutive days I played golf. It became apparent to me that the real difficulty with retirement is that you never know when you're finished. I was dying of boredom. I unretired.

I'd begun to invest in various businesses. I bought a bowling alley, a roller-skating rink. I invested in a Palm Springs hotel. I took a position in a savings and loan. I had some stock in a television-picture-tube manufacturing company, and I bought fifty thousand shares of National Theatres and Television.

National Theatres had been a division of Twentieth Century-Fox spun off in 1952, when the government prohibited movie producers from distributing their own films. National owned and operated almost 250 movie theaters, and its primary subsidiary, National Telefilm, syndicated TV programs like *The Sheriff of Cochise, Assignment: Underwater, The Third Man, The Play of the Week*. I thought it was a solid investment because National Theatres had assets of $40 million and its theaters produced a large amount of cash every week.

Because of my investment I was asked to join the company's board of directors. It was the first board of a public corporation I served on. I remember attending my first meeting. I was very intimidated. I looked around the long table. All these powerful men, I thought, men with outstanding reputations in the world of high finance, men who knew what they were talking about. I was a car salesman, a very good car salesman, but a car salesman. I decided I'd sit there quietly and maybe learn something. But as that meeting progressed I realized that I wasn't in fast company. These people weren't exactly speeding by me; in fact, I was sort of going by them. That gave me a lot of confidence.

National Theatres, I discovered, was a corporate pearl. Beautiful on the outside, but inside it was nothing but layer upon layer of oyster spit. Many of its theaters were decrepit, they were not

drawing well, and National Telefilm had lost $20 million in the
past two years and was bankrupting the company.

A few months after I'd made my investment the stock plunged
to an all-time low of 4⅞ths. Obviously, the president had to go,
but the board couldn't find a replacement. They asked me to run
the company for six months while they searched for a suitable
replacement. Why they asked me I don't know, but the former
president had lost $20 million in two years, so how much worse
could I do? I agreed to take the job for six months.

My first official act was to examine the payroll. I saw a name I
recognized and noticed he was being paid $800 a week. I didn't
know what he did to earn that much money, but I figured I ought
to find out. I strolled down the hall to his office. "Excuse me,
Pete," I said, "I was just looking at these figures and I see that
you're making eight hundred dollars a week."

"That's right."

"Well, what is it you do exactly?"

So help me, he replied, "I'll work for less."

Believe me, he did.

We quickly reduced overhead $25,000 a week by firing ex-
ecutives who were running money-losing divisions. We sold off
some of our "barns," large theaters located in decaying neigh-
borhoods, and redeveloped the land wherever practical. We went
where the population was going, to the suburbs, and built new
theaters in shopping malls and put up drive-ins. We began renting out our theaters for business meetings and promoted special
events like yo-yo contests to attract customers. To improve employee morale, I flew around the country visiting most of our theaters; I held contests for theater managers and awarded new cars
as prizes; I stopped booking the films of producers who demanded large up-front guarantees.

I also refurbished our refreshment stands, adding new signs,
mirrors, and bright lighting. Sixty-two percent of concession sales
are pure profit for the theater, and our stands looked as if we
thought we were doing the public a favor by allowing them to buy
popcorn and soda. I started selling hot dogs, hamburgers, sand-
wiches, assorted soft drinks. I stocked only large bars of candy
and doubled the price. I tripled the size of a popcorn bucket,
doubled the price, and added more salt to make it tastier as well

as to increase soft-drink sales. Our concession people never asked
a customer what size bucket he wanted; they just reached for the
large. I increased the length of intermission and flashed EAT POP-
CORN slogans on the screen. I brought in vending machines. We
raised the average moviegoer's expenditure on concessions from
17 cents to 29 cents per person, a 70 percent increase.

And then I raised ticket prices. I may well be the father of the
$5 ticket. Sorry.

At the same time I attacked our subsidiaries. National Telefilm
management told me they had to have another $5 million to stay
in operation. "And what if I don't give it to you?" I asked.

They were tough. "Then we walk."

Here's an important business tip to remember: Never make
threats when you've lost $20 million in two years. "There's the
friggin' door," I told them. "It's over."

"Uh, now let's wait up here a minute . . ."

They were out of business. My predecessor was like the man
who had lost $5 at the craps table, then spent another $10,000
trying to win it back. National Telefilm was bleeding the company
to death. I had to stop the hemorrhaging. It was better to swallow
the loss than to continue losing money.

I sold Cinemiracle, a process we owned that was supposed to
compete with Cinerama. That was losing $7,000 a week. I sold
our interest in Pacific Ocean Park, an amusement park. That was
losing $5,000 a week. I sold our headquarters in New York and
moved the company into two rented floors of a building in Los
Angeles.

While we were making subtractions I began adding companies
that would generate income. It didn't matter what industry they
were in; we needed profits. I bought Mobile Rentals, a manufacturer of portable business facilities. I bought CATV, a successful
cable-television system. I bought Mission Pak, a company that
produced and marketed candied fruit. My primary consideration
in every acquisition was, Where is tomorrow? What is the future
of the industry? Will it grow? Where will the industry be in five
years? In a decade?

I didn't know anything about portable offices, cable television,
or candied fruit. What I did know is that every business is the
same in the most important way—you cannot take more money

out of your pocket than you put in your pocket. Every business has to be run on that principle.

Except professional football, but I hadn't learned that yet.

One of the first things I did was change the name of the company to National General. When my corporate officers asked me why I'd picked that name, I told them that nobody will be able to figure out what a company named National General does. Anybody asks, I said, tell them we make generals. Actually, I picked that name because I didn't want to put a label on the company. I honestly didn't know in which direction we were going to go. National General became one of the first American conglomerates, large umbrella corporations owning numerous companies in unrelated industries.

I was interested in buying any company that made money and had the potential for substantial growth. My publishing career had been limited to loading books at a printing house and selling encyclopedias, but Bantam Books was a profitable company and I believed softcover books were ridiculously underpriced.

A number of groups were bidding for Bantam. A syndicate formed by Oscar Dystel, Bantam's president and a recognized publishing genius, had offered $36 million. I went to see investment banker Felix Rohatyn, who was handling the sale. "I don't want to negotiate," I told him, "I want the number. What's it gonna take for me to own the company?"

This was not the usual way of doing business, but I've always believed in being direct when negotiating for a company or a quarterback. "Gene," he explained, "I've got a lot of guys . . ."

"Please, don't tell me about a lot of guys. Just tell me what it's gonna take for me to make the deal right now."

He frowned. "Well, I guess if you give me a forty-nine-million, two-hundred-thousand-dollar bid, you've got it."

We shook hands. I had agreed to pay $49.2 million for Bantam Books. Now all I had to do was raise $49,200,000. National General certainly didn't have that kind of money.

That night I phoned Bill Thompson, an officer at The First National Bank of Boston, at his home. First Boston had loaned us $15 million to produce motion pictures and Thompson had offered to go for higher numbers if the deal was right. "Bill," I told him, "I've got a tremendous acquisition here." I went through

Bantam's profit statement and told him what I thought the future was. I sold him a used car. "But I've got to borrow some money from you."

"How much you need?"

"Forty-nine million, two hundred thousand dollars."

He coughed. "And, um, when do you need an answer?"

"By the time we hang up the telephone." He coughed again, loudly this time. "Bill, I either close tomorrow or I'm out. I need an answer now."

He chuckled. When you can afford to loan someone $50 million you can chuckle too. "I don't have sole authority to do it," he said, "but I think we can get you the money. Yeah, we'll do it."

Oscar Dystel thought I was completely insane for paying that much money for the company. I liked his way of thinking, and he agreed to run Bantam for me. As I still remind Oscar, I did overpay. When we sold Bantam we only got $125 million for it.

One of the first things I did after taking control of Bantam was raise the prices of softcover books. I may also be the father of the $3.95 paperback. Sorry.

Because of our aggressive acquisition program, National General began attracting media attention. *Time* called me "The King of Intermissions." The New York *Daily News* grouped me with Charlie Bluhdorn, Saul Steinberg, Jimmy Ling, Eli Black, and Harold Geneen, calling us, "the most controversial band of businessmen since the robber barons," and quoting an unnamed financial expert who claimed we ran "the kind of business that services industry the way Bonnie and Clyde serviced banks." That was kind compared to what *Forbes* called me. It was also a long way from "Cheaper by the pound than hamburger."

It was also unfair, I thought. When I saw a company that would be beneficial to National General, I went after it. I always paid a fair price and the stockholders always benefited. I bought companies to run them at a profit, not to dismantle them. And of the thirty or so companies I purchased for National General, the most controversial move I ever made was going after the Great American Insurance Company, the twelfth-largest insurance company in America.

An investment-banking firm brought Great American to my attention. They claimed it was substantially undervalued and pointed out that Great American kept a treasure chest of approximately $250 million in cash in the bank. They termed that "a surplus surplus." It was obviously a poorly managed company and a prime target for a takeover. There was only one problem—Great American was worth at least $600 million while National General was worth about $60 million. There was no way we could afford to buy them out.

Corporate takeovers had always been done the traditional way—with money. I devised a plan to gain control of Great American with paper and promises. I began by buying four-hundred thousand shares of the company, about 7 percent of the outstanding stock. Then I made an appointment to address the board of directors. At that meeting I explained that National General was extremely interested in Great American and suggested we reach some sort of peaceful accommodation. I could tell they were not receptive to my proposal when one member of the board fell asleep while I was making it. The board was openly disdainful. They responded by promising that if they had any interest in it at any time in the future they would certainly get back to me.

I didn't sit home waiting for my phone to ring. Instead I initiated one of the first "hostile takeovers" in the history of conglomerates—"hostile" meaning simply that this was against the wishes of management.

Great American stock was selling for between $30 and $40 a share. I offered stockholders the opportunity to trade a share of Great American for a package of stocks and bonds that would be worth as much as $60 a share—but only if I gained control of the company. In essence, I was trying to buy the cow with its own milk. If stockholders traded us their shares, they would profit considerably. If they didn't; the paper we were offering would have less value than cotton candy in a car wash. The term "junk bonds" was not yet in common usage, but that is exactly what we were offering.

I spent the next six months of my life on an airplane, traveling all over the country to convince the major stockholders, mostly mutual funds, that we could take over the company and run it far more profitably than current management was doing. Great American responded by bringing in a "white knight," a company they wanted to merge with—the white knight's chairman ended up offering me the opportunity to buy his company. Great American's stock went up enough to guarantee us a substantial profit on our four hundred thousand shares even if we didn't get the company. But we did: Stockholders tendered us almost 80 percent of the shares; the minnow had swallowed the whale.

Before National General took over, Great American's quarterly dividend had been about 70 cents a share. One of my first actions was to issue a special dividend of $55 a share, enabling us to transfer $180 million in cash to National General. That started a two-year investigation of conglomerates by the antitrust subcommittee of the House Judiciary Committee, and resulted in laws being passed that limited certain types of corporate takeovers.

Not everything I tried to do turned out as well. I bought exclusive rights to a closed-circuit color projection system called Talaria that had been developed by General Electric. The Talaria system was supposed to be able to project clear color-television images twenty-five feet by thirty-five feet on movie screens. While the system was being perfected I made deals with The Beatles, the Metropolitan Opera; I planned to broadcast Broadway shows, shows from London's West End; I even met with NFL Commissioner Pete Rozelle to convince him to schedule pro-football games that we could broadcast in our theaters every night of the week. Talaria was going to revolutionize the closed-circuit business.

I held an extravagant press party to introduce the new system. Everyone took seats in the theater for the premiere showing, the lights dimmed, the picture came on in living—black-and-white. Black-and-white? The color faded in and out. Schmucko, I thought to myself as I sank lower and lower in my seat, that's what I get for depending on GE.

Then we formed National General Productions to produce our own films. We made such memorable classics as *The Quiller Memorandum, Divorce, American Style,* and *The Stalking Moon*. We lost maybe $20 million. I decided we should stop making pictures and concentrate on the insurance business. The corporate executives running the film division disagreed with my decision to close down, and I had to fire them. They threatened to start a proxy fight for control of National General. "Take your best shot, fellas," I told them, "but don't forget to duck."

Both men left the company. One of them, Irv Levin, later went on to achieve recognition by buying the National Basketball Association's Boston Celtics and trading the team for the Buffalo Braves, then moving the Braves to San Diego. A seven-player trade was a condition of the deal. UPI reported that Levin claimed to have "raped" the Boston franchise, but the Celtics' new owner, John Y. Brown, responded, "In defense, all I can say is this is apparently his first rape case because what he doesn't realize is that he was the rapee, not the raped."

Minnie Pearl Chicken caused one of the classic cases of corporate indigestion. Minnie Pearl was a fried-chicken franchise operation. I bought it because I believed that for every industry giant like Hertz there had to be an Avis. Minnie Pearl was going to play Avis to Colonel Sanders's Kentucky Fried Chicken. My timing was awful, almost as bad as my chicken. The stock market collapsed just after I bought Minnie Pearl, and we couldn't raise enough money to go public. We lost $31 million. I had to decide whether to continue operating the company and maybe lose another $25 million, or go home. Believe me, when the accountants start giggling, it's time to shut the door.

I am one of the few people who can tell you from experience, it does not feel good to lose $31 million. In that situation the important thing for me to do was stay away from high windowsills and try to remember that I was playing for high stakes. Building a conglomerate was a balancing act, and as long as the winners outperformed the losers the conglomerate prospered. That $31 million loss was more than covered by the approximately $300 million Great American profit.

Oh, there were some other difficulties, like the time one of my executives neglected to make a $5 million interest payment on a loan and the bank called in our note for $120 million. We had to sell some subsidiaries and pay back $25 million before the bank would extend the note.

I stayed at National General twelve years. When I agreed to run the company for six months, National Theatres had visible assets of $40 million. When we sold out, our assets were valued at $1.1 billion. Our net worth increased from $8 million to $250 million, gross sales from $40 million to $600 million annually, and net profit from an $8 million-a-year loss to a $48 million profit. I played the corporate game for the highest stakes, and I won it.

Pro football, however, was a decidedly different game.

2

I learned quite some time ago that the poets were correct: Money can't buy happiness. But what it can buy, I also learned, are many of the things that make me happy. As soon as I started making a lot of money, I started spending it. I built one of the finest art collections in California, including paintings by van Gogh, Matisse, Miró, Modigliani, Picasso, sculptures by Rodin and Henry Moore. I had three Rolls-Royces, including one formerly owned by Queen Elizabeth, whose chauffeur came with it. My wife and I bought and refurbished the oldest mansion in Beverly Hills, located on six acres directly behind the Beverly Hills Hotel. We had tennis courts and a screening room. The house was furnished with Lord Nelson mirrors, a Marie Antoinette foot-bath, a lapis lazuli desk set that had once belonged to the Czarina Maria Alexandrovna of Russia, a Hungarian chess set studded with opals and garnets. We had our own Chinese chef. A second house in Palm Springs. An airplane. We had just about every type of expensive toy available, but did it make me happy?

You're damn right it made me happy. A boy from Matthews Avenue in the Bronx with a lapis lazuli desk set that had once belonged to the Czarina Maria Alexandrovna of Russia? Of course I was happy. But there was still one thing I wanted more than anything else—I wanted to own part of a professional football team.

I've had a lifelong love affair with football. I had even been at the Polo Grounds in New York watching a pro-football game when the announcement was made that Pearl Harbor had been attacked. Naturally, that was a day I'll never forget—"Tuffy Leeman Day," as the Brooklyn Dodgers beat the New York Giants, 21–7.

I had even played a little at NYU, which proved to me that I was one of those people who had the God-given ability to be a good fan. I was an end in the days when there was no such thing as a wide receiver, split end, tight end, or flanker; an end was an end, and on that team I was the end of the line. The best thing that could be said about my hands is that I had two of them.

My lack of ability didn't prevent me from loving the game, though. When the Rams moved to Los Angeles from Cleveland in 1946, I was one of the first people to purchase season tickets. I had barely been able to raise the $500 cash I needed as a down payment on my tract house in the San Fernando Valley, but nothing was going to keep me out of the Los Angeles Memorial Coliseum on Sunday afternoons.

Little more than a decade later I was trying to buy the team. There was a split between Rams co-owners Dan Reeves and Ed Pauley. Had Pauley won control of the club, he agreed he would sell me 1 percent of the team. That didn't work out. So I tried to buy a small piece of the San Francisco 49ers. That didn't work out either. So I tried to buy a piece of the Philadelphia Eagles. That almost worked out. Charlie and Herbert Allen of Allen and Company, my investment bankers, were offered the Eagles for $4 million. I was going to buy 10 percent of the club. But the Allens, in their infinite wisdom, decided that $4 million was a ridiculous price to pay for a pro-football team. I was getting so frustrated that I tried to buy a piece of the California Angels—and that was a baseball team. That didn't work out either. Gene Autry and Bob Reynolds outbid me.

Meanwhile, Texas multimillionaire Lamar Hunt was also trying, without success, to buy a pro-football team. But when the NFL turned down his application to purchase the Chicago Cardinals and move them to Dallas in 1960, he decided to start his own league.

Franchises in Hunt's new American Football League were priced at $25,000. For that $25,000 each buyer was practically guaranteed the right to lose hundreds of thousands of dollars in the following few years. It's difficult to put a value on something like that. Hunt sold ten franchises. Few people believed the league had any chance of surviving against the NFL. In fact, Wayne Valley, who bought the Oakland franchise, called the league "The Foolish Club."

Barron Hilton, son of Hilton Hotel chain founder Conrad Hilton, bought the Los Angeles franchise for that $25,000. I had met both Hiltons and tried to buy a small piece of the team. That didn't work out either.

Hilton was launching the Carte Blanche credit card at this time, so his new football team was named the Chargers. It turned out to be an appropriate name.

"To be truthful," Barron told the press, "I really don't know the difference between a three-point field goal and a three P.M. checkout time." That did not say a great deal about the way he ran his hotels.

Hilton did know enough about football to get out of the way. He hired fifty-year-old Sid Gillman as head coach and, a few months later, general manager. Gillman had been coaching college and pro ball since 1934, including five years as head coach of the Los Angeles Rams. He was a widely respected football man. In the language of football, as I was to learn, "widely respected" is a code phrase meaning he wins, but nobody likes him very much.

Gillman launched the Los Angeles Chargers by holding an open tryout camp. Two hundred and seven candidates showed up; as some of them left the tryouts they sold their football cleats to others coming in. Of the 207, one man made the team. The rest of the thirty-three-man squad was made up of NFL rejects and former college players not talented enough to have become NFL rejects. The first Chargers roster included great names such as Royce Womble, Bobby Clatterbuck, and Blanche Martin. They weren't great players, just great names. The fullback was Howie Ferguson, who had been cut by the NFL's Green Bay Packers. "Ferguson was very much like Packers fullback Jimmy Taylor," Gillman once said, "except that he didn't have Taylor's ability."

The 1960 Chargers won ten and lost four, winning the AFL's western-division championship. Unfortunately for Hilton, they did it in private. Attendance for the season averaged less than 15,000 a game. Only 9,900 showed up for the league championship game, which was 1,100 fewer than held season tickets. Hilton lost $910,000 his first year in business, which in today's dollars is equal to a hell of a lot of money. That was much more than he had paid his $25,000 to lose. At about the same time, Fidel Castro nationalized the Havana Hilton. "Given a choice," Barron said ruefully, "we would have preferred he take the Chargers instead."

Obviously, the Chargers could not compete with the Rams in Los Angeles. So when San Diego's city council voted overwhelmingly, 4–3, to increase the seating capacity of ancient Balboa Stadium from twenty-three thousand to thirty-four thousand, Hilton agreed to move the Chargers to San Diego. "We're now only fifteen miles from the Mexican border," he announced. "This is as far south as we can go."

The entire league was struggling. Just about every franchise was losing hundreds of thousands of dollars. After an exhibition game in Atlanta, for example, Kansas City's general manager had to wrestle the promoter for his share of the gate receipts. Supposedly, a reporter asked Lamar Hunt's father, billionaire H. L. Hunt, how he felt about his son losing $1 million in one year on the Dallas Texans. H.L. thought it over, then pointed out, "That means he only has a hundred and twenty years to make it profitable." Not everyone was as rich as Hunt, though. In fact, not anyone was as rich as Hunt. The only thing keeping the AFL in business was its television contract. ABC needed pro football on Sunday afternoons to counter the NFL games being shown on CBS.

Chargers attendance in San Diego was better than it had been in Los Angeles, but still not nearly high enough to prevent Hilton from losing even more money. "When we moved here," Hilton had once said optimistically, "kind friends told me that the only thing San Diegans would support was the zoo, and that I'd have to bring in a team of monkeys to draw fans."

Sid Gillman was doing a tremendous job on the field, though. He built a coaching staff that included offensive-end coach Al Davis, defensive-line coach Chuck Noll, and head scout Don Klosterman. His players included future Hall of Famers Ron Mix

and Lance Alworth, AFL Most Valuable Player Paul Lowe, record-setting quarterback John Hadl, star running back Keith Lincoln, and superstar linemen Ernie "Bigger Than Big Daddy
(Lipscomb)" Ladd and Earl Faison. The motto of the AFL in
those days seemed to be "the best offense is no defense," and no
team scored more points than the Chargers. Gillman installed the
"big bomb" offense, changing the traditional NFL philosophy of
"3 yards and a cloud of dust," to "30 yards, a lateral, and a cloud
of dust." The Chargers won five western-division titles in the first
six years of the league's existence. In 1963, they beat Billy Sullivan's Boston Patriots for their only AFL championship in a typ-
ically low-scoring 51–10 game.

Ironically, the better the team became, the more money Hilton
had to pay his players, and the larger his losses became. The year
after winning the championship, for example, the Chargers lost
$645,000. If the team had kept winning, Hilton could have gone
bankrupt.

He tried to get rid of the team, but nobody wanted it. He offered to sell the Chargers to a group of San Diego businessmen
for $700,000. They passed. He offered to sell 60 percent of the
club to San Diego multimillionaire C. Arnholt Smith for
$600,000. After deliberating for weeks, Smith turned down the
deal on the advice of an associate. The aide commented later,
after I'd bought the team for $10 million, "I dinged that deal. I
ought to jump out of a twenty-fourth-story window." The only
thing worse than recommending Smith not buy the club, of
course, would have been recommending that he should buy it.

At a Beverly Hills cocktail party in 1966, I learned that Conrad
Hilton was about to appoint his son president and chief executive
officer of the hotel chain, but was insisting that Barron get rid of
the football team so that he could devote his complete attention
to the hotel business.

I immediately contacted Barron and started negotiating for the
Chargers. Our discussions took six months. The problem was not
the price—we agreed on that in a few weeks—but rather, how I
was going to finance the deal. I knew one way I wasn't going to do
it—with my own money. A number of banks with whom I'd built
a good relationship were interested, but after examining the
Chargers' financial statement they turned me down. Barron fi-

nally agreed to hold my notes himself, thereby adhering to the classic business axiom: Never let a fish off the hook.

I put together a large group of investors and, in August 1966, bought the San Diego Chargers for $10 million. That was the largest amount ever paid for a professional football team. Although I'd once dreamed of setting sports records, this was not the particular record I'd had in mind. We put $2 million down, with the balance payable over eight or nine years. Theoretically, we would be able to pay for the club from its profits. Once again, I was buying the cow with its own milk. Of course, this does presuppose the cow gives milk. This later became known as my Flat Earth Theory.

My vice-chairman at National General, Sam Schulman, and I each bought 20 percent and became the general partners. We would run the club. I spent $25,000 of my own money and borrowed the rest of the $200,000 in cash I actually had to put up from a bank. The bank would not let me use my interest in the Chargers as an asset, however—apparently they knew more about sports than I did. I had to sign a note to Barron Hilton for the remaining $1.8 million I owed.

Sam and I sold percentages of the club to just about anyone we could talk into it. Eventually, we had nineteen limited partners. Barron kept 20 percent of the team for himself, and his father kept 10 percent. My best friend in Los Angeles, the late Gene Wyman, took a small piece. I think that was his way of proving his friendship. Former President Kennedy's press secretary, Pierre Salinger, took a bite. Frank Rothman, perhaps the finest attorney in the country, took a bite. Even Barron supplied an investor. "You've gotta meet this fellow," he told me, "he's gonna be the next president of General Motors." So John Z. DeLorean became a limited partner. Getting the AFL to approve the sale of the franchise was a formality. They wouldn't have cared if I had three eyes and wore skirts to meetings, as long as my check cleared.

My dream had finally come true: I owned a pro-football team. Had I been just a little bit smarter, I might have remembered that Dr. Frankenstein's dream had also come true.

There were people who thought I was crazy to pay $10 million for a football team—my wife, my family, and all of the friends I couldn't sell pieces of the team to, for example. I thought it was a very good deal. In reality, I only had to put up $25,000 of my own money. Everything else was financed, meaning catch-me-later. I had agreed to that price on the assumption there was going to be a merger between the AFL and NFL. Although I hadn't been aware that merger discussions were taking place while I was negotiating with Hilton, I believed there would eventually be a merger. In 1965, when the AFL's contract with ABC had expired, NBC had signed a five-year, $36 million contract with the league, guaranteeing each team $660,000 a year. NBC had even advanced some clubs $250,000 to enable them to sign high-visibility draft choices. NBC desperately needed to ensure the survival of the AFL. Otherwise the network would have to go back to religious programs, or worse, cultural programs on Sunday afternoon. Once the NFL accepted the fact that the AFL could afford to stay in business, and was financially able to survive a bidding war for the top players, there had to be a merger. The war was costing both leagues too much money. As far as I was concerned, I was really buying an NFL franchise.

The value of an NFL team was difficult to calculate. In 1962, an NFL franchise had been sold for $7.1 million. The Atlanta Falcons, an NFL expansion team, had been created and supplied with players a year before I bought the Chargers at a cost of $8.6 million. So the way I figured it, I was buying a controlling interest in a team worth a minimum of $8.6 million for $25,000 cash. Seemed like a good deal to me.

And even if the merger did not take place immediately, I still thought it was a good deal. The money that NBC had paid the Chargers in 1965 had enabled Hilton to make a $300,000 profit, the first time the team had been in the black. In addition, the city of San Diego had voted to construct a $27 million, fifty-two-thousand-seat stadium to replace Balboa Stadium. That meant the Chargers would have an additional eighteen thousand seats per game to sell.

Besides, buying the team was not just another business deal for me. Minnie Pearl was strictly business; I liked fried chicken, but watching people eat it was not my idea of excitement. I bought the Chargers primarily because I loved pro football and wanted to be part of it. Making money was not the bottom line; I was not against making money—I expected to make money—but I bought the team to have fun.

The most fun I had with the team was selling it for $80 million.

The day we bought the Chargers, Sam Schulman, our banker Al Hart, and I flew down to San Diego on Barron Hilton's private DC-3 and spent the day signing hundreds of documents. Then we turned over the checks and went to dinner with Hilton, coach Sid Gillman, and Al Davis. That was one of the most enjoyable nights of my life. It must have been—I even thought Al Davis was pleasant.

I shall never forget the newspaper headlines the morning after we closed the deal: PIERRE SALINGER AND LARGE GROUP BUY CHARGERS FOR $10 MILLION.

When I bought the team, I didn't really know how I would function as an owner. A player played, a coach coached, an owner owned. I intended to find out rather quickly, however.

Days after we closed the deal, the Chargers happened to be playing a preseason exhibition game against Lamar Hunt's Kansas City Chiefs in Anaheim. It was my first game as an owner, and naturally I was very excited. Getting ready to go to that game was about as great a feeling as I've had. Sam Schulman and I got our wives into the backseat of my car and took off for the ballpark. As soon as we got on the freeway, our wives started complaining. Neither of them knew anything about football, and neither of them wanted to go to a football game in August. "You guys are crazy," they said. "Don't you have enough problems already? Can't you find something better to do with your time? What do you need a football team for? And why do we have to go to the game? And . . ."

Sam and I listened husbandly for a while, but finally I'd heard enough. "Look," I said firmly, "it could be worse, you know. We could have mistresses." .

Without a pause, my wife responded softly, "Yeah, but at least we wouldn't have to watch."

We lost that game, 31–21, but I really didn't care. That was *my* team on the field, being coached by *my* coach. I'd had many wonderful experiences in the business world, but this was the first time I'd ever had the opportunity to root for one of my companies. Believe me, it's difficult to cheer for the construction of a portable office. Nobody buys tickets to watch them make candied fruit. Actually, we almost won the game in the final moments. With the score still 24–21, *my* quarterback, John Hadl, threw a 32-yard touchdown pass to *my* tight end, Jacque MacKinnon, putting us ahead. But the referee called a holding penalty on one of Gillman's offensive linemen, negating *my* touchdown. *My* coach, Sid Gillman, went crazy, running up and down the sideline raging at the official. The nicest thing he said to him was "How can you possibly make a call like that? You stink, you know that, you stink!"

The official said nothing—he just picked up the football and marched off a 15-yard penalty. But as he put down the ball, he turned and faced Gillman. "Hey, Sid," he screamed, "how do I smell from here?"

I probably knew more about football than I had about any other business I'd bought. I considered myself an expert football fan—I must have been, because I read every football story in the newspapers and I'd never known a sportswriter who wasn't an expert. I knew all the rules, the positions, I understood basic strategy— X's and O's, as we called it—I knew which were the strongest teams, I could identify some of the star players by uniform number, and I knew that running a football team was not that different from running any other business. Just as in the insurance business, the movie-distribution business, or the fried-chicken business, the objective is to identify the most talented employees in the company, pay them well, then get out of their way and let them do the job they were being well paid to do.

I would usually move very slowly when taking over the operations of a company. Employees are understandably anxious when management changes, and I tried not to do anything that would add to that anxiety. I would bring in my accountants and let them analyze the financials, I would try to get some understanding of the way previous management had run the company, and try to figure out how they had been successful or why the company was performing below capabilities. The only immediate changes I would make were the obvious ones. When I took over Great American, for example, I discovered that the five top corporate executives had a private elevator, with a full-time private elevator operator, reserved exclusively for their use. It would take them up to the fifth floor in the morning and bring them down in the evening. The first thing I did at Great American was put that elevator into general use. Eventually, of course, I made other changes; I got rid of the expensive china and silver in the private dining room, I sold the entire headquarters building, and finally moved the company from New York City to Los Angeles. But eliminating that private elevator was the only tangible move I made for quite some time.

Few businesses provide such easily perceived results as a sports franchise—they do not post scores in the candied-fruit business. The Chargers had been eminently successful on the field. Knowing Barron Hilton, that success was obviously due to Sid Gillman. So my first action as owner was to give Gillman a new five-year contract as head coach and general manager, with a substantial raise.

Gillman and I agreed that he would retain absolute control of the team itself, on and off the field. He would select his players and coaches and be responsible for negotiating their contracts. We also agreed that neither one of us would make a trade without the consent of the other. I would be responsible for running the business side of the organization, although both of us would attend owners' meetings. Basically, then, things would continue much as they had been.

Before attending the opening game of the regular season at Balboa Stadium, I opened our press guide and memorized my players' names, faces, and positions so I could chat intelligently with them. There are no press guides for insurance executives, but if there had been, I would have done the same thing before meeting Great American's management. My intention was to reassure the employees that new management intended to treat them with respect and, in turn, expected to be treated with respect.

The first player I met when I walked into my locker room was all-pro tackle Ron Mix. "Oh," Mix said sullenly, "you came to see the animals, huh?" So much for mutual respect.

We won our first four regular-season games my first year. I was obviously a very talented owner. Owning a football team was turning out to be even more enjoyable than I had expected it would be; all I had to do was show up for games on Sunday and watch us win. I began thinking we had a real good shot at another championship.

Those first four games had been played at home, however. The fifth week we made our first road trip. We lost to the New York Jets and began a losing streak. That losing streak lasted twelve years.

The following week we played Ralph Wilson's Buffalo Bills on a miserably cold, snowy afternoon in Buffalo's War Memorial Stadium. There were no enclosed boxes in the stadium, and visiting-team owners were always seated in the same outdoor section. Bills fans knew precisely where those seats were located, and just after the opening kickoff began throwing snowballs at us. Snowballs! I couldn't believe it. I was used to going to football games in California, and nothing like that ever happened there; not that California fans are any less loyal, it's just that there is no such thing as a sunball.

We spent the entire game being cursed at and threatened, and ducking snowballs. I was very surprised that fans would treat the owner of the visiting team that way; I was even more surprised when I learned that that was nothing compared to the way I would be treated by other owners. That day in Buffalo could have been worse, I suppose; we could have won the game. Then we really would have been in danger. The final score was 17–17. As it was, Bills fans celebrated the tie by beating up their placekicker.

We won only three more games that season, finishing with a respectable seven wins, six losses, and that tie. Gillman told me not to be concerned—no team could win its division title every year.

We didn't come close to another division title for a decade. The Chargers, it became apparent, were the sporting world's version of a used car—shiny on the outside but just good enough on the inside to make it through the warranty period.

In an effort to keep his annual losses to a minimum, Hilton had spent very little money on the team. While other AFL clubs had been building for the future by drafting and signing talented college players, the Chargers had been winning with aging NFL veterans. As these veterans slowed down or retired, Gillman had nobody to replace them. The Chargers had spent almost no money on a scouting staff, so they were basically drafting players out of magazines. Actually, it didn't matter who they drafted, because they couldn't afford to sign them anyway. Eventually, they had begun selecting players nobody else wanted, because they had a chance to sign them.

The Chargers couldn't even hold on to their proven stars. At the end of the 1965 season, for example, Gillman had to trade away superstars Ernie Ladd and Earl Faison because their contracts were expiring and they demanded to be paid what other teams were offering top players. When Ladd was asked how much he thought he was worth, he replied, "A million dollars," or approximately $970,000 more than the Chargers were offering him. Obviously $1 million was ridiculous, but a $970,000 difference leaves a lot of room for negotiation. There had to be a middle ground somewhere. For Ladd, that ground turned out to be in Houston.

The complete collapse was still three seasons away. Through the end of the 1960s, the Chargers played well enough for me to believe that we were only a few key players and a few breaks from being a championship team once again. The worst thing that can happen to a team is to finish with a 9-5 record, as we did in 1968. It was not good enough to win (we finished third), but it was good enough to make us believe we were better than we were. We preferred to think that we had finished third from the top; we should have been admitting that we were second from last. So instead of starting a rebuilding program we continued trying to plug holes. I learned that the three worst words in the language of the sports world, besides "Blame the officials," are "If we'd only . . ." as in, If we'd only converted that third-down play. If we'd only gotten one more break. If we'd only held them . . .

Gillman was really running the club. I was living in Los Angeles and running National General. I spoke to Gillman on the phone several times every day, I had game films delivered to my house and looked at them over and over, I asked a lot of questions, and on Sundays I flew to wherever we were playing and watched the game from the sidelines. You spend $10 million, you can be on the sidelines too. The San Diego sportswriters began accusing me of being an absentee owner, which I denied, but that was really. what I was. For me, the Chargers represented an out-let from incredible pressures of the conglomerate world.

Those first two years were so enjoyable that in 1967 Sam Schulman and I purchased the Seattle SuperSonics of the American Basketball Association, a league that had been formed to challenge the National Basketball Association. *Déjà bounce,* I called it. I didn't know as much about basketball as I did about football, but it did not seem to be a very complicated game. The first person to touch the ball shoots it. Either that or the coach carefully diagrams a "set play," and *then* the first person to touch the ball shoots it. Sam was the basketball fan, and he took control of the Sonics.

I began getting more involved with the Chargers in 1969. Gillman usually handled contract negotiations, but that year our quarterback, John Hadl, had played out his option and was threatening to sign with another team. Hadl asked to deal person-ally with me. Having negotiated half-billion-dollar deals with some of the world's most astute businessmen, I thought I could probably reach an agreement with a young quarterback. I also felt that Hadl, that any of my employees, deserved the courtesy of a face-to-face meeting with the owner.

Hadl sent his agent to this personal meeting. I was tempted to allow my "agent," Gillman, to meet with Hadl's agent, and call it a personal meeting between me and Hadl, but I wanted to get the contract settled. I didn't have too much time for it anyway; I was busy appearing before congressional committees investigating conglomerates. The agent and I quickly agreed to general salary terms, but then the agent requested that a low-interest loan of slightly more than $100,000 be given to Hadl for investment pur-poses.

Being a somewhat experienced businessman, I asked the agent what collateral Hadl intended to put up. The agent smiled and said nothing. That might have been when I first began to suspect that the phrase "football business" was a contradiction in terms.

In November of that season Gillman resigned as head coach because of a stomach ulcer and chest hernia. In the language of football, "resign" is a code word meaning "he was given the choice of quitting, being fired, or having the fans blow up his house." In this case, however, Gillman really did resign, although he remained general manager. On his recommendation, offensive backfield coach Charlie Waller replaced him as head coach.

The year 1969 began what sportswriters affectionately referred to as the "De-Klein" of the Chargers. We suffered through seven consecutive losing seasons, including a record-setting eleven-game losing streak in 1975. That was another sports record I had never dreamed of setting.

The Chargers' losing streak lasted longer than Charlie Brown's all-stars'. Every season I would try something different to make us competitive again, but no matter what I tried, we continued to get worse. By 1971, for example, Sid Gillman's ulcer had healed sufficiently for him to replace Charlie Waller as head coach. "I believe his talent is wasted in any other capacity than coaching," I told reporters, a fact I felt his work as general manager had proved. Former Los Angeles Rams head coach Harland Svare, who had once anchored, then coached, the New York Giants' legendary defense, replaced Gillman in the front office.

As head coach in 1971, Sid Gillman came close to making medical history. The team finished 6-8, and played so poorly that he almost proved ulcers can be communicable.

With four games left in the '71 season, Gillman resigned, a real sports resignation that time—I fired him—and Svare finished the season as interim head coach. Svare and I announced that we were going to make an extensive search for a head coach. We hired Svare.

We decided to rebuild the team through trading. Working together, we made twenty-one trades in 221 days, smashing another NFL record. We obtained veteran stars like tight end John Mackey, defensive ends Deacon Jones and Lionel Aldridge, tackle Dave Costa, linebacker Tim Rossovich, and enigmatic Duane Thomas. We believed that many of these players were available because they were not able to get along with the management of their former teams, rather than because of a lack of ability. Most of them were considered "free spirits," or "flakes." Their reputations were such that our defensive team was nicknamed "Harland's Hoodlums." Rossovich, for example, was well known for eating light bulbs and spiders, although when we got him he protested that he had changed, pointing out, "I haven't set my hair on fire in at least a year." In spirit, they were all like Dave

Costa, who claimed, "When I was a kid my crowd was actually pretty conservative. We only stole things beginning with the letter *a*. You know, a car, a radio, a hubcap."

As it turned out, Svare and I were only partially correct: The primary reason many of these players hadn't gotten along with the management of their former teams was that they'd lost their ability.

We spent much of the 1972 season trying to locate Duane Thomas, who always seemed to be one city ahead of us. Rossovich opened his mouth in spring camp one day and a canary flew out. John Mackey reported overweight and the only thing he lost was his interest in playing football. And Deacon Jones promised that he was "not going to die until the San Diego Chargers win a championship," causing columnist Joe Falls to speculate that Deacon might have discovered the secret of immortality. We won four games, lost nine, and tied one, finishing last.

The first lesson of economics is buy low, sell high. I bought Sam Schulman's interest in the club that year, selling him my piece of the Sonics. The Chargers had finished last. I assumed that was as low as they could go.

In March 1973, my wife had a stroke while playing tennis and died. It was an incredible shock, and caused me to look carefully at my life. The situation with the Chargers had become so frustrating that running National General represented an outlet from the incredible pressure of the sports world. I've always believed in the philosophy espoused by the immortal film producer Spyros Skouras, who said, "The fish stinks from the head," and I was certainly the head Charger. Obviously, the time had come for me to either commit myself to the team or sell it. National General was one of the most successful corporations in America; the Chargers were one of the worst football teams. It was not a difficult choice. My nature has always been to accept the greatest challenge. Perhaps it's a need for adventure, perhaps it's the stimulation of risk, maybe it's just stupidity, but in this case I chose football.

At the end of the 1973 season, I sold my interest in National General, sold my home in Beverly Hills, and moved to San Diego. Running the Chargers became my full-time occupation.

In the corporate world, when a company is not performing well, the usual solution is to bring in new management. On a football field, the quarterback is the manager. I felt we had the nucleus of a good team, but were lacking a strong leader. So before the 1973 season I went out and bought the greatest quarterback in pro-football history, Johnny Unitas. Unitas cost me $600,000. Sportswriters complained that I had spent too much for him, but attendance had been falling steadily at San Diego Stadium and I felt I had to do something to regain the confidence of the fans. We sold 40,341 season tickets, the highest total in team history.

Unitas had been a legendary team leader. "Being in the huddle with Johnny Unitas," John Mackey, who had played with him in Baltimore, remarked, "is like being in the huddle with God." At that time, God was a few million years old, but it was a *young* few million years old. Unitas, however, was a worn-out forty-year-old. In the first game he played, he dropped back to pass and fell over backward.

I also brought in the first team psychiatrist in pro-football history. I did not do it in response to those people who thought I was crazy to pay $600,000 for Unitas. His name was Dr. Arnold Mandell, and his job was to try to figure out how best to motivate football players.

The Chargers proved that season that you cannot win in the NFL without a good defense *or* a good offense. We won two, lost eleven, and tied one, finishing last once again. With four games remaining in the season, Svare resigned. I replaced him with assistant coach Ron Waller, no relation to Charlie Waller.

At the end of the season Dr. Mandell also resigned, deciding that "professional football is not the place for a psychiatrist." A few months later I learned that Dr. Mandell had not only been giving motivational talks to the players, he had also been giving them amphetamines. Mandell had tried to prove that with a good motivational lecture, and a pep pill, a player will improve his performance.

This was the first major drug scandal in professional sports history. NFL Commissioner Pete Rozelle fined eight Charger players amounts ranging from $1,000 to $3,000, fined Harland Svare $5,000, and offered me the option of firing Svare or paying a $20,000 fine. I sent a check. Blaming the presence of drugs in professional football on Harland Svare was like blaming toxic waste deposits on Lassie.

That fine might well have been another pro-football record.

Fortunately, I had the support of my fellow owners. Cincinnati's Paul Brown called the Chargers "The sinkhole of the NFL." My dear friend in Oakland, Allen Davis, thought I should be thrown out of football. Under the circumstances, a team with a 2-11 record and a drug scandal, I did the only thing possible: I raised ticket prices. If anyone ever asks for the definition of the word *chutzpah*, it means raising the price of tickets to Charger games after the 1973 season.

Changes had to be made. I made Svare general manager again and hired former Los Angeles Rams head coach Tommy Prothro. Prothro had been criticized as being "too intelligent to be a football coach." I can now say with some expertise that Tommy Prothro was not too intelligent to be a football coach.

Tommy was perhaps the finest judge of football talent I've ever seen. Before accepting the job he told me the Chargers were in worse shape than an expansion team; we had very few quality players, no players we could trade, few young players around whom we could build, and none of the bonus draft picks given to expansion teams. It was not that observation that convinced me Prothro was an extraordinary judge of talent—we'd won only seventeen of forty-two games the previous three seasons, so it didn't take an expert to know we were awful—it was his ability to select and develop young players. The only way to become competitive, he explained, was to rebuild through the draft system. That meant suffering through seasons of mistakes young players were going to make.

I'd once tried to rebuild by trading for and buying big-name veteran players and ended up with a linebacker who ate canaries. I agreed to try it Prothro's way.

Fortunately, in Tommy's first season as head coach, we won only five games and finished last again. That third consecutive last-place finish put us in a strong position for the 1975 draft. Our losing record also enabled us to continue playing young quarterback Dan Fouts, who had been our third pick in the 1973 draft. Fouts, who was to eventually quarterback the Chargers to three consecutive division championships, turned out to be among the most courageous players I've ever seen—and undoubtedly some of his bravery was learned standing behind our offensive line in those early seasons.

Prior to the 1975 season I hired Johnny Sanders from the Rams' front office as my assistant and Tank Younger, also from the Rams, as general manager Harland Svare's assistant. Svare, Prothro, Sanders, and Younger had all once been members of the Rams organization. Anyone who thinks that is a coincidence probably also believes Neil Armstrong and Buzz Aldrin just happened to bump into each other on the moon. I'd spent a lot of years watching the Rams and had great respect for their organization. When I began looking for experienced administrative people, I looked north to Los Angeles.

The 1975 season proved that Prothro was absolutely correct. The Chargers' draft that year may well have been the greatest single draft in pro-football history. Six of our selections eventually became starters on our championship teams. But when we played them, we suffered. We suffered through eleven straight losses. We didn't win a game for three months. Nothing I'd ever experienced prepared me for the prolonged agony of that season. When we crashed a B-17, it was over in minutes, but a losing football season seems to last forever. I kept thinking there had to be something more I could be doing, something I hadn't thought of, some way to stop the losing streak. I'd had many frustrating experiences in my life (few people have ever been stuck with 330 brand-new Kaisers), but I'd always found that if I worked hard enough, if I was clever enough, I could solve the problem.

Prothro kept reminding me that we had committed ourselves to rebuilding through young players. "We've just got to have patience," he reminded me.

"We've just got to have patience," I told reporters. "We're committed to rebuilding through young players." But it was difficult for me to be patient, and I have to admit that my confidence in the process did waver on occasion. It occurred to me that I had hired a coach who had guaranteed that we were going to lose. I couldn't fire him for being correct. The real question I had to deal with was how long to stay with the rebuilding program.

That entire season could easily have been called a nightmare, but Dr. Mandell had already termed 1973 the nightmare season in a book he wrote, so 1975 was simply a disaster. Tommy tried out more than one hundred players. Average attendance fell to thirty-one thousand. I couldn't blame the fans for not buying tickets. It wasn't always easy for me to go to the games either, and I didn't have to pay.

San Diegans, fortunately, were able to see some humor in the situation. One night, for example, a policeman stopped Tank Younger for speeding. The officer examined Tank's driver's license, which was made out in his given name. "Paul Younger?" the policeman asked. "You Tank?"

Tank nodded.

"Here," the policeman said, handing back his license, "I've seen the Chargers play. You've got enough problems already."

"With a team like this," wrote columnist Jack Murphy, "losing is a lot more bearable . . . than it is in New York or someplace else. The weather is nice. The golf courses and beaches are open."

Our ineptitude was probably best summed up by the fan who hung a banner proudly proclaiming, WE'RE NUMBER 26! The only thing I had to be grateful for was that there were just twenty-six teams in the NFL.

It would be inaccurate to claim that I was getting as much joy out of owning a professional football team as I had once expected. But unlike 1973, when we were 2-11 and had no immediate prospects of improving, our 2-12 record in 1975 was the price we were paying for rebuilding. At least we had a plan. Of course, in the darkest moments, I couldn't help but remember that General Custer had also had a plan.

The following March Barron Hilton and other minority stockholders sued to remove me as team president, charging that I had personally "tarnished the reputation of and diminished the community respect for the Charger football company."

Supposedly, John DeLorean had claimed that the drug scandal had caused him great embarrassment.

I pointed out to them that I owned 63 percent of the stock in the Chargers and that the way I understood the law of the land, the majority rules. I also offered to buy Hilton a computer to enable him to figure out what constitutes a majority, then countersued for $15 million. Eventually, we all dropped our suits and paid our lawyers. The real law of the land, I had come to understand, is that you have to pay your lawyers.

We made three significant moves before the 1976 season. Harland Svare resigned and was replaced as general manager by Johnny Sanders. We hired offensive coach Bill Walsh from the Cincinnati Bengals and Prothro handed over control of the offense to him, and we traded aging and unhappy defensive lineman Coy Bacon to the Bengals for aging and happy wide receiver Charlie Joiner.

In August that year, we appeared in the first professional football game ever played in Tokyo, Japan. It had nothing to do with getting as far away as possible from our fans; rather, it was an exhibition staged by a San Diego businessman of Japanese extraction. For us, it was almost like playing at home—we lost to the St. Louis Cardinals and only thirty-eight thousand attended the game at Korakuen Stadium.

Walsh installed a free-wheeling, motion-oriented, big-play offense that proved perfect for the talents of Dan Fouts and Charlie Joiner. Our defensive team, led by 1975 draft choices Gary "Big Hands" Johnson, Louis "Load" Kelcher with his size 16 EEEE feet, and Fred Dean, matured rapidly. We won our first three games. That was the first time we'd won three consecutive games in six seasons; it was one more game than we'd won during the entire 1975 season. Naturally, our fans took it in stride—they left the ballpark during the third quarter of the third game to join the ticket line forming to buy tickets for the upcoming home game against my good friend Allen Davis's Oakland Raiders.

In 1975 we really hadn't been as bad as our record, and in 1976 we weren't as good as we seemed to be during those first three games. We finished in third place with a 6-8 record. There was no question that we were improving. We had a quarterback with an outstanding arm and a defensive line that could pressure the opposition quarterback. At the end of the 1976 season, for the first time in many years, we were looking forward to next season, and not just because it meant this season had ended.

We felt the same way after the 1977 season too. At the end of the 1976 season Bill Walsh accepted the job as head coach at Stanford University. There were some people within the Charger organization who wanted me to allow Prothro to resign and give the head coaching job to Walsh, but I felt we owed it to Tommy to let him finish what he had started.

The team was hurt badly in 1977 by Dan Fouts's agent, Howard Slusher. I've always believed agents were very important, like mosquitoes, because if agents didn't exist, no one would realize how wonderful life could be without agents. Actually, I don't dislike all agents. Some of them do an excellent job for their clients. But I was continually getting into disagreements with agents and the players they represented because I had this quaint idea that a contract was a legal document binding both parties to its terms. Call me old-fashioned, call me a cockeyed optimist, but I was one of those crazy guys who believed that when an individual signed a contract of his own volition he should honor it.

Although Mr. Slusher's client, Dan Fouts, had a valid contract, he became very upset when we acquired quarterback James Harris from the Rams, and demanded to be traded. When I made it clear I had no intention of trading him, Fouts announced his retirement from professional football. I wished him a great deal of luck in his new career, whatever it might be. I wondered if he might become a football players' agent.

Fortunately, besides Harris, we had obtained veteran quarterback Bill Munson from the Lions, and had selected quarterback Cliff Olander in the fifth round of that year's draft. We were stocked with quarterbacks. By the tenth game of the 1977 season, Fouts was still retired, Harris and Munson were both on the disabled list, and rookie Cliff Olander was our starting quarterback.

Ironically, Olander had quarterbacked the team for most of a preseason game in Oakland against Al Davis's Raiders. Davis was so upset that Tommy Prothro had the audacity to play a rookie against him, rather than a veteran, that he refused to pay the Chargers our share of the gate receipts. Davis complained that it was not fair to the Oakland fans for the Chargers to play an inexperienced quarterback (fans he cared so much about that a few years later he moved their team to Los Angeles). Commissioner Rozelle forced Davis to pay up. I'm not sure what hurt Davis more, having to part with the cash, having to follow a ruling of the commissioner, whom he really dislikes, or what happened in the tenth game of the season. In that game, with Cliff Olander at quarterback, we beat the Raiders, 12–7.

Fouts decided to come out of retirement the following week, but it was too late to salvage the season. We finished a disappointing 7-7. The positive aspect of that is that we had good reason to be disappointed; we had been capable of winning more games, which was a vast improvement over previous seasons.

Our first draft pick in 1978 was wide receiver John Jefferson. The man could fly, and if a ball was thrown anywhere within his zip code, he would catch it. With Fouts throwing to Jefferson and Joiner, with our defensive line more experienced, we felt we were ready to culminate our rebuilding program with a championship. We opened the season by defeating the Seattle Seahawks, 24–20. Our next game was against Al Davis's Oakland Raiders.

Over the years I'd come to understand that Al Davis had a personality problem. He didn't have one. There are certain people in this world who aren't really happy unless they are unhappy. I've always felt that Al Davis, on the other hand, isn't really happy unless he is making other people unhappy. Within the league he had developed a reputation as someone who created problems. However, in the language of football, he was well respected for his knowledge and ability. There had been some great Raider teams. In the twenty-five games the Chargers had played against the Raiders since I'd bought the team, we'd won only three and tied two. The Olander game was the first time we'd beaten them in the regular season since 1968. I was really looking forward to playing them again. For the first time in almost a decade I thought we were clearly the better ball club. I thought this game would be a good indication of how good we really were. It turned out to be the most bizarre football game I'd ever seen.

With ten seconds left in the game we were winning, 20–14. The Raiders had the ball on our 25-yard line. With the clock ticking away the final seconds, Oakland quarterback Kenny Stabler faded back to pass. Our linebacker, Woodrow Lowe, hit him. In desperation, Stabler flipped the ball underhanded. It hit the ground. I thought the game was over. But Raider Pete Banaszak batted the ball forward 10 yards closer to the end zone. I still thought the game was over, but I noticed that a lot of players were running around on the field. Next, Raider Dave Casper kicked the ball into the end zone and fell on it. I started looking around for penalty flags. I expected to see more flags on the ground than in front of the United Nations. There were none. The officials signaled touchdown. Oakland kicked the extra point and won, 21–20.

I was standing in my private box—I had to stand; the toilet had overflowed and there was about two inches of water over everything—in absolute disbelief. Clearly Stabler's attempt to pass had to be ruled either an incomplete pass or intentional grounding, meaning he'd thrown the ball away to avoid being tackled with it. Instead, the officials ruled it a fumble. Even if it had been a fumble, Banaszak had batted it forward, an illegal play. Even he admitted that. The officials ruled he had been attempting to recover Stabler's fumble, which wasn't a fumble in the first place. And Casper? His play was about as legal as spending the money someone else had stolen from a bank.

We protested. We requested that Stabler's pass be ruled incomplete and the final score revert to 20–14. The league informed us that it is not possible to protest an NFL game. The final score stood. The league did apologize, however, admitting that the officials had ruled improperly on the play. That game became known as "The Holy Roller."

That loss hurt us. We lost our next two games and it was obvious that the season was getting away from us. Tommy Prothro decided he had had enough. He resigned, and was replaced by former San Diego State University and St. Louis Cardinals head coach Don Coryell.

Coryell's high-powered offense made Bill Walsh seem conservative. Coryell's teams were a throwback to the original AFL concept of "30 yards, a lateral, and a cloud of dust." His teams passed on every down, from anywhere on the field, at any time. "Air Coryell," as it became known, was simply his version of the strategy we'd used in touch-football games back in the Bronx, "Everybody go long." Vince Lombardi used to say that only three things could happen when you passed—an incompletion, an interception, or a completion—and two of them were bad. Coryell's philosophy was that if you bought three lottery tickets, you could live with two losers if the third ticket won the $1 million first prize.

Coryell's offense was so complicated as to be almost impossible to defense. Unfortunately, it was also too complicated for most football players to understand. Without a quarterback as intelligent as Fouts, it would not have worked. It was a mark of how much I'd learned about the *X*'s and *O*'s that I almost understood what Coryell was doing.

Air Coryell resulted in eight wins in our last thirteen games, including a last-minute 27–23 victory over the Raiders in Oakland. That was the first time we'd beaten the Raiders there in a decade. We finished the year with nine wins and seven losses, our first winning season since 1969.

With a coach like Coryell, there is one type of player a team is not going to select as a top draft choice—defensive. In the draft the following spring, with only seconds left before the Cleveland Browns had to make their selection, they agreed to trade us their number-thirteen pick for our numbers twenty and forty-seven. We immediately selected tight end Kellen Winslow. There are relatively few "impact players," people who can immediately become starting players and make a difference. Kellen Winslow was an impact player, and the final piece in our rebuilding scheme. Winslow, in fact, might well be the greatest tight end in pro-football history. Ironically, it was Tommy Prothro, working for the Cleveland Browns, who agreed to trade us their pick.

The next three seasons were the payoff for the years of misery. Air Coryell delivered three consecutive American Football Conference divisional championships. During those three years we won more games than any team in pro football. In 1980 and 1981 we came within a playoff victory of going to the Super Bowl. "Chargermania," defined as a desperate need to wear a Charger T-shirt, wave a Charger banner, and sing the Charger fight song while attending a Charger game, took over San Diego, and every home game from 1979 until I sold the team in August 1984 was sold out.

Our 1981 AFC playoff game against Miami was certainly one of the most exciting football games ever played. In Miami's incredibly humid, almost 90-degree heat, we took a 24–0 lead. The Dolphins came back to go ahead, 38–31. With minutes left in the game, we scored to tie it at 38–38. Then, with only four seconds on the clock, Kellen Winslow leaped into the air to block Miami placekicker Uwe von Schamann's 43-yard field-goal attempt and send the game into sudden-death overtime. First team to score wins. Gut-checking time. Six minutes into the overtime, our placekicker, Rolf Benirschke, missed a field-goal attempt from the Dolphins' 27-yard line. Miami immediately drove down to our 17-yard line—and von Schamann missed again. Finally, thirteen minutes and fifty-two seconds into the overtime period, Benirschke kicked the game-winning field goal. Kellen Winslow was so exhausted he had to be carried off the field. He'd caught a playoff-record sixteen passes for a record 166 yards, and blocked an attempt for the game-winning field goal.

The following week we played the Bengals in Cincinnati for the league championship; the winner would go to the Super Bowl. The temperature at game time was 9 degrees below zero with winds gusting to 35 miles per hour, equaling a windchill factor of minus 59 degrees. That was a turnaround of 139 degrees in one week. It was so cold that the stadium pipes froze. Steam rose from the Ohio River. Commissioner Rozelle considered postponing the game, and decided to play only after the Army Medical Corps assured him it would be safe. The weather also froze our passing game, and we lost, 27–7. There was some consolation, though; everybody survived.

Our success on the field led to serious problems off the field. All this time I had been suffering under the delusion that a football team could be run like a business, that expenses should have at least some vague relationship to revenues. In fact, football is a business about as much as genuine imitation leather comes from the hides of imitation cows.

In most industries, success is rewarded by increased profits. Not in pro football. Under the NFL's system of revenue distribution, all teams receive an equal amount of television income and playoff money, and gate receipts are split 60 percent to the home team and 40 percent to the visitors. Winning or losing does not substantially affect revenue. Basically, a team will get the same amount of money whether it has a winning or losing record. The New Orleans Saints, for example, who have never been in a playoff game, have received as much money from the playoffs and Super Bowls as have Dallas and Pittsburgh.

Therefore, winning creates an entire new spectrum of problems. A losing team generally loses because its players aren't very good. Bad players cannot demand large salaries, which is good for the bottom line. Better players can demand more money, however, which is bad, unless an owner cares more about winning than profits. The payroll of a winning team is going to be substantially higher than that of a losing team, while the losing team may actually have greater revenues, depending on the comparative size of its stadium and attendance. So, it costs money to be good, it costs more money to be better, and the best teams can actually lose money. When the Chargers became a championship ball club, I had the same opportunity to learn that lesson.

Before the 1981 season both wide receiver John Jefferson and defensive end Fred Dean demanded that I renegotiate their contracts. One year earlier I'd added incentive bonus clauses to Jefferson's contract, and now he wanted those clauses guaranteed. Dean just wanted more money. I refused both requests.

Meanwhile, the same sportswriters who a few years earlier had criticized me for spending too much money to obtain Johnny Unitas, were criticizing me for being too cheap. When it became clear that Jefferson and Dean would not play unless I renegotiated their contracts, I traded both of them. Instead of winning the league championship with an 11-5 record, as we'd done in 1980, we won it with only a 10-6 record.

I feel certain we would have won our fourth consecutive championship in 1982, had there been a normal 1982 season. But after two games that year, the NFL Players Association, led by Ed Garvey, went on strike. Garvey's major demand was that the owners give the players 55 percent of their gross income. Without the players, Garvey contended, there would be no professional football.

Of course, the same thing could be said about the footballs.

The strike lasted eight weeks. Eight terribly long weeks without football. Eight long weeks without suffering every Sunday. Eight weeks without worrying about replacing injured players, without hassling with agents, without having to read about drug problems, without having to deal with players' personal problems, without people calling to complain about their seat location. Actually, I discovered, eight weeks without football was not that terrible.

I survived quite well without football.

When the players returned, having compromised on their demands, we played an abbreviated schedule. We finished in second place, with six wins and three losses. In the unique Super Bowl tournament that year, we beat Pittsburgh, then lost to Miami.

My feelings about the game of football were changing, and my feelings about the business of football had already changed. In 1981, Davis had sued twenty-six other owners for attempting to prevent him from moving the Raiders to Los Angeles. The fact that the NFL constitution, to which he had agreed, forbids any team from moving to a new city without the approval of other owners, did not bother him. The fact that the Raiders' fans had been among the most loyal in professional sports also did not bother him. And not only did Davis sue the league, he also sued me, Los Angeles Rams owner Georgia Frontiere, and Commissioner Rozelle for $160 million, claiming we had conspired to prevent him from moving to Los Angeles.

The judge threw the conspiracy case out of court, as Davis apparently forgot that he needed evidence to prove his contention, but Davis won his suit against the NFL. During that trial I spent four hours on the witness stand one morning and, just after a recess had been called, suffered a serious heart attack. I spent almost two weeks on the critical list.

The players' strike, the lawsuits, the immense drug problems facing pro football, the avaricious agents, the lack of loyalty of the players, the selfishness of my fellow owners, and finally the heart attack; it was all taking its toll. And then I discovered the joys of horse racing.

In 1976, I had married again. I'd first met Joyce many years earlier, when she had been working at National General and I had fired her boss. When we met again many years later, she was unmarried and working as a stockbroker and I was a widower. The timing was right, the woman was right, so I married her. It turned out to be the right thing to do.

A few years later some friends of ours were buying some breeding horses and asked if we were interested in investing in those horses. I thought it would be a pleasant hobby for Joyce. Personally, I didn't enjoy horse racing; I could never figure out what to do between races.

That all changed the first time one of our horses won a race. It was incredible. After the race the horse's agent didn't call me to try to renegotiate for a larger stall or better oats, he didn't threaten to keep the horse out of the next race, and the horse didn't object to a drug test.

Suddenly, horse racing became more interesting. I began to like it even more when I realized that in horse racing you don't have to play defense.

Soon, Joyce's pleasant hobby had exploded into the 250-horse Del Rayo Racing Stables, and we had built the finest new training ranch in the country. And as my interest in horse racing increased, my interest in football waned. I knew the time had come to sell the team.

The buyer was Alex Spanos, a California real estate developer who had previously purchased a small interest in the team. The price was $80 million.

Thank you, Alex.

In the nearly two decades I spent in professional football I did everything except coach the team, and there were moments when I had to resist the urge to do just that. I hired and fired, I negotiated, I drafted, I scouted, I helped plan strategy, I helped make the rules, I brought in the first podiatrist in football as well as the first psychiatrist—so I tried to change football from head to toe, and finally, I got San Diego in the Super Bowl. Not the team, the city. One of my final accomplishments was to convince my fellow owners to play the 1988 Super Bowl there.

I didn't get San Diego in the Super Bowl, but I did get the Super Bowl in San Diego.

After all the years I spent in football, would I consider myself an expert? I bought the Chargers for $10 million and I was expert enough to sell them nineteen years later for $80 million. Call me anything you want.

3

Less than a month after we'd bought the Chargers, Sam Schulman and I attended our first AFL owners' meeting. Like every other sports fan, I had just sort of assumed that the owners of professional sports franchises were a group of highly motivated, intelligent gentlemen, captains of American industry, men who had achieved extraordinary success in the business world and therefore knew how to run their franchises in a businesslike fashion. People who knew what they were doing. It took me precisely one meeting to realize you don't have to be smart to be rich.

The meeting began at 8:00 A.M. As I had when I attended my first National Theatres board of directors meeting, I expected to sit quietly, listen, and learn. I had really been looking forward to this meeting; for the first time, I was going to play a part in the decision-making process of professional sports.

By 9:30 A.M. I knew we were in trouble. It had taken that long to decide exactly what we would be discussing if we ever finished deciding what we would be discussing. We hadn't reached any decisions; we were still arguing over the agenda. Every time one owner stood up to voice his opinion, two other owners instantly disagreed. And no matter who said what, and who disagreed with him, Al Davis of the Oakland Raiders would disagree. I glanced at Sam. He smiled weakly. We knew this was going to be a long day.

And, as it turned out, a long night. We were still sitting in that room at 11:00 P.M. And just as at that first National Theatres board meeting, instead of listening and learning, I was standing and shouting. We were arguing about something—it could have been a rules matter, it could have been details of the proposed merger with the NFL—I really don't remember. It could have been anything, because we argued about everything. Whatever the issue was, it required a unanimous vote to pass, and Wayne Valley, who owned the Raiders, and Al Davis, his partner, were the only ones against it. They were adamant in their position. They wouldn't even consider another point of view. Finally, in exhaustion, in frustration, I shouted at Valley, "Jesus, Wayne, don't be such a goddam stubborn sonofabitch!"

Wayne flipped over the table and came after me. Fortunately, before we could get into a fistfight, calmer owners stepped between us. Valley pointed a warning finger at me and started screaming, "Don't you dare call me a goddam sonofabitch, you no-good . . ."

Occasionally, I've learned, even I can be wrong. It's possible. Buying Minnie Pearl was a truly humbling experience. And in this case, whatever I meant, I certainly should not have said that to an owner over six feet, three inches tall. So I apologized. "I'm sorry, Wayne," I told him, "I shouldn't have called you that."

Wayne had calmed down too. "All right, Gene," he said graciously, "I accept your apology."

And, for a few seconds, a calm descended over the meeting. Then Sam Schulman, who is perhaps five feet, nine inches tall, said softly to Wayne, "Well, I still think you're a goddam sonofabitch." Annnnnnnddd . . . we were off! Valley and Davis took off after Sam, but Sam could move pretty quickly for a vice-chairman. He made it to the safety of the bathroom, slammed the door behind him, and locked it.

I stood there for a minute, watching Valley and Davis pounding on the door, screaming threats at Sam, daring him to come out of the bathroom. And suddenly a terrifying thought occurred to me: I've just signed a note for $1.8 million and these are my partners. I'm dependent upon people who are trying to break down a bathroom door so they can beat up my vice-chairman. At the countless board meetings I'd attended I'd seen arguments, threats, even bullying, but I'd never seen board members trying to kill each other. It was immediately apparent to me that professional football was a forced partnership with people not of my choosing, some of whom I would not have invited into my home, at least not if I were unarmed.

There are twenty-eight teams in the National Football League. The Green Bay Packers team is a public corporation, owned by the good people of Green Bay, Wisconsin. The other twenty-seven teams are privately owned. Or, as Colts owner Bob Irsay so delicately informed the citizens of Indianapolis, Indiana, at a "Welcome Colts!" rally after he'd moved the team there, "It's not your ball team or our ball team, it's my family's ball team. I paid for it and worked for it."

Fortunately, most of the owners of NFL franchises are dedicated to doing what is best for the entire league. First each of them decides what he believes is best for the entire league, then he tries as hard as possible to make sure the league does it.

As a group, NFL owners are about as magnanimous as three kings trying to share one throne. When you get all twenty-eight owners in a room, and give each of them one vote, you are going to be in that room for a very long time.

After the NFL and the AFL agreed to merge, for example, three of the then sixteen NFL teams had to join the ten-team AFL to equalize the divisions. Naturally, this being for the good of professional football, there were numerous volunteers. "I'm going to do everything possible to stay with my NFL friends," said Minnesota Vikings owner Max Winter, echoing the feelings of most NFL owners. "This is the biggest fight of my career."

After two long meetings, exactly no NFL teams had volunteered to join the American Football Conference. "When all the owners are in one room, it leads to polarization," explained Dallas Cowboys president Tex Schramm, "and that makes agreement almost impossible."

Commissioner Rozelle met privately with many of the owners, then convened a third meeting. When it began, on a Wednesday morning, Rozelle announced, "This is going to be the final meeting on realignment. We're going to stay right here until we get it done." By "here," I assumed he meant New York City. That was my mistake; "here" meant in the National Football League offices at 410 Park Avenue.

Actually, Rozelle allowed everyone to return to their hotel rooms Wednesday night. But that was it. Thursday afternoon the blankets and pillows arrived. It was at that point I turned to Sid Gillman, my head coach and general manager, and told him, "Sid, this is what separates the owners from the general managers. Whatever you do is okay with me." Then I flew back to California to run National General.

With the exception of the elderly founders of the NFL, George Halas of the Chicago Bears and Art Rooney of the Pittsburgh Steelers, everybody else stayed in the NFL offices until Saturday night. They slept on the floor, on couches, on desks. Finally, the realization that Rozelle was really going to keep them in his office until an agreement was reached, plus a bonus of $3 million, was all it took to convince Art Modell of the Cleveland Browns, Carroll Rosenbloom of the Baltimore Colts, and Art Rooney to volunteer to join the new conference.

As time passed, I discovered that the men, and woman, who control NFL franchises are called owners because they are used to getting their own way. Each of them runs a business worth in the neighborhood of $60 million to $70 million, which is a pretty exclusive neighborhood. Each of them is a celebrity in his or her home city, constantly being quoted in the newspapers, interviewed on television, asked to participate in every important civic function, named to the boards of numerous charitable organizations, and invited to most exclusive functions. The owner of the city's NFL team is considered a community leader, his opinion is solicited on various local matters, and he never, ever, has a problem getting the power table at the best restaurant in town.

And then, twice each year, these same people are put into a room with twenty-seven equal partners, told to raise their hand when they want to speak, and asked to put aside their personal desires and act in the best interest of the National Football League. There is about as much chance of that happening as there is that my racehorse, Tank's Prospect, will be asked to sing the lead soprano role in a horse opera staged at La Scala. Some of the owners of NFL teams don't know the meaning of the word *compromise.* And it wouldn't surprise me if a few of them couldn't spell it either.

The truth is that it does not require an IQ test to become either a parent or the owner of a professional football team. Individuals have become owners of NFL teams in a wide variety of ways, almost none of them having anything to do with knowing something about football. Rankin Smith, for example, inherited a fortune and bought the Atlanta Falcons because his college roommate, Georgia Governor Carl Sanders needed someone who lived in Atlanta and could afford to purchase 51 percent of the team to make a presentation to the NFL. "I tried to ask a few questions," Smith recalled, "and got nowhere. They just kept telling me, 'You don't have to worry about that.' I didn't know anything about football." After obtaining a franchise, Smith proved he knew nothing about football by suggesting that the number of prime seats located on the 50-yard line could be increased by laying down two fields crosswise, one running east-west, the other north-south, and switching fields each quarter.

Jack Kent Cooke began as an encyclopedia salesman in Canada and eventually built a vast communications and sports empire. In addition to buying the Washington Redskins, he also owned the Los Angeles Kings in the National Hockey League, the Los Angeles Lakers in the National Basketball Association, and the Los Angeles Wolves in the extinct United Soccer League.

Leonard Tose inherited his family's huge trucking company. He bought the Philadelphia Eagles when former owner Jerry Wolman declared bankruptcy. Leonard then used his experience in the trucking industry to good use and drove the Eagles into the ground.

Georgia Frontiere inherited the Los Angeles Rams when her husband, Carroll Rosenbloom, drowned. Rosenbloom had originally owned the Baltimore Colts, but when Rams owner Dan Reeves died, Carroll convinced Bob Irsay, a heating-and-air-conditioning contractor, to buy the Rams, and then the two men traded franchises. Now, I know that Carroll was an extremely persuasive man, but the Rams for the Colts?

Billy Sullivan was a college-football publicist, printing salesman, and oil-company executive, who took his $8,300 life savings, borrowed $16,700, and bought the Boston franchise in the American Football League. "Billy took eighty-three hundred dollars," another owner once commented, "and parlayed it into a thirty-million-dollar debt."

Joe Robbie, a Miami lawyer, managed to convince a group of investors and banks to put up most of the money needed to create the Miami Dolphins franchise, allowing them to receive most of the tax benefits while he became the sole general partner. I never have any sympathy for anyone who goes into business with a lawyer.

And then there is Al Davis, who litigated Wayne Valley out of control of the Oakland Raiders. Valley had originally hired Davis as coach and general manager, then pushed him hard for AFL commissioner. After the merger was agreed upon, Valley asked Davis to return to Oakland in his former position. As part of the deal, Wayne offered to sell Davis 10 percent of the team based on its book value, $185,000, which was considerably less than its actual value, and make him the third general partner. So, for $18,500, Davis bought 10 percent of the Raiders and became an owner. "Perhaps the biggest mistake I've ever made," Valley told me, "was in misreading his character. When he was our coach and general manager, he was an absolutely first-class individual. The day we made him a general partner, he changed. The same day. It was remarkable. It was like Dr. Jekyll and Mr. Hyde. Eventually, Davis went behind my back and made an agreement with our other general partner to give himself extraordinary powers to run the team. We ended up fighting for the Raiders in court. I finally had the opportunity to buy the San Francisco 49ers, so I gave up the Raiders. But before I put my money down on the 49ers, I realized I didn't miss football at all. The fun had gone out of the game for me."

The personalities of the various owners were as different as the way they obtained their teams. I met Lamar Hunt, for example, at the same meeting at which Valley and Davis chased Sam Schulman into the bathroom. During a morning meeting the day after that incident, we took a break to contact our offices. I walked into a bedroom and found Lamar Hunt, fabulously wealthy Lamar Hunt, lying on a bed, his feet up, talking on the telephone. I noticed Lamar had a large hole in the sole of one shoe, so I called Sam over and pointed it out. "Look at this guy," I said loudly, "with all his money, he can't even afford to get his shoes fixed." Everybody laughed, including fabulously wealthy Lamar Hunt.

The next day we took a break at about the same time and again I walked into the bedroom and again Lamar Hunt was lying there with his shoes on the bed—and I saw that he had had a new half-sole put on the bottom of the worn shoe. His other shoe, however, had not been resoled. "What's this, Lamar?" I said, "How come you only had one shoe fixed?"

The answer made perfect sense to him. "Well, Gene," he pointed out, "only one shoe had a hole in it."

If Lamar had had less money, people would have called him cheap, but because he was so wealthy, he was considered "good with money." He had a very limited wardrobe, just a few suits, and when I asked him why, he explained, "I can only wear one suit at a time."

Once, I remember, Lamar and I were boarding a commercial flight together. I turned to go to first class and, to my surprise, he turned right to go back to the coach section. "Why are you sitting back there?" I asked.

As always, his answer made perfect sense. "Both ends get there at the same time," he said.

Ironically, Lamar Hunt, who was certainly among the wealthiest owners, was the most frugal, while Leonard Tose, one of the least wealthy owners, was probably the most extravagant. Leonard was always sending presents to people. One Christmas, for example, a large box arrived from him. It contained four dozen pairs of socks, socks in every conceivable pattern and color, and every single pair was the wrong size.

Leonard had an extensive wardrobe and was meticulous about his clothes. During the Davis versus NFL trial, our attorneys asked the owners to dress conservatively when in court, so that the jury would not think of them as a group of rich men taking advantage of poor, beleaguered Al Davis. Leonard showed up for the trial wearing a white suit, a white shirt, white tie, white socks, and white shoes. Then he sat in the front row.

One night I met his ex-wife at a dinner party and she told me the story of their relationship. "We met on a blind date," she explained. "I opened the door and here was this man standing there with flowers in his hand. He looked at me and his very first words were 'Let's get married.' I suggested that we have dinner first. But two weeks later we were married.

"For thirteen years he called me every single day to tell me how much he loved me. Then one night, he just didn't come home. I never heard from him again. Six weeks later his driver arrived to pick up Leonard's clothes. Of course I gave them to him—after carefully cutting one leg off every pair of his trousers."

That might have been the ex-wife who tried to have him declared mentally incompetent during their divorce trial.

On another occasion I was in New York for a Chargers game and spent some time with Leonard and the lovely lady he'd been living with for two or three years. Two months later I saw him again at an owners' meeting, and asked how she was. "Oh," he said, shrugging, "I had to put her on waivers." He paused, then sighed and added, "But nobody claimed her."

Unfortunately, Leonard was a very heavy gambler. Worse, he was a bad gambler. That is a terrible combination. Some people claimed that the real reason casinos had opened in Atlantic City was just to be close to Leonard's money, and there were rumors that he had lost as much as $1 million in one night. Certainly, his gambling losses contributed to his decision to sell the Eagles.

Art Rooney, one of the most respected owners—real respect, not football-type respect—was also a contributor to the betterment of the horseracing industry. In fact, Rooney, Billy Sullivan, the Bidwill brothers in St. Louis, the Mara family in New York, all owned pieces of racetracks. At league meetings, Mr. Rooney was like the television commercial for that brokerage concern—when he got up to speak, everybody listened. Mr. Rooney, unlike most other owners, cared more about the league than about his own team. At one meeting, his son, Dan, who was actually running the Steelers, proposed a change in the draft rules. I don't remember the specifics, but the proposal had been lobbied around the league and it looked as if it were going to pass. Perhaps two or three teams were against it. Just before the commissioner took a vote, Mr. Rooney stood up and started speaking. He began by saying that he was very proud of Dan, and that he was doing a fine job running the team. He continued to compliment Dan for about five minutes, then said, "But you know, I've been around here a long time, and he's only starting in the league. And in this case, he's wrong. Pittsburgh is going to vote against it."

Votes changed faster than Leonard Tose could change suits. The proposal was defeated.

There were always a lot of nun stories told concerning Mr. Rooney, who was a serious Catholic. Once, when leaving a racetrack after winning eight or ten thousand dollars, he met a nun who had been out collecting for her church building fund. Not only did Art Rooney drive her back to the church, he gave her his winnings for the building fund.

The only other man who commanded the same kind of respect at the meetings was NFL co-founder George Halas. Halas, who owned, ran, and coached the Chicago Bears, never forgot those early days when the NFL struggled weekly to pay its bills. Dick Butkus, who starred for the Bears for many years, used to say that Mr. Halas threw nickels around as if they were manhole covers. Once, Butkus told me, he was standing next to Halas in a men's room and there was a dime in one of the urinals. Halas looked at it, then reached in his pocket, took out two quarters, and flipped them into the same urinal. "What the hell'd you do that for?" Butkus asked.

"Well," George Halas replied, "I sure wouldn't go in there for a dime. But for sixty cents . . ."

In many ways, Boston's Irish Billy Sullivan is a lot like Art Rooney. He's a gentleman, a devout Catholic, and one of the most energetic men I've ever known. I was told that he gets up at five o'clock every morning. I never saw him at that hour, of course, because at least one of us was always asleep. Supposedly, he spends those early-morning hours dictating as many as one hundred memoes and responses to letters. Billy is the only person I've ever heard of who answers his junk mail. He is not the slightest bit shy about expressing his opinion—he is one of those people who takes so long to say hello that by the time he finishes he has to start saying good-bye.

Billy's son, Chuck, a Patriots vice-president, has been widely criticized for the financial beating he took promoting the Jackson Family tour, featuring Michael Jackson. Evidently, Chuck guaranteed the Jacksons a fee based on the assumption that the tour would sell out. It did not, costing the family millions of dollars. Naturally, I would not have made the same mistake. Naturally.

After all, I'm the man who was smart enough to turn down American publishing rights for the Beatles' music.

Not everyone received the same kind of respect at meetings as Art Rooney and George Halas. Nor did they deserve it. In the early 1970s the World Football League was formed to challenge the NFL, much as the AFL had done slightly more than a decade earlier. Although we were all aware of the existence of the WFL, and wary, there was no real fear that they would be able to compete with us over a prolonged period of time. But unexpectedly, in the middle of a meeting, one owner stood up and declared that he had done extensive research into the origins of the WFL and had discovered that that league was definitely and conclusively a communist plot. The only thing he hadn't figured out, he admitted, was whether it was a Russian or Chinese communist plot.

At another meeting we were discussing the advisability of allowing radio receivers to be put into the quarterbacks' helmets, as is done with race-car drivers, so that the coaches could communicate with them. One owner was against it, reminding us that the Russians were capable of intercepting those signals. If the Russians were capable of tapping the signals from American embassies around the world, he continued, it would be no problem for them to tap into a quarterback's helmet.

I believe it was Art Modell who wondered how the Russians would interpret Ken Stabler's signals.

The Atlanta Falcons' Rankin Smith could always be depended on to say something . . . something. He once confided to reporters he had no doubt that "someday, somehow, we'll win the Super Bowl. And then you know what will happen? They'll want us to win it every year!"

Before the NFL adopted its balanced schedule, which prevents the weaker teams from playing too many strong teams in one season, we were always arguing about the makeup of the schedule. One season the Falcons' schedule was rated the most difficult in the league. That did not bother Rankin, however. "The real reason we play the toughest schedule," he decided, "is because we don't play us!"

Bud Adams is another owner who picked the right father. He's a nice man, but he was always soliciting other owners to invest in his projects. Usually it was some sort of oil venture, but once, I remember, he was promoting a soft drink that was going to compete with Gatorade. There were people who invested in his ventures, and perhaps made money, but I was not one of them. Lamar Hunt probably didn't invest either. I always filed Bud Adams's solicitations under *I*, meaning, "I never want to see this again as long as I live."

The Colts' Bob Irsay was certainly the most unpredictable owner. There was absolutely no way of figuring out what he was thinking about. And when Irsay finally did say something, there was no way of figuring out *why* he was thinking about it. At one meeting we were in the middle of a discussion about some minor change in the league by-laws when Irsay asked to be recognized. Pete Rozelle called on him, he stood, and tried to convince everybody to buy their own airplane. Airplane? Airplane. He rambled for fifteen minutes about the delights of owning your own airplane, then sat down and never mentioned it again. The oddest thing was that no one else seemed to think it was strange.

As amusing as I find some of Irsay's antics, I suspect he gets at least a mild chuckle when he remembers that I paid him $600,000 for a statue of Johnny Unitas. Of course, I didn't know it was a statue when I bought it, but it couldn't move, so it must have been a statue. Actually, a few months after we'd made the deal, Irsay called me and asked permission to speak to Unitas. Naturally, I was curious why he wanted to talk to my quarterback. "What do you want to talk to him about?" I asked.

"None of your goddam business," Irsay snapped.

I always react well to that sort of response. "Screw you," I told him, "you can't talk to him."

"Forget it, then," Irsay replied, "I'll talk to Bart Starr instead." He hung up and never mentioned that again either.

On Irsay's behalf, I must say that after Carroll Rosenbloom had borrowed the Baltimore Colts' 1971 Super Bowl trophy to display it in his Los Angeles home, then neglected to return it, Irsay spent $11,000 to have a replica made for the city of Baltimore—which he then took with him when he moved the team to Indianapolis.

Carroll Rosenbloom was one complex individual. Very smart, very tough, often very nasty. Carroll always gave you the feeling that if you crossed him, he was capable of slitting your throat, then donating your blood to the Red Cross blood drive. At meetings he could be particularly irascible. If he didn't get his own way, he'd stand up and start screaming loudly, "This is wrong, this is wrong, and you people are all wrong. I won't stand for this, you can't do it and I will not agree . . ." Then he'd storm out of the room, his face crimson with anger, and order his attorney, Ed Hookstratten, to go into the room and represent the Rams. Hook would walk into the room and find twenty-seven furious men glaring at him, practically ready to kill him, and he would have absolutely no idea what was going on. "So," he'd say as casually as possible, "what's happening?"

I always thought Carroll was a bit paranoid, although only he knew if he had good reason for it. I know that once the Rams were scheduled to play on Yom Kippur, a Jewish High Holy day, and Rosenbloom accused Rozelle of anti-Semitism. Carroll then demanded that the expenses of Rozelle's office be examined by an accountant. Carroll could also be very petty.

Officially, he drowned while swimming in the ocean. I don't believe it. I knew Carroll reasonably well. He had had open-heart surgery and was told to swim for exercise, but he was a very poor swimmer. Even when he swam in his pool he always, absolutely always, had an aide by the side of the pool watching him just in case he got into trouble. So the possibility that he would go swimming alone in the ocean, on a day when storm warnings had been posted, in treacherous surf, is difficult for me to believe. Maybe it did happen that way, maybe the Russians would have intercepted Ken Stabler's signals—I doubt anyone will ever know.

Rosenbloom's funeral was produced and staged as if it were a play. Actually, it was closer to a variety show. It took place in a large tent erected in his backyard. People entertained. Jonathan Winters was the master of ceremonies, host, conductor, director. Can you imagine how excited Winters must have been when his agent called and told him he'd been booked into a major Hollywood funeral? Winters began the funeral by saying that he knew Carroll would want the day to be funny and lively. Carroll Rosenbloom? Winters must have been hallucinating. Funny? Carroll Rosenbloom? Then Winters started telling jokes.

I don't believe he was as funny as Howard Cosell. Howard gave a passionate eulogy, speaking with great warmth about his good and close friend Carroll Rosenbloom. However, he somehow neglected to mention that at a dinner at my home maybe three weeks earlier, Carroll had almost ripped out Howard's heart and fed it to him on a platter. They were vicious with each other. Of course, it would have been interesting to see Carroll trying to find Cosell's heart.

Carroll's wife, Georgia, showed up late for the funeral. There was a good reason she was late, she explained to the mourners—she had been detained in the house talking to Carroll.

Georgia inherited the team, becoming the first female owner of an NFL team. This put a great deal of pressure on Leonard Tose, who could not open his mouth without cursing. At the first meeting of the executive committee that Georgia attended Leonard didn't even flinch. In response to a remark made by another owner, Leonard suggested he "Go f--- yourself," then immediately turned Georgia and said, "Pardon me." And that is the way he continued—every time he cursed, he stopped, looked at Georgia, said "Pardon me," then continued. Eventually, though, Georgia became one of the boys.

I first met her at a league meeting in Arizona while Carroll was still alive. Many of the owners were attending a tennis-and-dinner party. During cocktails, I was standing in a small room when I heard this somewhat pleasant singing coming from the next room. How nice, I thought, live entertainment. I went inside and there was Georgia, standing in front of Carroll, and to the tune of "Mr. Wonderful," she was singing the immortal song "Mr. Rosenbloom."

Carroll, this gruff, at times vicious man, was sitting there transfixed. That was the best argument ever made for choreographing owners' meetings.

Later I found out that Georgia would perform anywhere, anytime. When she opened the refrigerator and the light went on, she started singing. I like Georgia, and after she inherited the team she worked to become quite knowledgeable about football. The fact that she was the first woman in what had been exclusively a men's club did cause a few minor problems. For example, she did suggest giving her players ballet lessons because she thought it would help their movement and dexterity. And her new husband, Dominic Frontiere, insisted on playing in the NFL's spouses' tennis tournament, threatening to charge the league with discrimination if we didn't let him play. "I'm the spouse of an owner," he claimed, correctly, and eventually won the tournament.

My relationship with Georgia could best be summed up by a statement I made while testifying in the Davis versus NFL trial. Georgia's attorney, Joseph Cotchett, asked me about a statement Georgia had admitted making to me. "I absolutely do not remember such a statement," I said under oath, then added, "but not to be disrespectful, counselor, and to be perfectly frank, there are times when I don't pay too much attention to what your client says." I did not say what times, however.

On numerous occasions, owners' meetings threatened to dissolve into playground fights. The NFL is a multibillion-dollar business and practically every decision made at these meetings affects that business. People often hold strong, opposing views on issues, voices get raised, and attorneys begin consulting their fee schedules. And at those times, Cleveland Browns owner Art Modell, a very funny man, could always be counted on to put everything into perspective. What sets him apart from other owners who say funny things is that he does it intentionally. At one meeting, for example, we were discussing a serious, somewhat complicated financial matter, and tempers were just beginning to warm up. "Gentlemen, gentlemen," Art said softly, and the room quieted. "Before we make a decision, I think we should remember that the most important thing the National Football League has going for it is its integrity. We've built this league on integrity, we preach integrity, and every action we take has a bearing on the way people perceive professional football. I don't think I can overestimate the importance of having people continue to believe that we conduct our business with integrity, because once we have them fooled on that, we can get away with anything we want to!"

During another meeting, Ralph Wilson was giving a report on an insurance matter. Ralph Wilson is a very bright man, an insurance expert, and the report he was giving was important. Now, I can't speak for anyone else, but personally I have never been able to work up the same kind of excitement for insurance policies that I can for things like, oh . . . thoroughbred horse fodder. Insurance *companies*, maybe. Insurance policies? I find the subject boring. So, Ralph droned on for perhaps half an hour. Around the room heads were dropping onto desks as if this were a high school physics class. Finally, Ralph began his summation. And just as he did, Art Modell shouted from the back of the room, "'Scuse me, Ralph. I'm sorry, but I just came in and missed what you had to say. Would you mind repeating it?"

There is a substantial difference between laughing with some-one, as we do with Art Modell, and laughing at someone. Which brings us to my very good friend Allen Davis of the Los Angeles Raiders. Every tale must have its villain. Every Peter Pan must have his Captain Hook. Every tenant must have a landlord. Every divorced man must have his ex-wife's attorney. The National Football League has Al Davis. Davis has a reputation as a rebel, and he is certainly respected for his football knowledge, but I've found him to be one of the truly dislikable human beings I've ever known. And when you've been in as many businesses as I have, for as long as I have, that covers considerable dirty ground, coach.

Davis and I are about as well matched as Amos and Costello. To me, professional football is a business and an avocation. I never wanted to hurt anybody. To Davis, it is a war. In fact, to Davis almost everything is a war. During the Davis versus NFL trial, for example, attorney Joe Cotchett asked Davis if he had been accurately quoted by a national sports magazine in which he discussed the strategy he pursued against the NFL prior to the 1966 NFL-AFL merger: "Let's see what you told them," Cotchett said. "The same article, you said: 'Blitzkreig. Expediency. Panzers. Wehrmacht.' Where does that come from, by the way, those words?"

"As you probably know," Davis responded, "I'm very interested in foreign affairs and that comes from . . ."

Cotchett interrupted him to continue reading from the article: "'Bang. Boom. I admired them.'"

Finally, Davis protested, claiming, "That's not my language. That's not my language."

"You were not quoted accurately here?" Cotchett said.

"No," Davis said, "I don't use the words 'Bang. Boom.'"

"(Laughter)," the court transcript reads, but that does not accurately describe the scene in the courtroom that day. Later during questioning, my good friend Al Davis was again quoted from the magazine, commenting about the German army: "I admired them. . . . I didn't hate Hitler. He captivated me. (But) I knew he had to be stopped . . . he tried to take on the whole world."

Worrying about communist-inspired football leagues was one thing, but being captivated by Adolf Hitler? This man was one of my partners in the National Football League. I had to do business with him. The one thing that always amazed me was that many sports fans admired the man. I always felt that whoever was doing his publicity deserved at least a nomination for the Pulitzer Prize in fiction.

At league meetings Davis would often sit directly in front of Pete Rozelle, whom he hated, a copy of the league constitution on his desk, constantly biting his fingernails, brushing back his hair, waiting to find something to complain about. He usually didn't have to wait too long; whatever we were discussing, he would find something to complain about. Whatever it was. For example, after the commissioner, Art Modell, and I had negotiated a five-year television contract for a total price of $2.1 billion, Pete Rozelle got up in front of the executive committee to announce the details. He began by suggesting everyone take out a pencil and paper. No one except Pete, Art, and myself knew the figures, and we knew everyone was going to be surprised. They were expecting an increase, but no one suspected it would be a 250 percent increase. Pete began reading off the numbers. There were a few oohs and ahhs. Finally, when he reached the bottom line, the entire room burst into applause. That was the largest contract in the history of sports broadcasting.

Not everyone applauded, however. Davis complained that $2.1 billion was not enough money. He said that the negotiating committee had left money on the table. He claimed that he could have done better. He went on and on, complaining about details. Finally, Leonard Tose interrupted him. "Hey, wait a second, Al," he said, "let me ask you a question. Are you saying we can't take the f------ money?"

(Laughter.)

The first of our almost two decades of confrontations took place during the AFL meetings concerning the possible merger with the NFL. After buying the Chargers I learned that secret talks had been taking place between the two leagues. Obviously, a merger was the best thing that could happen for the AFL. It would mean complete public acceptance, the end of the salary war for players, larger attendance, and the opportunity to share in the NFL's lucrative television contract. I had 52,000 seats in San Diego's new stadium that I needed to fill. I didn't have to have my degree from NYU to figure out that Vince Lombardi's Green Bay Packers were going to be a better draw than Ralph Wilson's Buffalo Bills. AFL by-laws required that a vote to merge be unanimous, but I was not overly concerned about that. No owner in his right mind would vote against a merger, would he?

That's what I assumed too.

Davis was against the merger. As Wayne Valley later explained it to me, Davis felt he was responsible for the merger taking place, and he wanted to serve as commissioner of the combined leagues. As AFL commissioner, Davis had been a highly visible figure, encouraging AFL teams to try to sign NFL quarterbacks. Perhaps that strategy did speed up the merger timetable, but discussions between various NFL and AFL owners had been in progress long before Davis had been elected AFL commissioner. "I was on the phone with Davis when it was announced that Pete Rozelle would be the NFL commissioner," Valley recalled. "Al was really upset. 'I deserve to be commissioner,' he insisted. I reminded him that I'd had a difficult time getting him the job as AFL commissioner in the first place, he'd just gotten elected by one vote, and since then he'd succeeded in alienating three or four of the people who'd voted for him. And even if all the AFL owners supported him, which they did not, they still would have been outvoted by the sixteen NFL owners. Davis didn't listen, he just kept repeating that he deserved to be commissioner. I don't think he ever forgave Pete Rozelle for that."

Davis never admitted he was against the merger because he was jealous of Rozelle. Instead he came up with endless reasons why he was against the merger. He strenuously objected to the fact that we had to pay the NFL a $20 million indemnity over twenty years, amounting to $100,000 per club a year. "That's ridiculous," he said, "why should we pay them anything?"

"Are you kidding?" I told him. "We're gonna be part of the NFL. We're gonna get part of their television package. The minute the merger's completed, we go from six hundred thousand dollars a year in television revenue to two million. Who cares about a lousy hundred thousand?"

Davis cared. He had numerous reasons why we shouldn't merge, claiming we could put the NFL out of business if we fought them hard enough, long enough. Finally, Wayne Valley, who controlled the Raiders' vote, had heard enough. Oakland voted for the merger.

Within a few years, however, Davis had changed his mind about mergers. He wanted the NFL to merge with the World Football League. Unlike the old AFL, which had a large television contract, the WFL was having difficulty surviving: Their championship team had had its uniforms confiscated by a creditor, owners of another team had borrowed $27,000 from their coach—then fired him—and when the Detroit franchise declared bankruptcy they listed 122 creditors. Still, without permission of the NFL owners, Davis and Carroll Rosenbloom had met with representatives of the WFL. At the next NFL owners' meeting, Davis acknowledged that he'd met with WFL representatives, then he suggested we merge with them. His plan was simple: Each of the ten WFL teams would pay $12 million to join the NFL. They would buy their way in. He started writing figures on a blackboard, showing how many millions of dollars each NFL owner would put into his pocket. Take their money; that was his entire plan.

Once again, I found myself on the other side. I pointed out that if we continued to take in new teams we would eventually be splitting TV revenues between forty or fifty teams, as well as diluting our product.

Davis didn't care. I suspect he also wanted to be a hero to the WFL owners, who would eventually be entitled to vote for NFL commissioner. Obviously, Davis's plan was rejected.

By 1980, Davis was talking about starting his own league. When the NFL attempted to force the Raiders to stay in Oakland, Davis said, "I've been thinking about . . . starting a new football league. There are seventeen million cable-TV sets in the U.S. and seven million pay-cable stations. . . . We will be able to get good people, good players, and good management. . . ." I wonder who the commissioner of that league would have been.

Davis has been accused of many things by many people. Loyalty is not one of them. By 1986, he was testifying for the United States Football League in their antitrust suit against the NFL. Not surprisingly, the USFL sued only twenty-seven of the twenty-eight NFL teams. Guess which team they did not sue?

Perhaps Davis and I had our biggest fight at an owners' meeting in Scottsdale, Arizona, in the mid-seventies. At that meeting the executive committee, consisting of the then twenty-six owners, decided that all profits from the league's marketing and promotional division, NFL Properties, approximately $50,000 per team each year, would be given to our charity organization, NFL Charities, to be distributed to worthwhile organizations throughout the country. That meant that every time a fan bought a toy helmet with a Chargers logo on it, or a team jacket or plastic mug or bank, our share of the profits would go to charity. This was the league's way of giving something back to the fans who have supported it. As I remember it, every team, every owner, agreed to this plan. But when the time came to formalize the agreement, one club decided to withdraw.

All together now, guess which team did not participate? Guess which team is the only one of twenty-eight NFL teams that keeps its share of profits from NFL Properties?

When I learned that Davis had refused to sign the agreement, I got livid. I stood up and verbally attacked him. I called him every name I could think of, and every name Leonard Tose had taught me. But nothing I said seemed to bother him. He just sat there impassively. I realized then that Al Davis is the kind of man who, if you spit in his face, looks up at the sky and says it must be raining.

There was nothing the other twenty-seven owners could do. Davis was entitled to keep the money. Often, though, owners are asked to present checks from NFL Charities to local groups. Whenever I was asked to do so, I always made a point of explaining that the money was donated by "the twenty-seven participating teams in the National Football League."

Davis contended that the Raiders preferred to spend their money on local charities. That was the first time I'd ever heard of an office claiming that it gave at home.

Al Davis and I stopped speaking to each other after this confrontation, although Davis would occasionally talk to my son, Michael. After I suffered a serious heart attack while testifying against him in the antitrust/conspiracy trial, Davis called Michael to find out my condition. Michael told me, "He just wanted to make sure you were all right."

"Aren't you jumping to conclusions?" I asked Michael.

Obviously, Davis and I were not the only owners who did not get along. There are twenty-eight strong-willed partners in the NFL, and anytime two of them got together there was a potential personality conflict. In fact, with some of the owners, anytime one of them was alone there was a potential personality conflict.

Jack Kent Cooke and Al Davis did not get along, for example. Wellington Mara of the Giants and Al Davis did not get along. Art Modell of the Cleveland Browns and Al Davis did not get along. Leonard Tose absolutely could not stand Al Davis. At one meeting, I remember, Davis said something that irritated him, so he stood up and shouted at Davis, "Goddam it, Al, if there was a guy I could pay five hundred dollars to, I'd have you killed right now." That caused a debate among owners, some of whom thought Leonard would never spend the money and others who joked he would be overpaying.

Leonard also bitterly attacked Lamar Hunt, who was president of the North American Soccer League, for putting a soccer team in Philadelphia. Leonard was afraid that the soccer team would compete with the Eagles. He just ripped Lamar up and down; I thought he might hit him. Lamar remained calm during the whole episode. By that time he knew Leonard.

That soccer league also caused a problem between Miami's Joe Robbie and Hugh Culverhouse of the Tampa Bay Buccaneers. Culverhouse, the brightest of the new owners to come into the NFL while I had the Chargers, wanted to prevent NFL owners and their families from owning teams in any other professional sport. Robbie's wife owned the Ft. Lauderdale Strikers in the NASL and suggested Culverhouse mind his own business. Culverhouse contended that football was his business. Robbie also complained that Tampa Bay played too hard in its preseason games against the Dolphins, resulting in injuries. "I'm not interested in a cross-state grudge match for the championship of Florida," he explained.

Robbie also feuded with Houston's Bud Adams, who had once accused him of running the Dolphins "like a fruit stand."

Bud Adams and New Orleans Saints owner John Mecom lived in the same Houston neighborhood and had been friends for years. Then Adams fired his head coach, Bum Phillips, and Mecom hired him, claiming, "Bud did more for my franchise than I'd been able to do in fourteen years." I don't believe Adams thought that that was a tremendous compliment—Mecom's Saints had never had a winning season. A week later, after the Bum Phillips–coached Saints had upset the Oilers, Mecom added, "I'd have a moral hangover if I wished anything bad for them [the Oilers], but they have to realize that they need some leadership over there, and I don't mean on the field."

Mecom then complained that Adams wouldn't return his phone calls or respond to his messages. Perhaps it was Mecom that didn't get the message.

I suspect that Al Davis probably alienated Billy Sullivan by testifying against him when Billy was sued by his former co-owners. "He appeared in his Darth Vader costume," Billy said, referring to Davis's propensity for wearing black clothing, "and testified like Little Lord Fauntleroy."

If it is true that a man can be judged by the quality of his enemies, neither Carroll Rosenbloom nor his many enemies in pro football should be very proud. I don't think there were many people in football that Carroll respected. Rosenbloom went so far as to once accuse Pete Rozelle of fixing the officiating in a game played in San Francisco.

Al Davis has never missed an opportunity to criticize Rozelle. One season, for example, he complained to newspaper reporters that the league—meaning Rozelle—was forcing the Raiders to play four of their first five games on the road. The implication was that Rozelle was punishing him. The reality, as Davis neglected to tell reporters, was that he had written Rozelle a letter informing him that the Oakland Coliseum had been booked by the Oakland A's baseball team for four of the first five Sundays of the season, and therefore the Raiders would have to play on the road.

As commissioner, Pete Rozelle has tried to be diplomatic. "I differ with Al Davis," Pete admitted, "but it's not personal. . . . I accept what he said, that he does not want anarchy in the league

. . . [but] I believe his past actions indicate that, while he might want stability for the league, he wants anarchy for himself."

Although fights between NFL owners are often bitter, they rarely end up in court. But when co-owners start fighting over a franchise, lawyers start shopping for co-ops.

I was sued by my co-partners for mismanagement, a suit they eventually withdrew.

Wayne Valley and Al Davis fought for control of the Oakland Raiders, a battle Davis eventually won.

The Bidwill brothers in St. Louis had a bitter fight for control of the Cardinals. Billy Bidwill ended up with the team, his brother Stormy got the family racetrack.

Joe Robbie was sued by one of the original investors in the Dolphins for mismanagement.

Max Winter of the Minnesota Vikings was sued by his minority partners.

Denver Broncos owner Edgar Kaiser was sued by his minority partners.

In Boston, Billy Sullivan was temporarily forced out as Patriots president by co-owners who also repossessed his company car, canceled his life insurance policies, and moved him out of his seats in the front row of the owners' box. They should not have messed with those seats. Never, ever, mess with an owner's seats. The car, the insurance, maybe, but not the seats. With the assistance of Commissioner Rozelle and several other owners, Billy regained control of the team. Then he borrowed $8 million and bought out his unhappy partners. A few years later those partners sued, claiming Billy had paid them less than full market value for their shares in the team. The court ruled for those partners and that judgment, combined with the losses from the Jackson Family tour, forced Billy Sullivan to put the Patriots up for sale.

The football used in the NFL, "The Duke," was named after Giants co-owner Wellington Mara. Wellington and his nephew Tim each own 50 percent of the team. They don't get along at all. They don't speak. They don't sit near each other at meetings. It is very difficult to run a business successfully when two equal partners do not talk to each other. In that type of situation you end up with a hospital that advertises twenty-four-hour automobile repairs, or the Giants. Until recently, the Giants hadn't been competitive for almost three decades. Pete Rozelle had to intercede to help select their latest general manager.

Leonard Tose agreed to sell the Eagles to a syndicate that included his daughter, an Eagles vice-president who was really running the team, for $42.1 million. His daughter was to purchase 20 percent of the team, using money loaned to her by other members of the syndicate, to be repaid primarily out of her share of the team's profits. But before Leonard signed the final papers, he learned that another potential buyer had offered $52 million for the Eagles, an offer that his daughter must have forgotten about, because she didn't mention it to him. He repudiated his original agreement. Everybody sued everybody, and Tose eventually had to pay his daughter's group $1.75 million to drop their lawsuit so he could complete the sale to the other buyer.

Now, I certainly don't want to accuse Leonard of being a bad businessman, but how many people who are trying to sell something worth $50 million end up having to pay the people who are trying to buy it?

On the other hand, *he* didn't buy Minnie Pearl.

Perhaps the best thing that can be said about the entire episode is that Al Davis did not testify.

These were my partners. A man who spends $1.75 million trying to sell his team. Another man who wanted to increase the number of seats on the 50-yard line by laying down two fields crosswise. A woman who wanted to give her players ballet lessons. An owner who believed that the communists had decided to start a professional football league. Another owner who would spend every morning preaching the virtues of Alcoholics Anonymous—it had to be in the morning because by the afternoon he was soused. We had owners threatening each other, we had owners suing each other, we had owners hitting each other. And, most of all, we had my good friend Al Davis.

Obviously, not every owner was disruptive. Some of the men who owned teams in the National Football League were among the finest gentlemen, as well as the best businessmen, I've ever known. People like Art Modell, Hugh Culverhouse, the Rooney family, the Halas family, Leon Hess, Max Winter, Herman Sarkowsky, and many others, are quality individuals. But if

Michelangelo had painted even a small section of the Sistine chapel ceiling with Day-Glo paint, that is the section that would have attracted the most attention. The same is true of my partners.

As I look back on the thousands of hours I spent with these people, the good times as well as the terrible times, one thought comes to mind: Thank you, Alex.

4

During the formative years of the American Football League many clubs struggled to survive, among them Harry Wismer's New York Titans. In order to keep its New York franchise in business, which was vital for the prestige of the league, the AFL funded the team. Finally, at an owners' meeting at the Waldorf-Astoria, league officials told Wismer they were taking the Titans away from him. Wismer was irate. He yelled, he screamed, he threatened. And when he finished, he marched defiantly to the door, grabbed the knob, and promised, "I'll see all of you in court!" Then he yanked open the door, whirled around, and stomped into the coat closet, knocking himself down.

That meeting had all the elements of the numerous owners' meetings I attended: arguments over financial matters, threats of lawsuits, and an owner hitting himself in the head.

Every year the owners of the twenty-eight NFL teams or their representatives meet for one week in March. And every year the owners of the twenty-eight NFL teams or their representatives fail to complete their scheduled business during that one week and have to meet again in the summer.

The meetings were held in a different city each year. The site was carefully chosen based on meeting-room facilities, availability of hotel space, and local amenities. Places where we could get serious work accomplished. Places like Honolulu, Hawaii, Palm Springs, California, Scottsdale, Arizona.

There are two types of sessions at league meetings, open meetings and executive meetings. Open meetings were supposedly limited to the team owners and one other person, but eventually expanded to include the owners' relatives, close friends, relatives of close friends, people who wanted to come in out of the sunshine. Open meetings went on forever, so we finally enforced the limit of two people per club. We had fifty-six people in the room, which meant we only had about sixty opinions, as some of those people could never make up their minds.

In executive meetings each club was represented by one person—except the Giants, whose co-owners did not speak to each other, so both of them attended. Confidential matters, such as drug problems, lawsuits, and television contracts were discussed in executive meetings. They also went on forever.

While at National General I had chaired some very difficult board meetings. When I fired my two top executives for refusing to stop making terrible movies, for example, they threatened to start a messy proxy fight. When we took over Great American I had to deal with a hostile board. At the first board meeting, one prominent member asked coldly, "Mr. Klein, exactly how much stock did you really get?"

"I'll tell you what," I suggested, "if you don't believe my public statement, I'll let you go into the vault and count the f------ shares!" I then politely informed the other members of Great American's board, whose terms still had two or three years to run, "Gentlemen, you don't have to resign. You don't have to do anything. But I want you to know that I now own eighty percent of the stock in this company. If you want to stay on the board, don't make any mistakes with my money." After that, we got along about as well as cats and Chinese cooks.

So I know my way around a boardroom. But even the most difficult board of directors meeting didn't compare to an ordinary meeting of the NFL owners. Generally, the members of a corporate board work in harmony for the good of the company. And, even if sometimes they are out of tune, they at least sing the same song. At one time, when men like George Halas, Art Rooney, and Dan Reeves ran their clubs, that was true of the NFL. Those

people considered the good of the league first and their own organizations second. Today, unfortunately, there are too many NFL
owners who consider the good of their own organization first and
the good of their own organization second.

The problem is that several NFL owners don't look at professional football as a business. Normally, people buy a company because it has the potential to be profitable. But the men who can
afford to buy a pro-football team have already made their fortunes
in other industries. It's not imperative that their team make a
profit. They bought their teams to have fun and, in many cases,
for ego fulfillment. Until they gained public recognition by buying a football team, they were just another guy on the street with
a hundred million dollars.

I have a considerable ego, I admit it. Anyone from the Bronx,
New York, who appears on TV dressed in a cowboy outfit to sell
used cars can't claim to be shy. But when I bought the Chargers I
made an effort to run the team as a business. I tried to keep
expenses down and raise income. However, there were people
who had so much money they tried to win at all costs. I never
objected to those people; the people I didn't care for were those
people who tried to win by spending double and triple all costs.

Since winning was what mattered most to these owners, it was
difficult for them to understand that they could compete with
other owners on the field while working together in the meeting
room. Remember, none of these people had made his money in
rocket science. They just didn't trust the other owners. In fact,
some owners suspected that everything done at a meeting was
just another means of trying to screw them on the field. For example, as a way to cut scouting expenses, the NFL set up a central scouting bureau to rate college players. Most teams agreed to
participate in the scouting bureau because they were afraid they
might lose some slight advantage. And then just about every one
of them bolstered their own scouting departments because they
didn't trust the scouting bureau.

I hadn't been in the AFL long enough to mistrust my fellow
owners when we merged with the NFL. That first owners' meeting after the merger was like a convention of people suffering
from communicable diseases. Suspicion hung in the air like crepe
paper at a high school prom. The NFL people, who felt they had

been forced into a merger, would barely speak to us. Their hand-shakes had all the firmness of boiled marshmallow. But we knew we had to work together, or at least sit in the same room to-gether, so we tried to forge a conciliation. The night before Lamar Hunt's Kansas City Chiefs were to play Vince Lombardi's Green Bay Packers in the first Super Bowl, Barron Hilton hosted a celebratory dinner. Everyone was on their best behavior, and the open bar helped considerably. By the end of the evening we were actually beginning to get along. It was a fragile peace, how-ever. Suddenly, the wife of one of my co-partners in the Chargers grabbed the microphone and shouted joyfully, "Go, Chiefs, go!"

Ever hear the story of the late Harvard grad who walked into an old-west saloon and announced, "I think men who wear boots look like sissies"?

That room got so quiet so quickly you could have heard a pin drop—right into someone's back. So much for harmony.

Not that the NFL owners got along so well among themselves. The day after the Packers had defeated the Chiefs, Lombardi walked into an NFL owners' meeting and was greeted with a standing ovation. It was a great moment, he once remembered, "because normally the bastards wouldn't even talk to me."

This mistrust makes it tough to get anything important done in the meetings. For example, every year we would debate the number of players we were going to carry on our rosters. The league constitution mandates a thirty-three-player roster, but that number is changed annually. We usually settle at about forty-five players, although one year we did carry forty-nine. Winning teams have more quality players, and want to keep as many of them as possible, so they always vote for the largest possible ros-ter. Losing teams want small rosters, so that the better teams will have to cut more players, making quality players available. When the NFL players went on strike I felt we could use the issue of roster size to prove to them we could maintain a tough, united front. Smaller rosters would mean fewer jobs for players as well as a reduction in salary expenses. So I got up at the meeting and practically begged my fellow owners to show a united front and adopt the smallest feasible roster. "Please," I said, "for once, let's not be selfish. If the players see we can't even stay together on something like this, they won't believe we'll be able to stick together on more important issues. Here's our chance to show them once and for all that we're serious . . ."

The Washington Redskins, one of the best teams in the league, voted first. As soon as I finished my impassioned plea, their representative stood up and voted for a forty-seven-player roster. That was two more players than we already had!

Normally at a meeting, the commissioner and his staff sit at a long table in front of the room. The other owners or their representatives sit opposite that table. There are no assigned seats. I always sat in the first empty chair I found. Al Davis usually sat in the front row, just to be sure the commissioner could see him.

Davis always sat with his assistant Al LoCasale. The two of them are referred to as "Big Al" and "Little Al." "Big Al" Davis is about five feet, ten inches tall and weighs maybe 145 pounds. "Little Al" LoCasale is only about five feet three, but until he lost a considerable amount of weight, must have scaled over 200 pounds. Tank Younger once attended an owners' meeting with me at which Billy Sullivan and Chuck Sullivan got into a fight with Davis and LoCasale. The Sullivans kept screaming, "Big Al did this, then Little Al did that, then Big Al said this, then Little Al repeated what he said . . ." Finally, Tank turned to me and asked, "How did they decide which one was going to be Big Al?" People who weren't familiar with Davis and LoCasale were always confused because Big Al really should have been "Skinny Al" and Little Al should have been "Bigger than Big Al."

The meetings were run just like any other business meeting attended by a group of people, some of whom didn't trust each other and some of whom didn't know what they were doing. Every team had the right to submit proposals to the membership up to thirty days before the annual meeting. These proposals would automatically be put on the agenda. At the meeting, the proponent would make his pitch and, if his proposal was seconded and approved by a three-quarters majority, twenty-one votes, it would pass.

Before taking an official vote, the commissioner would take a poll, a sample ballot. "This isn't official," he would tell everybody. If the poll indicated that the proposal had no chance of passing, the commissioner would offer whoever proposed it the courtesy of removing it from the agenda. This is the corporate version of crawling back into your hole. Most people did. But if the sample vote was close, 20–8, for instance, the commissioner would open up the floor for debate. And more debate. And more debate. There was no time limit on discussion, and even that didn't seem long enough for some people. Some discussions seemed to go on forever, and just when we thought we had heard everything, someone would get up and start talking about airplanes or Alcoholics Anonymous.

A lot of lobbying would go on before we voted officially. There would be some arm-twisting and some vote-trading, but by far the most valuable currency was a preseason game. Owners make up their own preseason schedules. They can play whichever teams they want, wherever they want to play them, and make whatever financial arrangements they choose to make. Thus, teams with large stadiums who draw well in preseason games are particularly desirable opponents. Those teams can, and do, use the promise of a preseason game to influence those votes that are important to them. Fifty-five thousand filled seats can make a man see the wisdom of another opinion.

A proposal, debate, and a vote—that's the way a meeting is supposed to be run. And sometimes they were. But I remember asking my general manager, Harland Svare, what he thought after attending his first owners' meeting. "I was pretty surprised," he admitted. "I expected to walk in and see organized chaos. There was nothing organized about it."

Throughout every meeting, owners would be standing up, sitting down, walking in and out of the room, going to the telephones, loudly carrying on private conversations, and, on occasion, somehow managing to fall asleep. Leonard Tose would be cursing. Bob Irsay would be rambling on about something no one quite understood. Carroll Rosenbloom would be either charming someone or threatening them. Max Winter would be sitting quietly. And, in the front row, Al Davis would be biting his fingernails, brushing back his hair, leafing through his copy of the constitution, and constantly interrupting Pete Rozelle to complain, "You can't do that, you can't do that!"

The high-pitched engine roar of the bombers I flew during World War II eventually caused my hearing to deteriorate. I need a hearing aid to participate in normal conversations and even with my hearing aid I have great difficulty understanding high-pitched voices. That hearing aid has always been a detriment to me—except during owners' meetings. When Bob Irsay got up to speak, *fffttt*, I turned that baby right off. Couldn't hear a word he said. Davis started ranting, *fffttt*, forget it, Al, I can't hear you. One day Art Modell saw me turn the thing off during a particularly long and tedious speech. Afterward he came over to me and asked, "Where can I get one of those things?"

For obvious reasons, the NFL made changes with the speed of a racing glacier. For example, it took us only a little more than a decade to agree to play a sudden-death period when a game was tied at the end of regulation time. Every year, at every meeting, someone would propose playing overtime periods until either team scored, and every year at every meeting other owners would cite numerous reasons why it wouldn't work:

"Overtime periods would screw up the network's Sunday night schedule."

"It'll increase the number of injuries because players are exhausted after playing four quarters."

"The National Hockey League doesn't do it and they have a lot more tie games than we do."

"Everybody should really consider buying their own airplane."

"The game has always been played like this, so this must be the way it's supposed to be played."

"The North American Soccer League doesn't do it, and they have many more tie games than we do."

"Our agreement with the Players Association doesn't permit it. No question but they'd file a grievance."

"F--- you with that idea and the f------ boat that brought you."

"Why wouldn't you want to own your own airplane?"

"Theoretically, a game could go on forever."

"You can't do that, I'm telling you, you can't do that."

Eventually we got the twenty-one votes necessary to implement the rule. We agreed to limit overtime to one period. Games tied at the end of that period would end as ties. Some fans believe the rule we adopted is unfair, because the team that wins the coin toss and gets the ball first has a tremendous advantage. If they score, the game ends without the other team having an equal opportunity. We thought about that a long time before reaching an important conclusion: too bad. Life isn't always fair.

Like many other owners, I made certain proposals year after year. Most of the changes I suggested concerned opening up the game for more offense. As a member of the NFL's broadcast committee, I often met with network representatives. The one thing the networks always wanted was more scoring. Nobody watches football games to see interior linemen block, they pointed out, with the possible exception of the parents of interior linemen. Higher-scoring games made better television shows and resulted in higher ratings. In 1977, for example, NFL teams averaged only 17.2 points per game, the worst offensive showing in thirty-five years. TV ratings suffered because of that; in fact, NBC requested, and received, a small rebate. "We're in the entertainment business," I told the owners at a meeting of the executive committee, "and we've got to do something to increase scoring." The fact that the Chargers traditionally depended on a high-scoring offense had nothing to do with my feelings at all. My proposals were strictly for the good of the league.

To make it easier to complete a pass, we proposed changing the rule that permitted defenders to bump pass receivers anywhere on the field, even before the ball was thrown, to a rule that allowed them to hit receivers only within 5 yards of the line of scrimmage. This proposal had nothing to do with the fact that the success of the Chargers depended upon our passing attack. My proposal was strictly for the good of the league.

In addition, I wanted to liberalize the holding rules for offensive linemen, allowing them to provide better protection for the quarterback. This proposal had nothing to do with Air Coryell. It, too, was strictly for the good of the league.

To make it easier to run, we proposed moving the hash marks, those white dashes marking every yard on both sides of the field, closer to the center of the field. After each play, officials place the ball in the middle of the field or on the nearest hash mark. These marks were located so close to the sideline that a team was forced to run its plays toward the other, wider side of the field. Essentially, we were squeezing the field, a big advantage for the defense. By moving the hash marks closer to the center of the field, we would open up the entire field. Anyone who ever saw a Don

Coryell–coached team would know this proposal was strictly for the good of the league.

These proposals would certainly increase scoring, which would be for the good of the entire league. That was why those teams with powerful offenses supported them, while those teams that relied on defense were against them. Nobody wanted an airplane.

Eventually, many of those proposals were adopted. Scoring increased, our ratings went up, and we were able to negotiate the largest television contract in sports history. I'm not going to claim my proposals led directly to that multibillion-dollar contract—I'm Klein from the Bronx, not Davis from Brooklyn—but without question they helped our television ratings. The fact that the Chargers happened to win three consecutive AFC western-division championships, while Dan Fouts became the greatest passing quarterback in the NFL, was just a pleasant coincidence.

Besides, rather than changing those rules, we simply could have adopted Art Modell's proposal for increasing the ratings of *Monday Night Football:* "If they want scoring, why don't we just let the Chargers play every Monday night? Nobody can stop them from scoring, and they can't stop anybody."

I also wanted to increase the number of regular-season games. We were playing six preseason games and a fourteen-game regular-season schedule. That was like showing an hour of coming attractions before showing an hour-and-a-half movie. Six exhibition games! Exhibition games are even less important than *The Battle of the Network Circus Stars*—they must be, because the networks aren't interested in broadcasting them. And we were playing six of them.

Football fans were objecting to being forced to purchase full-price tickets for these games when they bought their season tickets. I didn't blame them. I didn't refund their money, but I certainly didn't blame them. I didn't want to play fewer games, which would reduce our revenue. What I wanted to do was make the games we played more meaningful. That meant either assigning some value to exhibition games or including at least some of them in the regular-season schedule.

Since each team is permitted to sell the television rights to its exhibition games to local stations and keep all the money, those teams with lucrative TV deals didn't want to change things. Those teams who didn't have a good broadcasting contract were sincerely concerned about the welfare of their fans.

As a compromise, I suggested counting exhibition games as half-games in the regular-season schedule, or using preseason records to break ties existing at the end of the season. The general consensus was that we should leave the schedule alone.

Then someone pointed out that adding games to the regular-season schedule would make our television package more attractive and lead to a more substantial contract. That general consensus fell apart faster than a Quality Motors guaranteed used car. I pushed for two exhibition games and eighteen regular-season games. We settled for four exhibition games and a sixteen-game schedule.

Not every proposal I made was adopted. Every year, I proposed giving coaches the option of attempting either a one- or two-point conversion after a touchdown. Next to the quarterback taking the hike and falling down to run out the clock, a play that rarely appears in team highlight films, the extra-point kick is the most meaningless play in football. For professional placekickers, it's automatic. And every time I said that in a meeting, someone would remind me that one or two games almost every season are decided by a missed point-after-touchdown attempt. Going to a professional football game expecting to see it decided by a missed extra-point kick is like going to the ballet to see Baryshnikov trip. It happens too infrequently to matter. But giving coaches the option of kicking for one point or running or passing for two points would add a new element of excitement to the game.

The first time I suggested this to a head coach he looked at me as if I were threatening his life. "What do you want to go and complicate things for?" he asked.

Complicate things? It couldn't have been the math—he wasn't a genius, but even he could add two points to a total rather than one. He just didn't want to give fans another opportunity to criticize his decisions. "Look at all the controversy it would add," I said. "Don't you want people talking about the game?"

"'Course I do," he told me. "I just don't want them saying, 'Did you see that stupid horse's behind go for the two points yesterday?'"

Few of my fellow owners seemed to feel as strongly about the concept as I did. I'd bring it up every meeting, and every meeting they would block my personal attempt for an extra point.

To say nothing about the mandatory-drug-testing proposal I also made every year, because nothing is precisely what many owners in the NFL wanted to do about the league's drug problem.

In addition to attending these meetings, owners also serve on league committees. They're assigned to these committees by Pete Rozelle, usually based on their expertise. If it has to do with insurance, for example, Ralph Wilson will be a member. The standing committees include the Broadcast Committee, Legislative Committee, Competition Committee, Coaches' Pension Committee, Meeting-Site Committee, Long-Range Planning Committee, Finance Committee, Hall of Fame Committee, NFL Films Executive Committee, Management Council Executive Committee, Preseason Committee, Pro-College Relations Committee, Retirement Board, NFL Properties Executive Committee, even a Super Bowl Ring Committee. In addition, we would set up special committees to deal with matters not covered by the standing committees, such as the Rozelle Compensation Committee. We had more committees than Bill Cosby has commercial endorsements.

I served on the Rozelle Compensation Committee and the Broadcast Committee. The Rozelle committee was charged with negotiating the commissioner's contract. I assumed I was assigned to that committee because of my long and varied experience as a negotiator. The Broadcast Committee supervises all relations with the networks and negotiates our television contracts. The big-money committee. That was the committee I wanted to work on.

When the two leagues merged, NFL teams were getting slightly more than $2 million a year from CBS, while AFL teams were receiving $660,000 from NBC. At a meeting soon after the merger, George Halas said he doubted each team would continue to get as much as the NFL teams had been getting because so many new teams had been added. I disagreed with him. In fact, I told him, I thought we could get substantially more than we were getting. Mr. Halas replied politely that I didn't know what I was talking about. "Mr. Halas," I said, "I certainly respect your opinion, but I've been in the television business a long time. If you really feel that way, here's what I'll do. I'll buy your TV rights for the next five years for the same two-point-two you're getting right now. You want to sell your rights to me?"

He didn't know if I was serious or not. I was absolutely serious. He thought about my offer for a moment, smiled, and shook his head. "Young man," he said, "no, I don't think so. I believe you may be right."

I assume I was put on the Broadcast Committee because of that confrontation, plus my experience as a TV cowboy.

When Pete Rozelle became NFL commissioner in 1960, the league office was located in Philadelphia and the staff consisted of two men and an eighty-year-old Kelly girl. The former commissioner, Bert Bell, often ran the NFL from his kitchen table, dressed only in his underwear. Under Rozelle's leadership, the value of an NFL franchise has risen from about $1 million to $70 million. I think everyone associated with professional sports acknowledges that Rozelle has been the most valuable sports executive in the last three decades.

Well, perhaps not everyone. Not to mention Al Davis's name.

Normally, the chairman of the board, the man who runs the business, is the boss. He is free to take whatever steps he believes are necessary for the good of the company. In professional football, Rozelle is an employee. Each of the owners sitting in front of him is his boss—although Well Mara and Tim Mara are only half a boss each. In practical terms Rozelle has about as much chance of satisfying those owners as I had of convincing Lamar Hunt to part with $1,000 for one of my 330 brand-new Kaisers. At some point in his career, Rozelle has undoubtedly made decisions that alienated each owner. His genius, I believe, was to alienate them one at a time. The key to controlling a board is to stay friendly with one more than a majority.

I think the commissioner has been eminently fair and forthright. I think he has been far-thinking. I think his understanding of public relations has been extraordinary. I think his use of television to promote pro football has been brilliant. I also think he should not have fined me $20,000 for lax supervision during the Chargers' drug scandal. At least he took a check. So I was pleased to serve on the Rozelle Compensation Committee.

Actually, I helped negotiate two contracts for him. The first because his current contract was about to run out, the second to compensate him fairly for the job he was doing. How much is a commissioner worth? How smart is a defensive lineman? The answer is that there is no single answer. Rozelle selected an attorney to represent him. We met with this attorney and he gave us an outline of what the commissioner thought would be fair. We haggled a bit. We gave him more in some areas, less in other areas, but these were not tough negotiations. We gave him a good package. Then, at the next owners' meeting, in Seattle, I gave the committee's report. Everyone thought the agreement was a good one.

Well, perhaps not everyone. After I'd finished, Al Davis stood up and suggested we postpone the vote to give people time to consider the package.

"We're not postponing anything," I said. "I want a roll-call vote right now."

Davis then made a speech opposing the contract. We were giving Rozelle too much money, he complained. We were giving him too many benefits, we were being forced into this.

"Roll-call vote," I said. The final tally was either 27–0 or 27–1. I'm not sure of the vote; I am sure of the voter.

Within a few years it became apparent that we hadn't done a very good job. Rozelle was being substantially underpaid, considering his value to the league and his responsibility for its success. So, soon after closing the deal with the networks for $2.1 billion, we decided to extend his contract. It's amazing how generous a couple of billion dollars will make most people.

Not *all* people, however. There was a debate. Some*one* pointed out that Rozelle already had a valid contract with some years remaining. I pointed out that the chief executive officer of every major corporation has stock options in his company, or some other way of gaining, so that if the corporation prospers the CEO would be remunerated over and above his salary. "We've done very well," I said, "and it's no secret that Pete is primarily responsible for that . . ." Did I hear someone moan? ". . . yet he's gotten nothing except his salary. He's got no participation in ownership, no equity, no nothing, so we ought to give him some sort of compensation."

Leon Hess, Hugh Culverhouse, and I were asked to negotiate a new contract with Rozelle. Leon Hess said we would only take the job if the owners gave us absolute authority to make a deal. Period. "We don't want to negotiate a contract, then come back here and have a floor fight over its terms. You trust our judgment, fine. If not, find some other people." Since we were deemed reasonable men, everyone agreed.

Well, perhaps not everyone. The vote was either 27–0 or 27–1.

We negotiated a ten-year contract with Rozelle at an annual salary slightly higher than that of a starting quarterback and a first-round draft pick. Then we threw in a signing bonus worth slightly more than $1 million after taxes.

We didn't have to vote on it. I suspect that frustrated at least one individual.

The Broadcast Committee was arguably the most important of all league committees, if you consider the survival of the NFL important. We negotiated television contracts for the league, and the NFL had become almost totally dependent on the revenue from these contracts. Pro football needed television like Sonny needed Cher. Remember Sonny? Of course, television also needed pro football. Remember *Omnibus*?

Television thrives on action—that's why there have been many more successful series about detectives than about carpet salesmen. Football is a game of action. Baseball, on the other hand, is essentially a game of anticipation. The only thing a network executive wants to anticipate is the next commercial. Boxing and wrestling were the first popular TV sports, and football combined both of them. Even better, instead of being limited to two men in a ring fighting each other, the rules of football allowed twenty-two men to go after each other simultaneously. Pete Rozelle positioned football as an intellectual sport, but the reality was that nobody ever watched a football game to see Joe Namath think. In fact, the only way that most people would watch the two brightest men in the world on TV is if they were boxing, wrestling, or playing football.

During the time I was a member of the Broadcast Committee, Art Modell, Pete Rozelle, and I negotiated three contracts with the networks, as well as creating *Monday Night Football* and *Thursday Night Football*. As I told Halas, I'd had quite a bit of experience in television before being appointed to the committee. National Telefilm, a National Theatres subsidiary, had successfully lost millions of dollars producing and syndicating television series. I'd spent a considerable amount of time learning about closed-circuit broadcasting when we were trying to merchandise the Talaria system. I bought and operated a successful cable-TV system for National General. So I had experience with network, closed-circuit, and cable TV. And, of course, I was an experienced performer.

Until 1964, CBS owned professional football because it broadcast NFL games, and the NFL was pro football. CBS was paying the league a tidy $4.65 million a year for exclusive TV rights. Although few people remember, ABC, the weakest of the three networks, was paying the AFL $1.7 million a year, just enough to keep the league breathing. In 1964, when CBS's contract with the NFL expired, NBC and ABC bid seriously for those rights. CBS ended up paying $28.2 million for two years to keep the NFL.

NBC president Bob Kintner was a fanatical sports fan—NBC Sports people claimed that Kintner would phone and complain if his dog looked bored by a sports broadcast—and disappointed at his network's failure to get the NFL. Kintner immediately struck a five-year, $42 million deal with the AFL. This $8 million a year made the AFL a viable commodity and made a merger inevitable. As part of the merger agreement, CBS kept its NFL cities, giving it the larger TV markets and ensuring higher ratings. NBC got the AFL cities. ABC got the professional-bowling tour.

By 1972, pro football had boomed, becoming the most popular sports programming on TV. That year Rozelle, Modell, and I negotiated a four-year deal with CBS and NBC for $2.1 million a year per club. Four years later we were able to double that to $5.2 million a year per club. In 1980, we signed the historic $2.1 billion contract, which escalated to $16.2 million a year per club.

The incredible thing was that no matter how much money we got from the networks, it turned out to be just slightly less than some owners needed to make a profit. The final figure didn't make any difference; whatever it was, owners and coaches would find some way to spend it. John Mecom finally put his checkbook down, for example, when his head coach, Hank Stram, bought $20,000 worth of extra goalposts for a practice field, glow-in-the-dark parking signs for the players, and a $4,000 large-screen TV set for his office. When I sold the Chargers, we had one coach for every four players and a medical staff that could have run a small hospital.

Rozelle, Modell, and I rarely met as a committee with the networks. We'd see the television executives at social occasions and talk to them on the telephone. Pete was our point man. He did all the face-to-face negotiating, usually at lunch. He liked to do it in public places because it embarrassed the network executives to scream out loud. No matter what deal we made, though, we had to report back to the executive committee, the owners, for approval. And no matter what terms we presented, at least one owner would complain that we'd left money on the table.

Believe me, there were times we even took the table.

Rozelle, Modell, and I created *Monday Night Football*. The three of us met often, not just when a contract was due to expire. We were constantly looking for means to increase revenue without overexposing our product. To me, anything short of playing games in people's living rooms was not overexposure. If people wanted to watch it, I was willing to sell it. When I had been putting together the Talaria system I'd tried to convince Rozelle to schedule games every weekday night. We chose Monday because it came right after Sunday, which meant that the teams that played Monday night would still have almost a full week to prepare for their games the following Sunday.

We first offered *Monday Night Football* to NBC, our way of compensating them for the fact that CBS had the bigger cities. We didn't actually assume they'd roll an armored car up to 410 Park Avenue and shovel out pounds of money, but we did expect some interest. There was no interest at all.

CBS thought it was an interesting idea. "Interesting" is a code word in the vernacular of television executives meaning they would rather broadcast *The Best of Sunrise Semester* than whatever it is you're trying to sell to them.

That left ABC. ABC, the third network, the network that had no professional football. When I owned Bantam Books we'd gotten the galleys, the first printed proofs, of a hardcover novel entitled *The Godfather*. I read the galleys and told Oscar Dystel to buy the softcover rights, whatever the cost. I didn't have to be a publishing expert to know it was going to be a big book. But more than anything else, I wanted that book because I didn't want our competition to have it. We were the biggest mass-market publisher in the world. I wanted to stay that way. I didn't want to let our competition get a foothold. Our final bid was $400,000. We lost *The Godfather* to Fawcett by $25,000. It became the best-selling softcover novel ever published, and it practically kept Fawcett in business. To me, letting ABC get a taste of pro football was exactly like allowing Fawcett to outbid us for *The Godfather*.

ABC bought *Monday Night Football*. It gave them a foothold in pro football. Actually, there was only mild enthusiasm within the league for playing on Monday nights. Everybody wanted to take the money and watch somebody else play. They were afraid that having only five days to prepare for their next game would give their opponents an advantage. Finally, Art Modell and Leon Hess volunteered to play in Cleveland. Eighty thousand people attended the game, and television ratings were spectacular. As Howard Cosell remembers it, he had successfully created *Monday Night Football*.

The success of *Monday Night Football* led directly to *Thursday Night Football*. Remember Sonny Bono? Remember *Omnibus*? Remember *Thursday Night Football*? If *Monday Night Football* was a concept whose time had come, *Thursday Night Football* was the concept that stopped the clock. Other owners were not excited about the idea because it upset their training schedules; they only had four days to prepare for the game, which really was not enough, and ten days to wait for their next game, which was too many. The only reason they agreed to experiment with *Thursday Night Football* was that ABC was willing to pay several million dollars for it. ABC was not excited about the idea because it interrupted its regular programming schedule. The only reason ABC agreed to experiment with *Thursday Night Football* was that the executive committee was willing to take several million dollars for it—and ABC did not want to give weeknight football to another network. If *Thursday Night Football* was going to fail, it was going to fail on ABC.

I liked it. I was in the minority, however. Our ratings were better than most telethons, religious programs, gardening and cooking shows and late-night movies sponsored by Ginsu knives, but not competitive with other football broadcasts. The four-year contract we signed with ABC gave us the option of scheduling two additional special games each year, usually to be played on Thursday nights, for which we would receive $3 million each. We decided not to exercise that option, passing up $24 million. In all my years on the Broadcast Committee, that was the only time we left money on the table.

The primary function of the Broadcast Committee was to negotiate the overall contracts with the three networks. I've always loved negotiating, and the more zeroes I was negotiating for, the more I loved it. In these negotiations we were operating from a position of tremendous strength: We were selling something our customer needed, we were the only supplier, and we were selling in a competitive marketplace. For me, it was like selling candy to a baby. Both CBS and NBC knew that if they didn't meet our price for the Sunday games, ABC was anxiously waiting to bid; conversely, ABC knew that CBS and NBC would pay almost whatever we asked for prime-time weeknight football.

If the networks all decided to harden their bottom line, we had investigated the possibility of creating the National Football League Network, which would consist of independent and cable-TV stations. We discovered it would be possible to put this network together and do so profitably. The plan was not a new one: In 1965, CBS had turned down the NFL's suggested contract. Because NBC was locked into the AFL, and ABC had college football, the NFL was seemingly boxed in. Rozelle conceived the idea of a pro-football network, and when the study he commissioned showed it could be financially successful, the NFL owners voted to set it up. As soon as CBS learned of this decision, however, they quickly reached an agreement with the league.

The plan we had set up was a participation deal. Revenues would depend upon the number of stations that would carry our games and what they could charge advertisers. On paper, it seemed like a viable alternative. Of course, on paper, when I bought Johnny Unitas for $600,000 he was still a star quarterback. Nobody really wanted to find out if this football network would be profitable. A bird in the hand is always worth more than two in the bush, unless that bird craps in your hand.

The most difficult decision we faced every four years was figuring out how much to ask for from each network. We wanted to be fair, but it's easier to be fair when you're rich. The essence of a good business deal is that everybody profits. We wanted the networks to be prosperous, because we knew we'd eventually be going back to them for another contract. Before entering negotiations we carefully examined each network's financial position— how much they were paying for the rights, how much they were charging for commercial time, and approximately what kind of profit they were making. Then we'd project how much their advertising rates would rise over the life of the contract, how much additional revenue they could generate, and then we'd throw in a few million dollars for good luck and base our request—the difference between a request and a demand is who is defining it— on those figures.

I was always the hard-liner on the committee. I always wanted to ask for more than Rozelle or Modell did. We can always ask, I'd tell them. What are they gonna do? Buy bowling? I had a big advantage over the two of them—I'd sold encyclopedias during the Depression. I'd learned that the key to being a successful negotiator is being secure. You cannot be afraid to lose the sale. That's the bottom line, and it doesn't matter whether you're selling a $225 used Ford or the rights to televise pro-football games, you cannot be afraid to lose the sale. The first thing I did when I took over Bantam Books, for example, was recommend that we raise the price of some softcover books from the 50 or 95 cents we were getting to $1.95. Bantam's executives were almost uniformly against me. They gave me a hundred reasons why consumers would not pay $1.95 for a paperback book. I listened to every reason, then told them, "If they want the book, they'll pay a dollar ninety-five."

To me, the economics were simple. I'm the only person selling a particular book. If they want the book, they'll pay the price I put on it—within reason, of course. And if they don't want the book, I couldn't sell it to them for a quarter. We bought Dr. Reuben's *Everything You Always Wanted to Know About Sex but Were Afraid to Ask* and charged $1.95 for it. Our costs, including purchasing the rights, printing, and distributing, were about 35 cents a book, and would remain 35 cents whether we charged 95 cents or $1.95. The high price made the book seem even more appealing, and we discovered there was no consumer resistance at that price. We made an additional dollar profit on every book just by printing that price on the cover.

I felt the same was true for NFL games. The NFL was the only one selling them. If the networks wanted our games, they would pay our price, within reason. If they didn't want them, it wouldn't matter what price we put on them.

The networks knew I was a tough negotiator. Once, for example, my son, Michael, then a successful producer of television movies, was introduced to a studio executive. The man, whom he'd never met before, greeted him by warning, "If you're anything like your father, don't talk to me."

Michael laughed. He had been with me at enough meetings to know what the man was talking about. "What'd he do to you?"

"I used to be a negotiator for NBC," he said, and that was all he had to say.

I had to be tough: The people with whom I was negotiating were tough. I knew that whatever deal we ended up with, I was still going to be the owner of the Chargers, but their jobs were on the line every time we started talking contract. Network executives were intelligent, aggressive, stubborn, highly paid, and highly visible. They either made a good deal or found another job. There was a high turnover among network executives.

Our most difficult negotiations took place in 1980. Months before we were to present our requests to the networks, Commissioner Rozelle and Art Modell came out to my home in Rancho Santa Fe, California. We spent a week formulating our plans. Each of us examined the same figures and each of us reached a different conclusion. As usual, I wanted to ask for the most money: I wanted to triple the expiring contract, I wanted to ask for $2.5 billion.

We were reasonably sure the networks wouldn't want to pay that much.

Deciding how much to ask for from each network was not simply a matter of determining a final figure and dividing by three. CBS still had the National Conference games, which included most of the major television markets, and usually meant higher ratings, as well as a Super Bowl every other year. NBC had the American Conference, which gave them a full schedule of Sunday games, as well as a Super Bowl every other year. ABC had *Monday Night Football* and the professional-bowling tour.

The networks were not going to pay us $2.5 billion because they liked us. They probably liked us about a billion dollars less than we wanted to be liked. But television networks operate under exactly the same principle by which I ran my companies: Put more money in your pocket than you take out. I knew that the only way we'd get the money we wanted was to prove to them they could pay it and still make a profit.

Our strategy was to divide and conquer. We knew if we could convince one network to sign up for the big money the other two would be in a weaker negotiating position. We wanted to pick them off one at a time.

CBS would be the most difficult because we expected to get the most money from them, so we decided to save them for last. ABC was going to pay the least. The commissioner met with ABC first.

The least was not a little. The least was a lot. It was a lot more than they expected to be charged. In order to make it palatable, we put together a package they could not possibly turn down. Because ABC had not been broadcasting pro football when the leagues merged, they had been shut out of the Super Bowl rotation. We knew how desperately ABC president Leonard Goldenson and Roone Arledge wanted a Super Bowl, for the prestige as well as the profit. We also felt ABC's commitment to *Monday Night Football* had earned them the right to participate. Until these negotiations, we'd always offered the networks four-year deals, giving CBS and NBC two Super Bowls each. A cornerstone of our negotiating strategy was to add a fifth year to this contract, and give ABC the odd Super Bowl. This is when the foothold they'd gotten by buying *Monday Night Football* paid off. For us as well as for them.

Actually, we didn't give them the Super Bowl. The only thing we gave them was the opportunity to pay us hundreds of millions of dollars. We felt certain they wouldn't turn down the chance to broadcast a Super Bowl. We haggled a bit, but eventually shook hands, and they sent us over some money. Most of these deals were secured by memorandum. If we waited for the lawyers to draw up and examine the contracts we'd have been off television.

NBC was in the middle position. I think "thrilled" would be a less-than-accurate way of describing NBC's reaction to our request. Perhaps "astonished," or "appalled," maybe even "incredulous," would be more accurate. But we were the only National Football League in existence, and we showed them, on paper, how they could make a sizable profit. They were tough, but the figures were there, and eventually we shook hands with NBC. That left the one great unblinking eye, the CBS Television Network.

Meanwhile, I was constantly getting phone calls from other owners; why is it taking so long? How much money are we gonna get? Can I afford a new airplane?

I'd tell each of them the same thing: "What difference does it make how much we get? Whatever it is, you're just gonna blow it anyway."

It's been said that the reason the CBS eye never blinks is that it's afraid that someone will take advantage of it while it isn't looking. CBS's negotiators were very tough people, but once we'd concluded our deals with ABC and NBC, I didn't think CBS had any real choice. CBS knew we would offer their Sunday games to ABC if they didn't come close to meeting our price. So their options were to either pay what we were asking or go back to televising the *Church Hour*.

Nobody wanted that to happen, with some possible exceptions from the Bible Belt. CBS and the NFL had had a long and excellent relationship; we'd benefited mutually from the growth of pro football. We wanted to be fair to our oldest customer, but we were also aware that we were in what I laughingly referred to as a business. I believed CBS would scream and shout and threaten to walk away and claim that the ratings of religious programs were going up, but that we would eventually make a deal that was good for both of us.

As always, Pete Rozelle was our point man. Rather than meeting formally in an office overflowing with attorneys, Pete would have a nice lunch with network executives and present our position. For CBS, this turned out to be one of the most expensive lunches in the history of food. Pete told me later that the CBS people had been extremely polite when he told them how much we wanted for the rights. When they fell on the floor, he said, they did so very quietly.

After a few weeks of negotiating with CBS, we'd reached an impasse. Pete called me and said that CBS's projections were substantially lower than ours, and that they were claiming they couldn't afford to pay anything near what we were asking.

Oh, they were using the old "We can't afford it" ploy. That was so old that Adam had used it when Eve asked him for a new fig leaf. Unless, of course, CBS really couldn't afford it. It was just a question of whose numbers were more accurate, and since we were both making predictions, there was absolutely no way of knowing that. I knew how we'd arrived at our figures, and they made good business sense to me. I felt CBS was playing a game of "negotiating chicken." If I hadn't played chicken when I decided to close Minnie Pearl, I certainly wasn't going to give in to the network. "Pete," I told the commissioner, "go ahead and make me the heavy. Tell them that I'm representing the owners and your job is to satisfy the owners and that I won't budge one dollar. Say whatever you want to say, but tell them that Klein told you that if you accept their offer, he was going to file a minority report recommending that we turn it down."

The delay in concluding negotiations was beginning to make some other owners nervous. My telephone began ringing more frequently. No one, however, suggested we might be asking too much. They didn't know what we were asking, but they did know it couldn't be too much.

Negotiations remained stalled. Then one day Gene Jankowski, president of CBS, called and asked if we might discuss the problem personally. I invited him out to my home in Palm Springs. When he arrived, we sat by the pool, watching golfers stroll by on the nearby course, and casually chatted about several hundred million dollars. His people had examined and reexamined the figures, Gene explained, and there was just no way CBS could pay what we were asking. Gene Jankowski is a very astute businessman and an excellent negotiator. But I must admit I wasn't moved to tears of sympathy for the network.

I had also looked at the figures. My bottom line added up differently from his bottom line. So, when he finished explaining his position, I asked, "Does that mean you don't want to televise the NFL?"

"That's not what I said, Gene. Of course we do."

"Well, then," I told him, "this is what it's going to cost you. We can sit here for a day, a week, or a month, but these are the numbers. This is equivalent to what the other shops are paying. You either take it or you don't." I was very firm. I did not give him the impression that those numbers were negotiable. That's where being secure, confident, even arrogant, comes in. Of course, Jankowski gave me the firm impression that CBS would not possibly accept those numbers. He too was secure, confident, even arrogant. That's what made negotiating with him so much fun for me. I'm not sure how he felt about it.

Our meeting was cordial, but finally Jankowski sighed and said, "I can't believe this, but I really don't think we're going to be able to make a deal."

Oh, the old sigh-and-walk-away ploy. "Well, I think you know I'm sorry about that. I want you to know that I have the utmost respect for CBS and for you, and this doesn't make me any happier than it does you, believe me. But I'm sure the network'll survive without the NFL and I know the NFL'll survive without CBS."

"What are you going to do?"

It was kind of him to be concerned about our welfare. "Oh, don't worry about that," I reassured him, "we'll figure out something. I wish we could have gotten together, but I appreciate your position and I hope you understand mine. If the numbers don't add up for you, there's nothing you can do. Personally, I think you're doing the right thing if that's the case."

He left without making a proposal, but at least we were dancing. I didn't think they would meet our asking price, but I suspected they would come pretty close. I refused to believe that CBS would be willing to give up pro football. That was the one thing they really couldn't afford.

Pete Rozelle called a few days later with Jankowski's new offer. It was in the ballpark, still in the bleachers, but in the ballpark. We came down a bit, they came up a little, we came down a little more, they came up even less, but eventually we reached an agreement. The final package was worth $2.1 billion, or about $65 million a team. In the final year of the contract each team would receive $16.2 million. I'd paid only $10 million for the entire franchise, and now I was getting $16.2 million for the broadcast rights for just one season. It seemed like a good deal to me.

The only person not satisfied with the final package was my good friend Al Davis. During the *USFL* v. *NFL* trial, while testifying for the USFL, Davis contended that we had actually left money on the table. He claimed we could have gotten even more money. Well, I searched that table pretty good. I even looked underneath. If there was any money there, I certainly didn't see it. Two point one billion dollars is a pretty good haul, but I believed both the league and the networks had made a good deal.

Okay, so I was wrong.

What happened was that, although our ratings temporarily sagged, then bounced back and turned out to be excellent, advertisers rebelled. They refused to pay the prices the networks needed to get in order to generate a profit. To sell all their commercial spots, the networks had to discount their rate cards. In effect, they had to put air time on sale. So, the Broadcast Committee was wrong. Everyone makes a mistake or two billion.

Unfortunately, this is going to make it very difficult for the league to negotiate its new television contract. In addition, all three networks are under new management: Capitol Cities, known to be a very conservative company, now owns ABC; General Electric, a company that still hasn't figured out how to get Talaria working, bought NBC; and Laurence Tisch controls CBS. Since the owners have found ways to spend every penny of their TV revenue, and have made commitments based on that income, if the new Broadcast Committee fails to get at least the same money from the networks, a number of teams are going to be in serious financial difficulty.

When I think of the difficult negotiations ahead, when I think of the impending financial problems, one thought comes to mind: Thank you, Alex.

5

Soon after buying the Chargers I drove out to our training camp to watch my team practice. The business aspect of the deal had been completed, and this was my first opportunity to really savor the ultimate adult male fantasy: The San Diego Chargers were a professional football team, and they were playing with my football.

The offense and defense were scrimmaging when I got there. I stood on the sidelines for a few plays, then ambled onto the field near my head coach, Sid Gillman. We were standing perhaps 10 yards behind the line of scrimmage. As the teams lined up to run another play, Gillman suggested, "Maybe we'd better step back a little."

Who'd he think I was, some wimpy business executive? I was the owner; it was my team, my practice field, my football. I could stand anywhere I wanted to stand. This was about as good a time as any to remind Gillman of that fact. "That's all right," I said, jamming my hands into my back pockets, "I'm okay here."

The quarterback began shouting signals: "Huthuthut . . ." His voice was loud and clear and very close. I felt like I was right in the middle of the action. Exactly why I'd bought the team. Then the ball was snapped.

The offensive and defensive lines smashed together. "RRRRG-GGGHHHH!" "AAAHHHHGGGG!" "NNNMMMMMMMAHG!"

The linemen sounded as if they were auditioning for the lead role in a monster film. The quarterback dropped back a few yards to pass. Gillman and I moved back a few steps. Blockers formed a protective pocket around the quarterback. It was just as I'd seen countless times from the stands, except that I was in the middle of it. We dropped back a few more steps.

Suddenly, a defensive player sprinted around the end of the line and started circling behind the quarterback—he was coming right at us. At us? At me! This player's eyes were riveted on the quarterback; we were just another obstacle to be swept out of his way. Nothing was going to stop him, certainly not an executive. I started backing up fast, very fast, faster than Gillman.

At the last possible instant, the player cut inside. Just as he was about to cream the quarterback, a blocker saw him, turned, and smashed a forearm into the side of his helmet, knocking him aside.

The quarterback threw the pass. It dropped incomplete.

Gillman blew his whistle. I breathed. On the line players began untangling themselves. For the first time I had some idea of the incredible force, the violence, the brutality, that occurs on every play. And these were teammates, friends—I couldn't even imagine what it would be like when they were playing against another team. And I couldn't wait to find out. This was just great. "All right, all right," Gillman shouted, clapping his hands, "let's do it again, and this time, let's try to get it right."

The offensive and defensive teams lined up again. It was my practice field, my team, my football—and it was also my life. I could stand anywhere I wanted to stand—and where I wanted to stand was about 15 yards farther back. And this is how I began my initiation into the world of professional football.

Every owner runs his franchise differently. Some are intimately involved in the day-to-day operations of the team, others rarely even show up for the games. I remember going into a team's locker room with its owner after that team had beaten the Chargers. A running back had played an outstanding game and I wanted to congratulate him. The owner searched unsuccessfully for him, but I spotted him stripping down in front of his locker. I walked over to introduce myself. The owner followed me over, then said, quite surprised, "You can't be so-and-so, you're not black." This owner had never met one of his team's better players.

About the only thing my good friend Al Davis doesn't do for the Raiders, on the other hand, is play. Once, when Wayne Valley and Davis were fighting for control of the team, the Raiders played in Kansas City. Lamar Hunt tactfully gave Valley and Davis separate booths from which to watch the game. In the first half of the game, by Valley's count, runners made twenty-eight trips from Davis's booth to the field, carrying plays to be used.

John Mecom went even further than Davis. He did play, in practice at least. Mecom used to work out with his Saints, once breaking a few fingers trying to catch a punt. For a businessman, broken fingers are a serious injury. Mecom also played the role of a third-string quarterback in the Charlton Heston feature film about pro football, *The Pro.*

When Jack Kent Cooke was still living in Los Angeles he had little to do with the operation of the Washington Redskins, but he would occasionally skate around the ice with his National Hockey League team, the Los Angeles Kings. Everyone believed that the Canadian-born Cooke enjoyed the Kings more than the Redskins, and I know he was frustrated by the Kings' failure to draw well. "There are eight hundred thousand Canadians living in the Los Angeles area," he once complained, "and I've just discovered why they left Canada. They hate hockey."

Owners choose to watch their teams play games from various vantage points. Normally, for example, Vikings owner Max Winter was very calm, very much in control. He made Ralph Wilson seem nervous. One Monday night, however, Minnesota was playing the Rams in Los Angeles and I went to the game. Max and I were sitting in the press box. Actually, I was sitting; Max was pacing back and forth. The Vikings were losing by a few points in the fourth quarter and Max was sweating. "I can't take this anymore," he kept repeating, "I just can't take it."

"Sit down, Max," I suggested, "just relax."

"I can't relax," he said. "How can I relax? I can't watch, I can't watch." And with that, he left the stadium and went out to the parking lot to listen to the end of the game in his car. The Vikings blocked a punt with seconds remaining and scored a touchdown to win the game, but Max never saw it. Ironically, Max couldn't enjoy the game because he owned the team; if he hadn't owned it, he probably would have enjoyed the game much more. So much for the pleasures of owning a professional team.

Bud Adams watches the Oilers' games from his glass-enclosed private box in Houston's Astrodome. Every time the Oilers scored, Adams would lead all his guests in a conga line. They would snake around the private box, holding onto the hips of the person in front of them. I suppose that was why Bud Adams was known as pro football's King Conga. (Fifteen-yard penalty for hitting the punner.)

Although most owners watch their teams from private boxes, some prefer to be on the field. When people complained that an owner didn't belong on the field, John Mecom replied, "If I'd wanted a seat in the stands, I could have bought one for twelve dollars."

The first few years I owned the Chargers I roamed the sidelines during our games. I learned that when you're six feet five and own a winning football team, you're generally referred to as "tall," but when you're six five and own a losing football team, you are what is known as a "big target." I didn't have to be on the sidelines to have people screaming insults at me—I could have had that anywhere. So, when we installed new skyboxes in San Diego Stadium, I watched our games from there, often going down to the field for the last few plays.

It was probably a good thing that I got off the field. I used to get so emotionally wrapped up in the games that I came close to losing control. One Sunday, I remember, we were playing Minnesota in a preseason game. It was a meaningless game. But just after our quarterback, Johnny Hadl, threw a long pass, a Vikings lineman smashed him in the face with an elbow. He just knocked him silly. It was a late hit and I was sure it was deliberate. Instantly, every player on our bench grabbed his helmet and started running onto the field. I took off with them. I was in the middle of the pack—we had a pretty slow team—when suddenly I thought, How crazy am I? Who am I gonna fight? I knew that if I tried to hit a professional football player wearing his protective equipment, one of two things was going to happen: Either I was going to get hurt, or I was going to get hurt bad. I stopped running and did what generals and owners are supposed to do. I started waving forward the players still behind me.

It's almost impossible not to get caught up in the excitement on the sidelines of a pro-football game. During the New Orleans Saints' first season, they were playing the Giants at Yankee Stadium when a brawl started. Owner John Mecom raced onto the field with his players. Giants rookie Freeman White took a wild swipe with his helmet at Mecom. Mecom deftly sidestepped the helmet, then dropped White to the turf with a single right hook to his stomach. If anyone ever catalogs *The Greatest Moments in Owner History,* this will have to be included. Believe me, there isn't an owner in professional football who hasn't had the urge to deck a player at some point. Usually, though, it's one of his own players.

Patriots general manager Patrick Sullivan was not quite as agile as Mecom. After New England had beaten the Los Angeles Raiders for the 1985 AFC championship, Pat got into an argument with the Raiders' Howie Long. Matt Millen then hit Sullivan with his helmet, bringing the all-time score to: Players with Helmets 1, Owners Without Checkbooks 1.

I was quite happy in my private box. I'd cheer, yell, curse, drink a little, eat a little, curse, entertain my guests, complain. I wasn't at all superstitious, although if I was sitting a certain way and something good happened, I'd probably stay that way until something bad happened. Of course, I was too sophisticated to believe that the way I was sitting made any difference, but you never know. There were times when I was pretty desperate.

The most difficult thing for an owner to do is resist the urge to coach his team. With the exception of my good friend Al Davis, George Halas, and a few other people, owners are not football experts. I certainly didn't have the qualifications to be a coach. I didn't have the experience to be a coach. I didn't have the knowledge to be a coach. I didn't have the temperament to be a coach. I didn't even want to be a coach—not when I could be the Monday morning quarterback.

I never told my coach what to do during a game, although once I did come close. In 1976, we'd obtained quarterback Clint Longley from the Dallas Cowboys. I really believed he could play. But my head coach, Tommy Prothro, didn't have as much confidence in Longley as I did, and didn't want to play him. Late in the season we were playing Denver in San Diego. We'd lost our last three games to bring our season record to 4-5. It was the fourth quarter, and we were losing, 17–0. I thought it would be a perfect time to put in Longley. It would have been a perfect time to put in Klein. What was Longley going to do, embarrass us? We didn't need him for that—we'd proved we could do that without him. The worst thing he could do was nothing, which was exactly what our other quarterbacks had done. But when we got the ball back, Prothro sent Dan Fouts back into the game.

Up in my private box, I was furious. I was yelling, screaming, cursing, just as usual. Finally, I couldn't take it anymore. I decided to call down to the field and order Prothro to play Longley. I reached for the telephone, and almost had my hand on it, when I saw my son, Michael, watching me. He knew exactly what I intended to do. Maybe he shook his head slightly, maybe I just imagined he did, but I knew what he was thinking: If I told Prothro who to play, what I was really telling him was that I'd lost confidence in his ability to run the team. I knew I was right, but I also knew Michael was more right. I'd spent my entire business career hiring executives and letting them do their jobs. I never told a foreman how to construct a portable office, a director how to make films, or Minnie Pearl how to fry chicken. So I was not about to tell Tommy Prothro how to coach a football team. At least I was not about to get caught telling Tommy Prothro how to coach a football team. I took my hand off the telephone.

Bob Irsay couldn't resist. He would sit up in a skybox with his assistant coaches calling plays down to the field. The assistant coaches finally got so irritated they pulled the plug out of the phone. Once, though, when Irsay couldn't get through to his head coach, Howard Schnellenberger, and he wanted Schnellenberger to put in quarterback Marty Domres, he went down to the field during the game and ordered him to do it. Howard Schnellenberger refused, and the two of them started screaming at each other in front of the entire team. In the locker room after the game Schnellenberger quit and Irsay fired him. Neither man had any choice. Irsay had destroyed Schnellenberger's credibility with his players.

The closest most owners get to actually coaching their team is hiring the head coach. I inherited one head coach, rehired him, hired five more, and eventually fired five of them. So that sort of makes me an expert on hiring head coaches. What makes a good head coach? If I knew the answer to that question, I wouldn't have had to hire six of them.

Perhaps Vince Lombardi had the right idea. In 1965, George Allen left the Chicago Bears and was hired by Dan Reeves to coach the Rams. At an owners' meeting, Bears owner George Halas told Reeves that "George Allen is a liar, a cheat, and a no good S.O.B."

Lombardi, sitting next to Reeves, heard that and turned to him and said, "It looks to me like you've got yourself a winning coach."

Reeves eventually learned what Halas meant. A few years later he told me, "It was more fun to lose under my previous coach than win with George Allen."

I tried one of practically every type. Sid Gillman was my old pro, the head coach with the most experience. He finished third in a four-team division each of the five seasons he coached for me. Gillman later became one of an elite group of men to be fired by three different professional football leagues. Harland Svare was a former star player, assistant coach, head coach, and football executive. He was also my friend. He led the Chargers to two consecutive losing seasons, including a 2-11-1 record in 1973. The best judge of raw football talent was former college and pro head coach Tommy Prothro, a brilliant life master in bridge, who helped rebuild the Chargers, but in doing so tied an NFL record with eleven consecutive losses. Our most successful head coach was Don Coryell, who once admitted, "Sometimes I can't even spell my own name," and was so obsessed with football that'd he literally bounce off walls while walking down a hallway. Coryell led the Chargers to three consecutive championships.

As a business executive, my primary function was setting corporate policy, then hiring people capable of implementing that policy. When hiring, we investigated the background of every candidate, I read their résumés and their letters of recommendation, I interviewed them, and in the end, it usually came down to playing a hunch. I just got a feeling about people. National General succeeded because we hired the right people, then let them do the job we hired them to do.

I thought I could do the same thing in pro football. Each time a head coach had to be replaced I'd sit down with my general manager and we'd make out a list of suspects. These were people who had an excellent reputation in football or men I'd met who had impressed me. The only qualification I demanded was professional coaching experience. I didn't believe a college coach could instantly make the transition to pro football.

For example, I didn't hire Don Coryell, who'd made San Diego State a national collegiate power, until he'd led Billy Bidwill's St. Louis Cardinals to the playoffs three out of five years. Most other owners agreed with me—the transition from college to pro was almost impossible, although there were exceptions. Joe Robbie once hired the University of Alabama's immortal Bear Bryant to coach the Dolphins. Bryant accepted the job on the condition that Alabama Governor George Wallace, the board of trustees of the university, and his family approve. The trustees agreed to release Bryant from his contract, provided that he could find a better coach to take over for him at Alabama.

For a man with Bryant's ego, that was like asking him to produce dry raindrops. Robbie settled for Don Shula.

Practically every man who'd seen a football game believed he was qualified to become a head coach. When Robbie founded the Dolphins, for example, he received applications for the job from a hotel clerk, a Pittsburgh trash collector, even an itinerant evangelist. When Chuck Sullivan was searching for a new head coach, he said that of all the applications he got, "the one that impressed me most came from an eleven-year-old girl in Swampscott." I was constantly getting letters from people who had coached Pop Warner league teams or high school teams to a number of consecutive titles and had been watching pro-football games for years and knew they could turn the Chargers into a winning football team. Occasionally wives would write, telling me that their husbands would make great head coaches, although one woman admitted she really just wanted to get him out of the house on weekends. But if a candidate did not have professional coaching experience, I wouldn't consider hiring him.

After narrowing down the list of potential head coaches, I'd invite the serious candidates in for a personal interview. The first question I'd ask was, What makes you think you can be a head coach in the National Football League? Too often, the answers sounded like these people had written the letters to me. One successful assistant coach told me sincerely, "Believe me, Gene, I know I can do a good job." When I asked him how he could be so sure, he replied, "I dreamed it." He did not get the job.

Only once did a recommendation help me make up my mind about a coach. After firing Harland Svare, I was considering former Rams coach Tommy Prothro as his replacement. Rams owner Carroll Rosenbloom told me that Tommy Prothro was absolutely the last man I should consider for the job. Coming from Carroll, I considered that a strong endorsement. I offered the job to Prothro the next day.

As a fan, I had always assumed there was some sort of complicated process that owners and general managers went through before finally selecting a head coach. In fact, there is no formula for picking a person to do a job, in portable-office building or in professional football. In the final analysis, it comes down to a gut feeling. Sometimes I was right, sometimes I was wrong. I hired Tommy Prothro instead of Don Coryell; Wellington Mara hired Allie Sherman rather than Vince Lombardi. The difference between portable-office building and football, however, is that fifty-two thousand people don't pay twenty dollars every Sunday to see if you've hired the right man to put up an office.

Fortunately, I was right more often than I was wrong about people, even about Ted, my first employee at Quality Motors. Except for the fact he was stealing from me, he did an excellent job. Only once did I make a really bad mistake in judgment. A very bad, very expensive mistake. In 1973, an art dealer sold me a Modigliani for $250,000. The dealer then requested my permission to let the painting hang in a museum show. I agreed. About a month later, he called to tell me he could resell it for $100,000 more than I'd paid for it. We split the profit evenly. The dealer then suggested we go into business; I would buy paintings on his recommendation, he would resell them, and we would split the profit. That quickly, I was in the art business. I trusted this dealer so much, in fact, that I tried to convince my son, Michael, by then a vice-president at Bear Stearns, to give up the investment business and become a partner in our art business.

We began buying paintings. Everything was fine until I visited the Los Angeles Museum of Art. Hanging there was another painting I'd bought, but the plaque beneath it attributed ownership to my dealer's gallery. Naturally, I informed the museum of their error. And that is when I discovered that my partner, whom I'd trusted, with whom I wanted my son to go into business, was a crook. He was selling the same painting to four, five, even six people. As long as he got enough money from his latest customer to satisfy a past owner, and as long as no one insisted on hanging it in his or her home, he could continue to sell it. So, compared to giving him several hundred thousand dollars to invest in paintings, hiring the wrong football coach was not such a serious mistake. It was certainly a less expensive mistake.

Once I decided who I wanted to hire, I never had a problem signing him. My philosophy, in business as well as in football, was that if you wanted something of value, you paid what it was worth. Unless, of course, you can make a better deal. The way I always negotiated, whether I was selling a used car or signing a head coach, was to ask the person to whom I was selling to name his price. How much would he pay, how much does he want. People tend to know exactly what they're worth, and if they'll be satisfied with less than I was willing to pay them, I certainly was not going to haggle. Usually, though, the salary they asked for was competitive with what other people doing a similar job were being paid. When I bought the team, head coaches in the NFL were getting $35,000 to $45,000 a season. By the time I hired Coryell, head coaches were being paid as much as $600,000—and assistant coaches were getting $100,000.

The old pro Sid Gillman already had a valid contract when I took control of the team, but after we'd won our first four games I extended his contract an additional five years and doubled his salary. Not that I was overly enthusiastic, but if the Chargers hadn't lost five of our next seven games, Gillman might still have thirty or forty years to go in his contract. As it was, he assumed his contract was for life. I did too, as long as he didn't live more than five years.

Every owner felt differently about the length of the contract a head coach should have. It had to be long enough to allow him to feel it was his team, but not so long that it allowed him to believe it was his team. When Robbie hired Don Shula, reporters asked him if he had guaranteed Shula enough time to turn the Dolphins into a winning football team. "Absolutely," Robbie said. "He's got all summer."

Probably the most accurate response to that question was given by John Mecom. When he hired Dick Nolan, he was asked how long Nolan had been signed for. "Long enough to win," Mecom replied. In Nolan's case, that turned out to be two and a half years.

During my first few years in football, Sid Gillman proved to be the best head coach I'd ever had; he was also the only head coach I'd ever had. Gillman turned out to be extremely impulsive; when he made a decision he would stick to it firmly, at least until he changed his mind. Then he'd stick to his new opinion just as firmly. He was liable to change his mind at any time, for any reason. Once, I remember, we drafted a center named Bill Lenkaitis in the second round. Gillman raved about his ability, claiming that he would make the team strong at the center position for the next decade. Lenkaitis made one bad play that completely soured Gillman on him; we put him on waivers and New England claimed him. Gillman had been right—the Patriots were strong at the center position for the next decade.

Since I had no comparative basis on which to judge Gillman, I thought every head coach in pro football had "ten players coming, ten players going, and ten in mind," as he often claimed. Gillman was a strong authority figure, a tough man, and he never let his players feel too secure around him. He wanted his players to be worried about keeping their jobs; he believed that made them perform better. His basic philosophy of coaching was "A professional football team is like my wife's wardrobe, constantly changing," and as long as he worked for me we were always "just one or two players away" from being a strong contender. As I later realized, those two players were Jimmy Brown in his prime and Superman.

Gillman and I got along very well for the first few years. He had me just where he wanted me—in Los Angeles. As head coach and general manager, he was running the team on a day-today basis, although we did confer on every move. Gillman did the perfect coaching job for me the first three years—each year he won one more game than the year before. "We're getting there," he kept telling me. We won seven games in 1966, eight games in 1967, nine games in 1968, just good enough for me to really believe we were improving, but not good enough for us to actually contend for the division championship. Finally, in 1969, when ten wins would have made us a serious contender, doctors forced Gillman to resign as head coach because of an ulcer.

Gillman, who told reporters, "I'll never coach the Chargers again," remained as general manager. Assistant coach Charlie Waller replaced him as head coach for a season and a half. When the team won only five games in 1970, Gillman's ulcer had healed sufficiently for him to return to the sidelines. Sure enough, in 1971 we won six games—although Gillman didn't survive the entire season as head coach.

The agreement that Gillman and I had made when I bought the team was that we would discuss every player transaction, and no moves would be made unless we both agreed. We had made a big trade for wide receiver Jerry LeVias, giving up two players for him. LeVias turned out to be a major disappointment. Gillman had him rated fifth on his depth chart; we only had five wide receivers. October 26 was the NFL's trading deadline; after 1 P.M. that day players could not be traded. One hour before the deadline I got a frantic call from Kansas City Chiefs coach and general manager Hank Stram. "Gene," he said, "I don't understand what's going on. I offered Gillman a first-round draft choice for LeVias and he won't give me an answer. He won't even return my calls. You think we can make a deal?"

A number-one pick for a wide receiver who had less chance of playing regularly than I did? The most important thing to do in such situations is to remain calm and try to complete the deal before they put Stram back inside the locked gates. "It's something to think about, Hank," I said. "Let me talk to Sid. I'll get right back to you. Don't go 'way." Please, please, don't move.

The deal was almost unfair. In fact, if I hadn't spent years as a used-car dealer, it probably would have bothered me. Instead, I buzzed my secretary: "GET ME GILLMAN RIGHT AWAY!" We called our training camp at La Mesa and I was told that Gillman was on the field with the team. "Tell him I want to talk to him, please."

I waited. Someone finally picked up the phone. "Sid says he'll call you back right after practice."

After practice? After 1 P.M.? After the trading deadline had passed? "You tell Gillman to get his ass on the phone right now." A few moments later Gillman answered. "I got great news," I said, or something like that. "Hank Stram wants to give us a number-one pick for Jerry LeVias."

I expected Gillman to be at least as enthusiastic as I was. "I don't think so," he said calmly, "I don't want to trade him."

Not trade him? He was last on the depth chart. "He's just playing on special teams," I pointed out. "Here's a chance to get something for him."

Gillman was adamant. "Look," he said curtly, "it's my job that's at stake. My reputation. I don't care what Stram offers, I don't want to make a deal."

I slammed down the telephone. It's no fun being the boss unless you can be the boss, but there was nothing I could do about this. I'd made an agreement with Gillman, no deals unless we both approved, and I never reneged on an agreement. But a number-one pick for a man who wasn't playing?

Gillman later explained that he was concerned about hurting the morale of the squad. "How would a draft choice help us this season?" he asked.

About as much as a player sitting on the bench, I thought.

Gillman and I didn't speak for several weeks after that. This was the final year of his five-year contract, and I really hadn't decided if I wanted to rehire him. I'd never fired a head coach, and Gillman was still the best head coach I'd ever had. Only five coaches in pro-football history had compiled better lifetime records than he had, and he'd won an NFL division championship, five AFL division championships, and one AFL league title. In a decade as head coach of the Chargers, he'd only had one losing season. I was mad at him, but I also knew that only one coach in the league wins the final game of the season. As it turned out, I didn't have to fire him, he fired himself.

For weeks, San Diego sportswriters had been reporting that Gillman's job was in jeopardy. I knew that had to be true, because

I read it in the papers. I really hadn't made up my mind. But with four games left in the season, Gillman called me in Beverly Hills and said he had to see me right away. I invited him over that afternoon.

Gillman obviously believed what he read in the papers. After we'd discussed the team for a while, he told me, "Gene, I've got to know what my situation is. I've got to know where I stand for next year."

I told him the truth: I hadn't made a decision. "Tell you what, Sid," I said, "let's wait till the season's over, then we'll sit down and talk about it."

Gillman did not want to wait until the season was over. "I want an answer now," he snapped. "Today."

Here's an important football coaching tip to remember: Never make demands of the owner when your team has four wins and six losses and you've finished third five consecutive seasons. "Okay, Sid," I said, "you want your answer, you got it. You don't come in here and put a gun to my head. You're through. It's over." Gillman wanted to discuss it, I didn't. I'd made my decision and intended to stick to it. Who did he think I was, a pro-football coach?

At a press conference following the announcement, Gillman claimed I'd fired him when he asked me to extend his lifetime contract. Of course, if I were really capable of that, I should have been in a higher league than the National Football League. Then Gillman concluded, in a statement that should have made him a hero to every attorney, "I've got a message for the youth of America. Whenever anyone says you have a lifetime contract, tell him, 'Thank you, but put it in writing, please.'"

I too have a message for the youth of America. When anyone says you have a lifetime contract, ask for a big advance.

When Gillman's ulcer had caused him to temporarily retire in 1969, we had elevated assistant coach Charlie Waller to the head coaching job. As I was living in Los Angeles, I didn't have extensive contact with Waller. And when Gillman was able to coach again, Waller returned to his spot as an assistant.

A few months later I was surprised to receive a bill from Waller for about $20,000. Coaches usually ask for a bonus when they're hired, or when they win a championship, but rarely when they get demoted. "When I was made head coach," Waller explained when I questioned the bill, "I didn't have a projection room in my house to look at game and practice films. So I built an extra room and it cost me twenty thousand dollars. Now that I'm not the head coach anymore, I've still got this room and I think you should pay me for it."

I'm sure he also bought a new suit when he was promoted to head coach, but I didn't think I should pay for that either. Waller eventually filed a formal complaint with the commissioner's office. I imagine he still has his projection room, but I know I didn't pay for it.

Among the many things I learned from Sid Gillman was that one man cannot function as both general manager and head coach. It's impossible for a general manager to negotiate contracts with his players, which often requires a brutal assessment of their ability, and then go down to the field and try to convince those same players that the general manager doesn't know what he's talking about. So when Gillman returned to the sidelines as head coach, I hired Harland Svare to replace him as general manager.

I'd first met Harland Svare in 1956, when he came into my showroom to price an MG. Svare was a linebacker in the middle of an outstanding professional football career. In my showroom, though, Harland proved that there is no defense against a brand-new MG. In the vernacular of car salesmen, he was what is known as a "cherry," meaning that salespeople would kill their little pet dogs to get to him first. As soon as he walked into that showroom, it was obvious that he was going to leave with that car, no matter how hard we tried to sell it to him. So I raised the price $500 and sold it to him. From that point on, I watched with pleasure as he starred on the great New York Giants teams of the late 1950s, then became a defensive coach with the Giants, and finally head coach of the Los Angeles Rams. When the Rams hired him he was thirty-one years old, the youngest head coach in the National Football League.

Three and a half years later he became the youngest head coach to be fired in the National Football League.

When I was searching for a general manager to take over that job from Gillman, Rosey Grier suggested I speak to Svare. Harland became the first head coach or general manager that I actually hired, and we became close friends. Gillman was fired as head coach with only four games left in the dismal 1971 season, and Harland and I agreed that he might as well take over the team for the remainder of the season while we searched for a permanent head coach. We knew that we wanted to hire someone who had professional coaching experience, like Harland. We wanted somebody capable of rebuilding our defense, like Harland. We wanted somebody who would be able to relate to the players, perhaps a former player, like Harland. We wanted somebody with whom both of us could get along, like Harland. We wanted somebody who was available immediately, like . . . Whoa! Hold it. Suddenly I had this tremendous idea—hire Harland Svare.

What did I really know about hiring a head coach? The answer was absolutely nothing. I was a fan, an expert fan, but really just a fan. Harland Svare was my friend; he was a man of honesty and integrity, and he knew a lot more about football than I did.

Actually, he was quite happy as general manager, and I had to convince him to take the job. When we announced that he had accepted the job on a permanent basis, reporters asked me about the length of his contract. Once again, I proved I had learned a lot from Gillman. "He's entitled to a shot," I said noncommittally, "and he'll have more than one year."

Actually, before Harland agreed to take the job, we discussed experimenting with a totally new concept in head coaching—no head coach. Instead of having one man in complete control, we thought about dividing the responsibility between a head offensive coach and a head defensive coach. As we discussed it, we realized that the only reason no one had ever done it before was that it wouldn't work. Which coach would decide whether to go for a first down on fourth and inches in the fourth quarter? Which coach would decide when to attempt an onsides kick? We realized that the reason the top man is known as the head coach is that when the team goes badly his head is the one that gets chopped off.

There were people who claimed I picked Harland Svare because I knew I could control him. That theory said that when Gillman ran the team, Gillman ran the team, and that I wanted to take over. The problem with that premise is that I controlled every person who worked for me, from theater manager to vice-president. That's one of the main advantages of paying the salary rather than being paid. I certainly wasn't going to hire a head coach who wouldn't talk to me. I hired Harland Svare because I believed he was the right man to run the team at the time.

Harland Svare turned out to be the wrong man in the wrong job with the wrong team at the wrong time. Other than that, I'd made a fine selection. When he took over the Chargers, the team was in shambles. Our veteran players were too old and most of our younger players weren't very good. We tried a quick fix, trading for established veterans, but I learned that when you have nothing very good to trade, that's usually what you get in return. We ended up obtaining more veterans who couldn't play in exchange for our draft choices, putting us in the position of having traded away our future for a disastrous present. We finished last in 1972 and 1973.

I don't think any coach ever tried to understand his players the way Harland Svare did. That was probably his biggest mistake. Harland believed a team was an extended family and, like any family, its members should be treated with kindness. Instead, he proved that the human element in pro football is about as important as a nameplate on an ocean liner.

Only once, in all the time he was with the Chargers, did Harland lose his temper. We were playing Dallas in 1972 and trailing at halftime, 31–0. In the locker room during the half, Harland finally let go. He grabbed three different players, threw them up against the wall, and slapped them around. That shocked the team so much that we came back in the third quarter and scored four straight touchdowns. Of course, we still lost, 34–28. After that game I gave Harland a five-year contract extension.

In 1973, the Chargers went 2-11-1, the worst record in our history. We also became involved in the drug scandal that led to my $20,000 fine. After each loss that season, the situation in San Diego got more ominous. SACK SVARE and HANG HARLAND signs appeared all over the stadium. The press was merciless. All four tires on Harland's car were flattened and he had to start parking it inside the stadium for safety. Once, when I was leaving the ballpark after another loss, people began rocking my car and slapping HANG HARLAND stickers on the windows. Harland's wife couldn't go out of her house without being insulted. I'd go into a Baskin-Robbins ice cream store and ask for a vanilla cone, and instead the salesperson would give me an argument. Can you imagine what it feels like to be booed at the gas station?

An optimist might say that at least people were showing an interest in the team, but to a realist it was obvious I had to fire Svare.

I'd told reporters that he was entitled to a shot—I didn't say he was entitled to be shot. Things had gotten so bad, I was seriously concerned for the safety of our players and coaches and owner. Pro football is an extremely violent sport, in the stands as well as on the field. Who could predict when some nut, who had had too much to drink, and was stimulated by the ugly mood of the crowd, might climb out of the stands and go after someone? As it was, a few fans were throwing beer bottles, liquor bottles, anything that wasn't bolted down, at our players and coaches. It became obvious that the situation had gotten out of control when our players had to put on their helmets after the game to get to the locker room. I think probably the only positive thing to be said about fans drinking at a ballpark is that it spoils their aim.

Harland and I were close friends—we're still close friends—and much of what happened was not his fault. I had hired him. The ultimate responsibility was mine. And I had to fire him.

The ideal way to fire an employee is to do so during an argument *he* initiates, even if you have to force him to initiate it. But Harland and I had never had a real argument. After that, the best way to fire someone is to convince him that leaving is really his idea. Harland is not a quitter. Then, there is always the possibility that the employee can be convinced he is being fired for his own good. In this case that was true, although it was for my good too. Harland was not going to believe that. That left honesty. Honesty is always the most difficult way. Telling someone that they are not good enough to do the job is one of the toughest things to do in business.

After we'd lost 19–0 to a bad Kansas City team, Harland and I sat down together. We spoke about some changes he was considering, and finally I had to tell him. "Harland," I said, "we just can't keep going like this. It isn't working. This is hurting the club, it's hurting you, I've just got to make a change." The fact that he would remain with the club as general manager made my task a bit easier, but not much.

Firing Harland was the best thing I could have done for him. He could leave his house again without being abused. He could go to the stadium without people cursing at him and throwing things at him. Plus the fact that he eventually became a millionaire by selling real estate in the San Diego area, which certainly would not have happened if I hadn't been wise enough to fire him.

Assistant coach Ron Waller took charge for the final six games of the season, making us the only pro-football team in history to have Waller-to-Waller head coaches. But I didn't hire Waller just to complete a bad pun. I hired him because it was an absolutely impossible job and somebody had to do it. Another Chargers assistant coach, former Green Bay star Forrest Gregg, complained that he should have been given the job.

"I would have given it to you," I told him, "but I like you too much. I didn't want to ruin your career." Not giving someone a promotion because I didn't want to hurt his career was a novel excuse, but in this instance an accurate one. "This team's going nowhere," I continued, "and if I gave it to you, it'd be a black mark against you." As it turned out, I was right. Waller lost five of six games, and Gregg eventually became a fine head coach at Cleveland. And Cincinnati. And Green Bay.

Ron Waller was a very enthusiastic coach. As head of our special teams, he had instituted an incentive award system for his players. If a special-team player tackled a ball carrier within our opponent's 20-yard line, for example, he would receive a color television set. Fortunately for our budget, we were so bad that we had people earning crystal sets.

I interviewed about fifteen candidates for Svare's job, among them Tommy Prothro, who had been a very successful college coach at Oregon State and UCLA, and had coached the Rams for two years. Before I offered him the head coaching job he told me bluntly, "The only way you can rebuild this team is to draft young players and play them. That means we're gonna lose. Believe me, it's going to be terrible, but that's the only way these people can get the experience they need."

"I'm behind you, Tommy," I told him. A day later he accepted the job.

We had been 2-11-1 in 1973; that didn't leave us a lot of room to be more terrible. If a business I owned had performed as badly as the team, I would have shut it down to prevent additional losses, as I did with National Telefilm and Minnie Pearl. But in pro football, losing does not cost a team a substantial amount of money. We still received our share of the television revenue, which was our primary source of income, and our salary structure actually improved as we replaced highly paid veterans with rookies. So, financially at least, losing was not an important factor.

When Minnie Pearl failed few people blamed me personally. But when the Chargers collapsed, everybody blamed me. I wasn't used to failing so publicly. It hurt. That, coming after the death of my first wife, made me decide that as long as I was going to get the blame, I might as well take the responsibility. At the end of the 1973 season I made my commitment to pro football. I sold my house in Los Angeles, I sold National General, moved to San Diego, built a house, built an office in San Diego Stadium, and took over day-to-day control of the team. I intended to turn the situation around and I intended to do it quickly.

We lost our first eleven games in 1975. "I knew we were going to lose," Tommy admitted, "but I didn't know we were going to lose this much."

I was still behind him, but I tried standing a little farther back. It was even worse than he warned me it would be. Eleven losses in a row. Even the New Orleans Saints had never lost eleven games in a row. For a game against the Patriots we drew only twenty-four thousand fans, our worst attendance in a decade. Fans were canceling their season tickets in advance. Normally, at the end of the season our public-relations department put out a promotional highlight film available to almost any group upon request. We had so few highlights that year we could have barely put together a highlight photograph. So we retitled our 1975 film *Charger Lowlights*, and included the misplays, blunders, and fumbles of the season. The real difficulty we had was in cutting down the running time of the film. It turned out to be funnier than some of the comedies we'd produced at National General.

I'm able to laugh at that film now.

The championships we would win a few years later were due primarily to the work done by Tommy Prothro during his more than four years as head coach. He built that team. He played our young draft choices, suffered through their mistakes, and accepted the criticism. But Tommy was an administrator, not a motivator.

Even in pro football a head coach has to inspire his players occasionally. Tommy believed professional athletes should be inspired by their paychecks. If Harland tried to treat his players as if they were part of an extended family, Tommy treated them as if they were the black sheep of that family. He just didn't believe in getting too close to his team, a philosophy he had learned while working for the great UCLA head coach Red Sanders, who said of his players, "I'm too busy coaching 'em to court 'em."

Tommy had this crazy idea that he could treat professional football players like adults. I don't know where he got that idea—certainly not from me. I remember one defensive lineman, for example, who took himself out of a game. As he trotted to the sidelines, Tommy went over to him and asked with concern, "What's the matter, something hurt, something broken?" Why else would a player take himself out of a game?

"No, nothing like that, coach," the player replied. "My stomach is sloshing."

Some veteran players were not used to being responsible for their own actions, and resented Prothro. One veteran star, finishing his career with the Chargers, told reporters, "There's nothing I wouldn't do for Tommy Prothro, and I believe there's nothing he wouldn't do for me. And that's how we spent the whole season, doing nothing for each other."

Tommy was just too honest for pro football. At the team meeting the day before we opened the 1975 season against the Pittsburgh Steelers, for example, he told the squad, "If each of you goes out there and plays the best game you'll ever play, if each of you plays over your head, and if each of them plays the worst game they'll ever play, the worst game of their lives, we still don't have a chance."

That's not a speech that is often included in collections of inspirational literature, but Tommy just didn't believe in telling his players something that everybody knew wasn't true. We couldn't beat Pittsburgh, and the next day we went out and proved it, losing 37–0. No one had to play the greatest game of his life for us to lose, either.

Tommy liked to pick his spots. The only time I ever knew him to make an inspirational speech was before the final game of the 1976 season. We were playing the Raiders, a team he really disliked because of their style of play. "I very rarely have ever asked a team to win a game for me," he said, "but I'm asking you guys today . . . because Oakland is a dirty, cheating ball club . . . and I hate them." Which goes to prove that inspirational speeches can be of tremendous value, as long as your players are bigger, stronger, and better. We lost that game too, 42–0.

By 1978, Tommy had become a victim of his own talents. "If I have an ability in coaching," he'd told me, "it's teaching, not strategy." Tommy had picked a group of aggressive, inexperienced young players and molded them into a team capable of winning championships. The fans, and the owner, expected them to win. But they didn't win, at least not with any consistency.

"There's a stick of dynamite here," one player complained to a reporter, "but no one's lighting the fuse." After the Packers beat us 24–3 to bring our record to 1-3, Tommy spent much of the evening alone, watching game films. Then he called me and said he felt that the team needed a fresh approach, "a rude awakening." I didn't try to talk him out of it. Tommy, my new general manager, Johnny Sanders, and I met at 5:00 Monday morning and Tommy offered to resign. I asked him to stay with the team and work with us in evaluating and drafting players. "You can have any title you want," I told him.

He considered it, then decided his presence would make the new head coach nervous, so he turned me down. Had he known who the new head coach was going to be, he might have felt a bit differently—spending a weekend at the Bates Motel wouldn't have made Don Coryell nervous.

Prothro had done an excellent job, but the job had changed. This was a team ready to win, and there was no question who I would hire to replace Prothro. In twelve years as head coach at San Diego State, Don Coryell had compiled a 104-19-2 record, including three undefeated seasons, then he'd coached the St.

Louis Cardinals for five years, getting them into the playoffs three times. I'd often wondered if I'd made a mistake hiring Svare instead of Coryell to replace Gillman, but I was an inexperienced owner at that time and I didn't feel confident enough to hire an inexperienced pro coach.

Coryell was a local hero, he was a proven winner, and he was unemployed, although technically still under contract to the Cardinals. I didn't have to hire Don Coryell; I didn't have to have any people in the ballpark during games either, which is what would have happened if I hadn't offered him the job.

Do fans influence the way an owner runs his team? Only if that owner wants to make money. They may be called fans, but they are really customers, and unless an owner is bothered by too much noise during games, he has to do everything possible to foster the emotional relationship between his team and these customers. Sometimes that isn't easy. In Atlanta, for example, Falcons fans forced Rankin Smith to fire head coach Norm Van Brocklin. After the team lost its first game under new head coach Marion Campbell, banners demanding, BRING BACK VAN BROCKLIN appeared.

In my situation, though, Don Coryell was the right man for the right job with the right team at the right time. Tommy Prothro resigned at 5 A.M. I immediately called Coryell. "This is Gene Klein," I said when he answered, "what are you doing?"

It was 6 A.M. "Not too much, right now," he said.

So much for formalities. "How'd you like to go to work today?"

Coryell knew why I was calling him, and decided to play hard to get. "Boy," he said enthusiastically, "I'd love to." By 10:00, I'd given the Cardinals a third-round draft choice for the right to sign Coryell. It was more than I wanted to give them, but less than they could have gotten from me. In this situation, I was the "cherry."

Don Coryell was the absolute opposite of Tommy Prothro. Tommy had been a subdued, conservative coach who stressed defense; Coryell's philosophy of football could be best summed up as "Give me the ball last." He seemed to believe that the primary function of our defensive team was to stay on the field long enough to give the offense a brief rest. I remember arriving at practice one afternoon and immediately thinking something had to be wrong—Coryell was working with the defense.

Supposedly, when Coryell was an undergraduate student at the University of Washington, he did a lot of boxing. He used a windmill style, charging across the ring, throwing a lot of punches, taking a lot of punches, hoping for the one-punch knockout. A lot of people believe this is where he got his basic football strategy. Of course, other people believe he got hit in the head too much.

Coryell was a tremendous inspirational leader. The day he took over he made a long speech to the team. Afterward, our team podiatrist, Dr. Richard "Feets" Gilbert, told me, "It was the most emotional talk I'd ever heard. By the time he finished he had the trainers and doctors ready to go out onto the field and hit people."

Players loved playing for him. He was so sincere that even if the things he said sometimes made no sense, they didn't care. On Saturday nights before every game, for example, the entire squad would gather for a talk, then split up into smaller groups to review strategy for the next day. "On those Saturday nights, we never knew what Coryell would talk about," Pat Curran, a former player who I appointed business manager, told me. "Even when we were listening to him, we weren't exactly sure what he was talking about. Actually, most of the time we were lost. Sometimes he'd talk about camping trips, sometimes it was about other cultures, one night he was talking about driving down a dark street. He always had us laughing, although I don't think he intended to be funny. These speeches were very good for us, because there's a tremendous amount of tension before a game, and he eased it.

"I remember the night before we played Seattle, for example. He was telling us about their quarterback, Jim Zorn. Zorn was a scrambler—he could really run, he could be tough on linebackers. Coryell got up and told the defense he wanted them to be just like killer dogs tracking down a rabbit. After that, every week he wanted us to be killer somethings. Once it was killer bees—he wanted us to sting the other team to death. And once, when we were going to be playing on a wet field, he wanted us to be killer ducks. Killer ducks.

"After he'd finished speaking, we'd break up into smaller groups. The assistant coaches would always begin by explaining, 'What Don was trying to say was . . .' It didn't really matter what he said; we understood what he meant, and we also knew he was genuinely behind every player on the team. He made us want to play better. There aren't a lot of coaches who can do that."

Coryell was obsessed with coaching football. I'd see him walking down the office hallway, lost in his own world, knocking pictures askew. When we passed I'd say, "Morning, coach," and he would just walk right by. He wasn't being rude, he just didn't hear me. Everything in his life was football. During the Iranian hostage crisis, he walked into a meeting room and someone asked him what he thought about "this guy Khomeini."

The Ayatollah Khomeini had been on the front page of every newspaper for weeks. Coryell looked at the man who asked the question. "Where's he play?" he replied.

He was always, absolutely always, looking for the slightest advantage. On New Year's Eve, 1981, we were flying to Miami for the AFC divisional playoff. We were thirty-five thousand feet in the air, two and a half hours from Miami. Suddenly, Don got this great idea—bananas. Bananas had to be delivered to every player's room. Getting those bananas became the most important thing in our lives. His theory was that it was going to be extremely hot on the field during the game and that the potassium in bananas would help prevent cramps. Pat Curran had the airline pilot call ahead and find the bananas. Where they got bananas on New Year's Eve I have no idea. I do know it cost us a dollar a banana. But they were waiting in the hotel rooms for the players.

I never professed to understand his methods, but I know the players loved him, and he won a lot of football games. So if my coach wanted bananas, I wanted bananas. And, in fact, it was incredibly hot on the field that day, the game went into overtime, and we won. It might well have been those bananas that made the difference.

On another occasion he came trotting over to me in practice and again, from the worried expression on his face, I thought something might be wrong. "Gene," he said, "I need to talk to you. Don't you think it would be wonderful if we could have Popsicles during practice?" He was not smiling. Don was the funniest man I've ever met who did not know that he had a sense of humor.

But if my coach wanted Popsicles, I wanted Popsicles. We got Popsicles.

One thing Don could never quite figure out was what time we had to leave San Diego when we went on a road trip. He wanted us to arrive at our destination at least a full day before kickoff, but he would get very confused equating kickoff times in various time zones to San Diego time. "We have to leave two days before the game," he'd decide.

"No, Don," I'd tell him, "we really don't have to."

He'd insist upon it. "We got to," he'd say. "Otherwise our bodies aren't going to be there, they're going to be thinking a different time."

"Bodies don't think time," I'd explain, although I knew he was trying to make sure our players would be able to adjust to the different time zones.

And then when we got to wherever we were going, he'd start changing the itinerary. Once, in Seattle, he changed our departure time to the stadium three times in one day. Unfortunately, he kept copies of only two changes; he missed the buses to the stadium. There were three buses and everyone assumed he was on one of the other two. He showed up at the ballpark an hour late.

Don would do whatever was necessary to win. For example, he doesn't really drink, but during a flight to Miami for a Thursday night game in 1980, we flew into a severe thunder-and-lightning storm over Oklahoma City. When we lost power in one engine, most people aboard got a bit nervous. In the vernacular of airplane passengers, "a bit nervous" means we were absolutely terrified. We had to make an emergency landing. That night, on the good, firm, hard ground, everybody drank. Coryell, Johnny Sanders, and my son, Michael, went off together. Coryell had two glasses of gin and he was flying without our airplane.

Eventually, we got to Miami, and the next night we beat the Dolphins in overtime.

The Saturday night before our next game, Michael called Coryell and asked him what he was drinking. "You know I don't drink," Coryell told him.

"You drank last week in Oklahoma City," Michael reminded him, "and we won the ball game. It couldn't hurt to have a glass of gin tonight." Some superstitions are more enjoyable than others; Coryell had a glass of gin, and the next day we beat the Eagles, 22–21. Michael immediately sent Coryell a case of gin.

Perhaps Coryell didn't like to drink, but if the team needed him to have a glass of gin, he was going to drink some gin. Every Saturday night for the remainder of the season Michael would call him. "I'm drinking Boodles tonight" (or whatever), Coryell would tell him, "and I find it has a very pleasing taste. . . ."

If my coach wanted to drink gin, I wanted to drink gin.

Perhaps Coryell couldn't figure out when to leave San Diego, but he was the most thorough coach I'd ever seen. Tommy Prothro hadn't had a special-teams coach, for example. In fact, he didn't even believe that kickers were football players, and wouldn't let them participate in team votes. Coryell broke down special teams into five separate units and gave the responsibility for each one to a different assistant coach. One assistant had kickoff coverage, another assistant had kickoff returns, we had punt coverage, punt returns, and finally, field goals and conversions.

During games, his concentration bordered on the fanatical. I remember seeing him come off the field after his first game as head coach. We'd lost to New England by five points, 28–23, but he kept repeating, "If only we could have gotten down there for a field goal, if only we could have gotten that field goal." If we had, we would have lost by two points rather than five.

When we lost a game, Coryell would practically have a tantrum. No matter how badly the team or an individual player had performed, he would blame himself for the loss. I never heard him publicly criticize a player.

His wife, Aliisa, was just as intense as he was. She would come to our games and cheer as loudly as she could for about one quarter. That was all she could take, a quarter, then she'd go home. She wouldn't watch the game on television or listen to it. If we won, Don would immediately call her; if we lost, he wouldn't. We used to take all the coaches' wives with us on road trips—it was just something that made the entire experience more enjoyable. Shirley Prothro always went with us, for example, but Aliisa Coryell never did. She just couldn't stand it.

So when Don Coryell says, "I'm not a genius. Sometimes I can't even spell my name," that has to be taken within the context of his obsession. I've known Don Coryell a long time now, and I'm sure that with practice, he could learn to spell his name.

Coryell won seven of our last eight games after he replaced Tommy Prothro in 1978, then coached the Chargers to the division championship game three consecutive years and the best record in football during that span. By that time I'd learned enough about football to be an active participant in the operations of the team. The years of losing made the years of winning all the more enjoyable. I'd go into a Baskin-Robbins and ask for a vanilla cone and the sales clerk would give me a long speech about how difficult it was to get tickets to a Chargers game. "Don't give me a speech," I'd tell her, "just give me a vanilla cone." Do you know how nice it feels to be cheered at the gas station?

My six head coaches, Sid Gillman, Charlie Waller, Harland Svare, Ron Waller, Tommy Prothro, and Don Coryell had six quite different approaches to the same game. Gillman loaded his team with veterans. Svare was the disciple of defense. Prothro believed in baby boomers. Coryell instituted his bomb squad. As I learned, philosophies of coaching football are like horror stories about the Internal Revenue Service—everybody's got his own. The most important thing an owner can do when selecting a head coach is to match his philosophy to the talent on the team. And that, of course, is what made it so difficult for me to choose a head coach; until we rebuilt with draft choices, we didn't have any talent.

There are certain traits, however, that most head coaches have in common: I've never known a football coach who wasn't paranoid. The more successful they were, the more time they spent worrying that an opponent's scout was going to hover above the field in a helicopter, or hide in a nearby tree or building with binoculars, and steal their formations and plays. The fact that no one has ever actually been caught hovering or hiding has done nothing to alleviate the concern. When George Allen coached the

Rams, for example, he used to have police dogs patrolling the perimeter of his practice field.

Sid Gillman made me put a screened chain-link fence around our practice field. One season he decided even that wasn't enough. "We're gonna practice at a secret location," he announced.

"Okay," I agreed, being new at football espionage, "where's that going to be?"

"I don't know if I want to tell you," he said. We ended up practicing at a Marine Corps training base. It was ridiculous. We didn't even have any secrets worth stealing.

Coryell was the most paranoid. In 1983, a fifteen-story office building was put up within sight of our practice field. Some of our players told Coryell that the building was owned by Al Davis, and that the only reason he'd built it was to spy on our practices. Don immediately wanted me to rent the top two floors.

We eventually convinced him that Al Davis had nothing to do with the building. In fact, it was owned by a man named Pat Bowlen—and a year later Pat Bowlen bought the Denver Broncos.

Coryell really had nothing to worry about—our own players had playbooks and even then some of them couldn't understand our offense, so whatever information other teams had wasn't going to help them.

As long as I owned the Chargers, I absolutely never, ever tried to spy on another team. It's just something that I would never do, unless, of course, I knew I could get away with it and it would be helpful. But football has just become too complicated for information about a play or a formation to make any substantial difference.

Before I bought the team, for example, I would hear stories about a pro-football team's playbook. These stories made it seem as if these playbooks, which included diagrams of the basic plays and formations used by a team, were more valuable than the players. Teams supposedly levied large fines against players for losing their playbooks. When a player was cut or traded, he was always told to report to the head coach, "and bring your playbook." As I discovered, a playbook is only slightly more important to a team than its cheerleading squad. When we cut or traded a player, we took his playbook, but we couldn't make him hand in his brain. He knew our plays, our formations, and perhaps most important, our terminology. He knew what signals the quarterback was calling at the line of scrimmage—that can be valuable. We did lose an occasional playbook, and we fined players for losing them, but there simply wasn't enough information in those playbooks to make as much difference as a mobile tackle.

In business, I personally hired those executives with whom I would be working, but I always let them hire their own assistants. I took complete responsibility for the people I hired, and I held those people responsible for the people they hired. In football, I hired the head coach, and I let that head coach hire his own assistants, although I did retain the right to veto any choice.

When I bought the team Gillman had six assistants: an offensive-line coach, an offensive-backfield coach, a defensive-line coach, a defensive-backfield coach, a linebacker coach, and the only strength coach in pro football.

When I sold the team Coryell had thirteen assistants: an assistant head coach in charge of passing, an offensive-line coach/offensive coordinator, an offensive-backfield coach, two special offensive assistants/special-teams coaches, a wide-receiver coach, a defensive coordinator, an assistant defensive coach/advance scout, a defensive-line coach, a defensive-backfield coach, a linebacker coach, a strength coach and a special assistant to the head coach. Plus an equipment manager. I suspect we would have had even more assistant coaches, but we ran out of titles.

A good assistant coach has to be a teacher. Assistant coaches work with a diverse group of athletes, some of whom are bright and articulate, some of whom are stuck for an answer when you say hello. A good assistant has to have the ability to deal with each player as an individual, and work to improve his specific abilities. We had numerous coaches who had ability and knowledge of the game of football, but just couldn't communicate. One defensive-line coach, I remember, just kept screaming at his linemen, "This is a game of real estate, you can't give up real estate, you understand that? Keep the real estate!" This coach just couldn't teach, and couldn't understand why his players kept surrendering real estate.

Harland Svare had an offensive assistant who was a total authority figure. He made his offensive plan and warned his players, "You will go out five yards and make your cut and then you will catch the ball."

The Chargers have had some well-known assistant coaches, among them Phil Bengtson, Al Davis, Joe Gibbs, Forrest Gregg, Jim Hanifan, Lamar Lundy, Chuck Noll, Jack Pardee, Ray Perkins, Bum Phillips, and Bill Walsh. Although many of our former assistants eventually became head coaches in the NFL, Walsh came closest to getting the Chargers job. Anyone who knows Bill Walsh realizes he is an intelligent, personable, knowledgeable man. Tommy Prothro hired him in 1976 to take complete control of our offense, which he did. Toward the end of that season, when it appeared that Prothro's job might be in jeopardy, Walsh told me he wanted the top spot.

I was tempted to hire him. I finally told him that Prothro had indicated to me that he wanted to lead the Chargers for one more season, to finish the job he had started. I told Walsh that I was committed to Prothro for one more season, but that if he stayed, he would be in line for the head coaching job.

I didn't know what his answer would be until the final game of the season. He didn't show up. The next time I saw Bill Walsh was on the TV news, accepting the head coaching job at Stanford University. I considered that a strong indication of his decision. Walsh eventually led the San Francisco 49ers to the Super Bowl.

The day a head coach is hired, he knows it is just a matter of time until he is fired. One of the things I like most about thoroughbred horse racing is that you don't fire horses, you put them out to stud. That means they spend the rest of their lives earning money by having sex. If I could have offered that opportunity to my head coaches, it would have been easier letting them go. Firing a head coach was certainly one of the most difficult things I had to do in football, with the exception of listening to Al Davis at league meetings and trying to get a vanilla ice cream cone without an argument at Baskin-Robbins.

Had I not sold the Chargers, eventually I would have had to fire another coach. Instead, when the time comes to retire one of my horses, I can do it with pleasure. And for that, I thank you, Alex.

6

Quarterback Bobby Douglass spent only one season with the Chargers, and didn't play very much, but I'll never forget him. In the final game of the 1975 season we were getting killed by the Cincinnati Bengals, 47–17. It was a bitterly cold day, it had been the worst season in our history, and we were losing by thirty points; everybody just wanted to run out the clock and go home. Jesse Freitas had quarterbacked the team most of the game, but with less than three minutes left, Tommy Prothro ordered Douglass to loosen up. And when we got the ball back, Tommy told him, "Go ahead in."

Douglass grabbed his helmet and dashed over to Prothro. "How do you want to work this, coach," he asked with great enthusiasm, "want me to go for the win or just tie the game up for you?"

There were probably close to a thousand football players with the Chargers while I owned the team, some for only a day, others for as long as a decade. A thousand players—that's a lot of dreams. Some of these players I got to know very well, some I never even met, and some I got to know very well and just wished I'd never met. Some, like Douglass, I remember because of one incident or one play; some, like Dan Fouts and Kellen Winslow, I remember because I had the privilege of watching them mature from talented rookies into pro-football superstars, some, like Charlie Joiner, I remember because of their great ability and the joy they brought to San Diego, and some, like Tim Rossovich and Fred Dean, I remember because there are certain things in life one never forgets, like natural disasters, automobile accidents, Tim Rossovich, and Fred Dean.

I never socialized with Chargers players, because if I invited one or two players to my home, forty-three or forty-four other players would be wondering why they hadn't been invited and exactly what I'd served. But I did try to encourage a warm relationship between the organization and the players. I wanted our players to feel that we were concerned about them as human beings, not just as replacement parts in a football machine. For example, one of our star players retired after my first season and I wanted to do something to help him adjust to life after sports. So when he found a liquor store he wanted to buy, the Chargers helped him with his financing. Naturally, he was very grateful.

A few weeks later I was watching game films with our coaches and noticed that the room was unusually hot—the two large fans we'd installed were missing. We eventually found them in the new liquor store; the player we'd helped put in business had borrowed them. That was not the warm relationship I had in mind.

I learned quickly that many star athletes had been so pampered throughout their lives that they had come to believe that what was theirs was theirs, and what was mine was eventually going to be theirs. One Saturday night the first year I owned the club, I got a panicky call from Sid Gillman in San Diego. "You've got to come down right away," he said, "We've got an emergency. So-and-so doesn't want to play tomorrow."

I drove down to San Diego early Sunday morning and went right to the ballpark. "What's the matter?"

"So-and-so won't play today unless he gets a Cadillac exactly like yours."

"What?" I was a new owner, and I was still naïve. I thought Gillman was telling me that I had to give this player a Cadillac or he would not fulfill his contract and play in the game that day.

"Look," Gillman explained, "we've got to win today and we can't do it without him. You've got to get him a Cadillac."

If this player had been an employee of my corporation, I would have given him the boot. But he was a defensive star and we needed him, so I gave him my Cadillac. I gave my car to this player. Many people would say I was crazy to give my car to this player, but anyone who has dealt with professional athletes knows how lucky I was that all he demanded was my car.

There is a widely held belief that all pro-football players are wild men, capable of doing almost anything at any time. After spending almost two decades in pro football I learned that that's not true—they're not *all* that way. Pro-football players are just like any similar group of mammoth, aggressive young men who happen to make their living running through or over people or bashing heads together. Some of them are smart, some of them don't know the meaning of the word smart, some are wild, and some are conservative, but most of them are just like everybody else—a complex mixture. The dirtiest player we ever had on the Chargers was a preacher off the field. During the game he'd be grabbing face masks, tripping, slapping people in the side of the helmet, blocking from the blind side; and after the game he'd once again become a soft-spoken, gentle man. People who knew how he played claimed the only reason he was a preacher was he needed a lot of extra time to ask forgiveness.

I think one reason football players have a wild image, aside from the fact that some of them set their hair on fire, eat light bulbs, and wrestle snakes, is that public attention is focused on them for their athletic ability long before they've had the opportunity to grow and mature as individuals. Many of the players who reported to our training camp, for example, were just kids, very big kids, but just kids. I'd watch rookies walk into the team dining room and spot that massive spread, and their eyes would just light up. We often had problems with our young people gaining too much weight their first few weeks in camp, simply because they'd never eaten so well in their lives.

For example, Pat Curran is a bright, witty man. But he grew up in a small town and played his college football at tiny Lakeland College. He was so naïve when the Rams drafted him that he thought being drafted meant he was on the team. He didn't know he had to make it. So when he reported to the Rams' rookie camp he brought his wife and all his belongings with him.

Pat Curran was simply naïve, but among the thousand players we had on the Chargers there were some people who really weren't very bright. It simply isn't necessary to be smart to be a successful pro-football player. How smart does a man have to be to put his body in front of a 235-pound fullback trying to run over him? It seems to me that a truly intelligent man would be smart enough to get out of the way.

Late one season we traded with the Rams for a wide receiver. In the divisional playoff game that year this player caught the game-winning touchdown pass with time running out. He saved the season for us—he was a hero. But when our training camp opened the following July he didn't report and we couldn't find him. Two days later a Rams official called. "Didn't we trade so-and-so to you last season?" he asked. We assured him that they had. "I thought so too," the official continued, "but he just showed up here. I think he forgot he had been traded."

This player had led us to the division championship, and then had forgotten he'd been traded.

Obviously, a lack of intelligence can affect the outcome of the game. One year, Tommy Prothro had two defensive tackles who had not been honor graduates of their universities. The way Prothro designed our defense, one of these tackles would go through the opponent's line first, and then the second tackle would go through the opening he created to get to the quarterback. To avoid confusion as to which tackle would go through first, Prothro taught them a "You-Me" call. The tackle calling signals would yell either "You," meaning you go first, or "Me," meaning he would go first.

The first time they used it in a ball game, the signal-calling tackle yelled, "You," meaning "You go through first, I'll follow you." The ball was snapped. The signal-calling tackle spun to his left, took two quick steps—and ran right into the second tackle coming from the opposite direction.

After the play had ended, the signal-calling tackle asked the other tackle, "Didn't you hear me call 'You'?"

"I did," the first tackle admitted, "but I couldn't remember if 'You' meant you were going through first and I was supposed to follow you, or if it meant that I was supposed to go through first and you were going to follow me." Prothro issued colored wristbands to both players and keyed their signals to the colors of these bands.

We were constantly trying to find ways to help our people remember our plays, particularly after Coryell installed his complex offense. We'd write key words on wristbands, on white tape; one player even wrote a simple code on the back of his hand with a ballpoint pen. And after he'd blown his blocking assignment, Coryell took him out and berated him. The player was upset too, but claimed that it wasn't entirely his fault. Perspiration had caused his notes to smudge, he explained, saying, "I just didn't figure on sweating that much."

There is a substantial difference between a lack of intelligence and a lack of common sense. Any discussion of players most likely to aspire to be a tackling dummy must begin with linebacker Tim Rossovich, who we got from the Eagles in exchange for a first-round draft choice. There were people who believed Rossovich couldn't be very smart because he ate objects like light bulbs and drinking glasses and razor blades and canaries and spiders, and on occasion he would run full speed across our training room and dive head first into our whirlpool tub. But Rossovich was actually very smart—before diving into the whirlpool, for example, he always made sure there was water in it.

Rossovich was wonderful to have on the team because, no matter what crazy thing any other player did, Rossovich would do something to keep things in perspective. One season, I remember, he broke his leg in a preseason game, an injury that led to the end of his career. He arrived at our homecoming banquet with his leg in an ankle-to-hip cast. He seemed to be having tremendous difficulty getting around—until a beautiful woman came into the room. At that point he leaped over a table, landing on the girl and knocking her to the floor. And as they were lying there, he asked, in a loud voice, if she would marry him.

Perhaps he didn't say "marry." I was just being polite.

Rossovich had probably learned how to dive head first into the whirlpool tub as a safety precaution, because he also enjoyed setting his hair on fire. Supposedly, one night when he was still with the Eagles, he knocked on the door of an apartment in which a party was going on. The hostess opened the door to find him standing in the hallway with his hair in flames. "Did somebody call for a match?" he asked.

The other guests rapidly extinguished the flames. When the

smoke had cleared, Rossovich looked around the room at the un-familiar faces and exclaimed, "Oh no, I must have the wrong apartment."

When Joe Namath was paid $10,000 by a shaving-cream com-pany to shave off his beard, Rossovich put his long shaggy hair and moustache up for sale at $5,000 each. "If a shaving-cream or razor company isn't interested," his agent suggested helpfully, "maybe we could get a lighter-fluid firm."

Football players for some reason seemed to have an affinity for unusual creatures. Rossovich ate spiders. Clint Jones, a running back we got from Minnesota, had four pet snakes, including two pythons, a Florida indigo, and a boa constrictor. Unfortunately, he was gone by the time we got Clint Longley, who spent his off-seasons wrestling rattlesnakes. "First you smoke the snake out of the hole with gasoline," Longley explained, "then you lasso it with this pole that has a noose on the end, then you just go ahead and wrestle it." And how do you wrestle it? "Very carefully," Clint said.

Some of the crazy things our players did were not funny, just crazy. We had a player who used his signing bonus to buy a customized van. He was riding with his girlfriend in this van one day—they were going about forty miles per hour—when she said something he didn't like. He reached across, opened her door, and pushed her out. Her arm was broken and she was badly bruised, but the thing she really had to be concerned about were the flash burns she suffered when the personal injury attorneys whipped out their business cards. In the vernacular of the negli-gence attorneys, this case is what is known as a "penthouse apart-ment." Eventually she did sue our player, but she offered to drop the lawsuit if he would marry her.

Isn't love wonderful?

Some marriages are made in heaven; this particular marriage was made on the San Diego Freeway. The only person who cried at their wedding was her negligence attorney.

Then there was our high draft choice whose dog was barking too loudly in the front yard, so he took out his gun and shot the dog. This player also used to throw beer cans and rubbish in his backyard, until his neighbors threatened to report him to the

My most difficult moment as a navigator in the Army Air
Force A.T.C., Army of Terrified Civilians, came when we
missed Scotland and started to land in occupied France.

My first inventory

I guaranteed
every car on my
lot—I guaranteed
that they weren't
stolen.

The most difficult part of selling foreign cars in Los Angeles in
the 1950s was remembering whether the engine was in the
front or the back.

When I bought the Chargers in 1966 they were the best team in the AFL, featuring stars like future Hall of Famer Lance Alworth. At that time I believed in wearing suits to the games and trying to run the team as a business. A few years later we were in last place, I was wearing T-shirts to the games, and I was still trying to figure out how to run a football team as a business.

At the Charger games I entertained everyone from the Russian cosmonauts to U.S. Presidents Richard Nixon and Gerald Ford. The cosmonauts thought the game was a test of pure strength, Nixon understood its complexities, and when Ford attended the toilet overflowed. Note that our shoes and trouser bottoms are not visible.

Who's missing in this picture? Here I am with Bob Hope, presenting a check to the U.S.O. from the twenty-seven participating teams in NFL Charities. Only Al Davis's Los Angeles Raiders, who claim to make local contributions, are not contributors to NFL Charities.

The best trade I ever made was flipping draft choices with the Cleveland Browns to obtain all-pro Kellen Winslow. This is just after Winslow had signed his first pro contract. Look at the smiles on our faces and guess who is paying and who is receiving.

When placekicker Rolf Benirschke contracted a rare disease, his life was in jeopardy. When he made what we believed might be his final visit to the stadium, he was appointed honorary captain and helped to the center of the field for the coin toss by Louie Kelcher. A season later he returned, and he eventually kicked us into three division championships.

While I owned the Chargers we obtained players in every conceivable fashion. We got Louie Kelcher, for example, on a ten-pound test line.

As owner, I could pretty much do anything I wanted to do. Here I am taking wide receiver Charlie Joiner home with me for safekeeping after we'd clinched our first division championship.

Here I am giving Dan Fouts a Most Valuable Player trophy in 1979 for being the first Chargers player to understand Coryell's offense.

Without question, Don Coryell is the most offensive coach in pro-football history. The Chargers' offense was so complicated that many of our own players didn't understand it—and they had playbooks and coaches to explain it. Note the Killer Ducks in the background.

When Barron Hilton moved the Chargers to San Diego in 1961 he was warned that the only thing the city would support was a zoo. When we started winning after a decade of losses San Diego's fans showed their appreciation by renting an outdoor billboard and an aircraft carrier.

On the sidelines with my son, Michael (center), and former L.A. Rams defensive end Fred Dryer. From my smile this must have been taken before the game.

All I have left after selling the team in 1984 are some wonderful memories, a few photographs, some game balls voted to me by the team, and $80 million.

board of health. So he bought a goat, and set him free in the backyard.

Of course we immediately got rid of these players, immediately after they stopped playing well. As I learned, the difference between an "unusual sense of humor," and antisocial behavior is the ability to sack a quarterback.

Any discussion of players most likely to play pro football without any padding at all must end with the inimitable "Mean" Fred Dean, so-called because in high school he reportedly threw a rival quarterback through a fence.

"It was just under the fence," Dean always contended.

Fred Dean was our second choice, the thirty-third pick overall, in the 1975 draft. He was a linebacker from Louisiana Tech and perhaps the strongest man I've ever known. Before drafting a player, we always did a background check. While investigating Dean, we were told that during a card game his sophomore year he'd accidentally been shot, then walked several miles to the training room to get aid. After we'd drafted Dean, Harland Svare went down to Louisiana to sign him, and asked about that story.

"Nah, that's not true at all," Dean assured him. "That wasn't no accident—they *meant* to shoot me. See, what happened was that I was playing cards with some guys and they caught me cheating, so they shot me. That's when I walked over to the training room to get fixed up. That's all that was."

We gave Fred Dean a $45,000 bonus to sign and he immediately bought a Lincoln Continental. But when he reported to training camp two months later, he was driving a beat-up old $800 Chevy. Fred saw the big new cars our other high draft choices were driving and announced that he was going home to get a job in the glass factory. When Tank Younger asked him why, Fred explained, "Everybody else got their new cars and look at this old piece I got to drive, and I even had to have a professor at school co-sign the paper for me so I could get this one."

Tank asked what had happened to the new Lincoln.

Fred told him that he had burned up the engine in the Lincoln, so he put in a new engine, gave that car to his brother, and bought himself a new Buick Riviera.

Tank asked what had happened to the new Buick.

Fred said he had totaled the Buick, so he had made a down payment on a new Pontiac Grand Prix.

Tank asked what had happened to the new Pontiac.

I believe Fred said he had totaled that car when he got hit by that ditch. He had then made a down payment on a new Ford LTD. Apparently, Fred Dean was the best thing that had happened to the American automobile industry since highways.

Nervously, Tank asked what had happened to the new Ford.

The Ford had been repossessed when he couldn't make the payments, Dean explained. And that is how he ended up driving the $800 Chevy. Tank and I figured out that at the rate Fred Dean was going, it would cost us $225,000 a year just to keep him in cars. We convinced him that he would have to work a lot of overtime to make that much money in a glass factory, so it was either play football or drive the Chevy.

Fred Dean eventually became one of the best defensive ends in football, but he would just drive us crazy with his problems off the field—figuratively, of course. One afternoon, for example, Fred didn't show up at practice, so Tommy Prothro sent Tank to Dean's house to find out what had happened. When Fred answered the door, Tank demanded, "Geez, Fred, what are you doing here? Why aren't you at practice?"

Fred actually had a good excuse. "It's like this, Tank," he explained, "I got up this morning and went down to start my car and it wouldn't start, so I quit football."

Tank paused for a moment to consider that, then asked, "What are you talking about?"

"Like I said, my car wouldn't start, so I'm retired."

Tank unretired him very quickly. Cars and women gave Fred more trouble than opposing linemen. While he was with the Chargers he was divorced twice and sued for paternity by a third woman, and sued by his second wife for $1 million in damages in a civil assault case. And those were only some of his problems. He had to go into debt to keep up his child-support payments and finally, in 1981, he walked out of camp and threatened to retire, again, unless we renegotiated his contract. I very rarely renegotiated a valid contract, and I never renegotiated a contract when threatened by a player or his agent. Instead, I traded him to the San Francisco 49ers for a second-round draft choice.

When the trade was reported, Chargers fans thought I'd cut off my end to save my bank account, but they didn't know how many times we'd helped Dean with his problems. We'd finally reached the point where we just didn't care if he played with us or not. He wasn't worth the aggravation. Of course, fans don't care about problems off the field; they care about winning football games. I know, I have been a fan a lot longer than I was an owner.

Dean was with the 49ers for four seasons, helping them win two Super Bowls. He didn't actually play four seasons—in 1984 he threatened to retire unless his contract was renegotiated and sat out most of the season. Finally, at the end of the 1986 season, Dean got his wish—the 49ers asked *him* to retire. And, after spending his entire career threatening to do just that, Dean refused. The 49ers had to release him.

In all the years I owned the Chargers, of all the players we had, one player stands out, or, more accurately, sits out. Duane Thomas. Duane Thomas was the best football player in the world, it's just that that world was not the same one in which all the rest of us live. Thomas was the strangest human being I've ever known.

Playing with the Dallas Cowboys for two seasons, Thomas had proved he was one of the best running backs in football. But he had had all kinds of problems in Dallas, including being convicted of possessing marijuana, and when he refused to report unless the Cowboys renegotiated his contract, they decided to get rid of him. My son, Michael, had become friends with Thomas, and was convinced that all Thomas really needed was a little understanding and a lot of money. We knew that if he played up to his capabilities he would be a tremendous asset to the Chargers, so we started negotiating with Cowboys general manager Tex Schramm and his assistant, Sid Gillman.

The Cowboys demanded running back Mike Montgomery and wide receiver Billy Parks in return for the right to negotiate with Thomas. I thought that was a high price, but I'd spent five seasons watching Gillman judge players—if he wanted Montgomery and Parks, they probably weren't as good as I thought they were. On July 29, 1972, we made the deal.

As soon as I finished talking to Schramm, I sent Michael over to the Cowboys' training camp in Thousand Oaks, California, to get Duane Thomas on the first plane to San Diego. About an hour later Michael called me with some good news and some bad news. The good news was that Tex Schramm had gotten the tele-typed confirmation from the league office making the trade of-ficial; the bad news was that Thomas had disappeared about a half hour earlier.

In retrospect, the good news turned out to be the bad news, and the bad news was really good news.

We couldn't find Thomas for three weeks. Then, on August 17, he walked into our training camp. On August 17, he also walked out of training camp. "What happened?" I asked Svare.

"It was the strangest thing I've ever seen," Harland said. "He just stared at me."

"What do you mean?"

"Just that. He stood about two inches away from me, face to face, nose to nose, and he just stared at me. He never said a word, he just stared. Then he left. It was scary."

He disappeared again, although we kept getting reports that he had been seen in Dallas or San Diego. In early September a fan reported seeing him in downtown San Diego. "Are you Duane Thomas?" the fan asked.

"I'm everybody," Thomas evidently replied.

That same day two teenagers recognized him. "You're Duane Thomas," one of the kids said.

"I'm Escondido," Thomas said, apparently referring to the small city about thirty miles from San Diego.

The next time we heard from him was on September 19, when he finally reported to camp. At a hastily arranged press confer-ence, he was asked why he had waited so long to report. "That's a good question," he responded. "In the first place, I haven't thought much about that question. I don't have an answer."

Another reporter asked Thomas if he had anything to say to the people of San Diego. "Hello," Thomas said. Well, that certainly turned out to be the wrong answer.

The following morning he left camp again. This time we caught him at the airport, trying to borrow $94 to buy an airplane ticket back to Dallas. I told Harland to try to convince him to meet me in Palm Springs to discuss his contract. "All right," Harland said, "but you'd better watch out. He's gonna come out there and stare at you."

That is exactly what he did. He stood no more than six or seven inches away from me and just stared into my eyes. He didn't say a word, he just stared. I asked him a few questions. He continued staring at me. "You got anything you want to say to me?" I asked again. He continued staring at me. "Okay, if that's the way you feel," I said, as if we'd actually had a conversation. "That's all, go ahead back."

In a normal situation, I would have realized that Duane Thomas was a troubled man and had nothing more to do with him. But pro football is not a normal situation. I had managed to convince myself that football players were artists and thus had to be treated differently from other people. It was either believe that, or accept the fact that I was running a child-care center for overdeveloped children. And once I started accepting what would have otherwise been unacceptable behavior in an effort to build the strongest team, I left myself open for everything else that happened.

In professional sports, this is what is known as being competitive.

After Thomas left Palm Springs, we didn't see him again for two months. Then, unannounced, he showed up just before we were to play the Cowboys. By that time, our record was 2-4-1 and we'd lost three successive games. If he wanted to play, we wanted him to play. He dressed for the game, ran out onto the field with the team, and then sat down, cross-legged, beneath the goalposts, staring straight ahead.

While the team went through its pregame calisthenics, Thomas sat immobile. Just staring. The team finished its workout and returned to our locker room for a final meeting. Thomas just sat there, beneath the goalposts, staring.

I was watching this from my private box. "What's he doing?" people kept asking me. What could I tell them? Staring? Finally, the rest of the squad came back out onto the field. Thomas still hadn't moved. When the band started playing the national anthem, we had him half-carried, half-dragged off the field. He didn't play a single down for us that season.

One of the many things I had learned in professional football was the importance of hope. Hope against all odds, hope when we knew we had no chance, hope that miracle might happen and change what an otherwise realistic human being knows is a hopeless situation. And so, even after Duane Thomas had been carried off the field staring, I still had hopes we would be able to convince him to play for us the following season.

Before the 1973 season began we tried to arrange a meeting between Muhammad Ali and Thomas, hoping that Ali might be able to convince Thomas that he was wasting his prodigious talents. Ali was training in San Diego for a fight—I believe it was with Kenny Norton—when Harland went to his training camp to try to arrange the meeting. Harland was watching Ali's workout when Norton walked in. Ali snapped; he leaped out of the ring, yelling, screaming at Norton. Ali's handlers had to hold him back and finally drag him into his dressing room still screaming. Harland heard metal chairs being thrown around inside the dressing room. Whew, he thought, this probably isn't the best time to ask him a favor. But Angie Dundee, Ali's trainer, had been expecting him, so he walked inside. Ali was calmly toweling off. "How you doing?" Ali asked pleasantly. "Boy, it's getting tougher and tougher to sell tickets."

Because of his antiwar views during the Vietnam War, Ali had been prevented from boxing for three years. We wanted him to explain to Thomas how difficult it was to regain athletic skills after a long layoff. "No question the layoff hurt me badly," Ali told Harland. "As long as this doesn't have anything to do with negotiating a contract, I'll talk to him." Harland assured Ali it didn't, then called Thomas's new agent, former AFL star Abner Haynes, to set up the meeting. At that time Ali was the most prominent sports figure in the world. Who wouldn't want to meet with him?

Thomas. He didn't show up for the meeting.

If Thomas hadn't been such an outstanding football player, by this time I definitely would have begun to believe he was just a jerk. But in the vernacular of the sporting world, a jerk capable of gaining 1,000 yards rushing in a single season is a "complicated individual." Complicated? Thomas was the Rubik's Cube of athletics.

The owner who puts up with this type of behavior is the jerk.

Abner Haynes was a bright, decent man, and a few days after the Chargers had opened the 1973 preseason camp, we agreed on a new contract for Thomas. Haynes promised Thomas would be at practice the following morning.

Forty-five minutes before the squad took the field the next morning, Harland was stunned to see Thomas dressed and working out by himself. He went through an unusual series of loosening-up exercises that seemed to be a combination of calisthenics, yoga, and medieval torture. When the team began scrimmaging, Svare put in Thomas at running back. "It was the most amazing thing I've ever seen," Harland told me later, his voice literally shaking. "He'd never been to a single team meeting, but he shifted into every one of our formations as if he'd been running them all his life. He didn't miss one. Then he started running the plays as if we'd designed them especially for him; every time he got his hands on the ball he broke through the line. Gene, this was the best performance I've ever seen on a football field, I mean the best. This guy is solid gold."

The next day I went to the workout to see for myself. Again, Thomas arrived forty-five minutes early. When practice began, he was even better than Harland had described. He was a superb runner, a superb receiver, a superb blocker. His presence seemed to raise the level of play of the entire team. That night he even attended his first team meeting, although as far as Harland and I were concerned, he didn't have to do anything he didn't want to do. I began to appreciate the fact that Thomas was truly a misunderstood, complicated individual.

The third morning the same thing happened—he showed up early and dominated practice. I knew what it felt like to discover the Holy Grail. At the end of the morning workout we stopped for lunch. Duane got into his car and drove away. Afternoon practice began at 2:20. When he hadn't returned by 2:10 we began to get a little nervous. 2:15. 2:25. Practice began without him. Soon afterward, he strolled onto the practice field. He was not wearing his equipment. Svare saw him and shouted, "Hey, Duane, get in here."

Thomas glared right through him. "Quit hassling me, man," he shouted back. "What are you hassling me for?" Then he continued his leisurely, somewhat wobbly walk around the field.

Although Thomas had not been overly hostile, he'd challenged Svare in front of the entire squad. If we allowed him to get away with that, Harland would have lost the respect of every other player. He would have lost control of the team. We had no choice. We had to get rid of him. A day or so later we traded him to the Redskins.

Players like Duane Thomas come along only once in a lifetime. Fortunately. But it's important to remember that troubled players like Thomas make up a small minority in pro football. For every Thomas there is a Charlie Joiner, who caught more passes than any receiver in NFL history, while at the same time becoming such an important member of the San Diego community that fans honored him with "Charlie Joiner Day" while he was still an active player. And for every snake-wrestling, glass-eating, girlfriend-throwing flake, there is a Rolf Benirschke.

Placekicker Rolf Benirschke is the most courageous football player I've ever known. We picked him up on waivers in 1977 after he had been drafted, then cut, by the Oakland Raiders. In that instance Al Davis really did turn out to be a friend. Benirschke immediately established himself as one of the most reliable field-goal kickers in the NFL. In 1978, he made eighteen of twenty-two attempts, second-best in the league. During that season he began suffering severe stomach pains, but doctors couldn't find anything wrong with him. When he opened the 1979 season by hitting four field goals in four attempts against Seattle, we figured his physical problems had disappeared.

Those were the only field goals he was to make all season. He began losing weight and strength and his stomach pains returned worse than before. In late September he entered the hospital, and was diagnosed as having chronic Crohn's disease. Doctors operated and removed a large part of his colon. I remember calling his hospital room one night and his father, an internationally renowned pathologist and conservationist, answered the phone. I told him who I was and asked how his son was doing.

His voice breaking, Dr. Benirschke said, "We don't know if he's going to make it." A moment like that puts football, business, Duane Thomas, everything, into perspective. Rolf barely survived that crisis, and his weight dropped from 174 to 123 in a matter of weeks. Because part of his colon had been removed, he had to wear a small external pouch on his abdomen to collect body waste.

In mid-November he unexpectedly walked into our locker room before an important Monday night game against the Steelers. Some of our players were so horrified at his gaunt appearance that they could barely look at him. A few people thought he had come to say good-bye. Louie Kelcher, our all-pro defensive tackle, suggested to Don Coryell that Rolf be named the honorary captain for the game, meaning he would have to go out to the center of the field for the traditional coin toss. When Coryell agreed, Rolf hesitated. "I don't know if I can walk that far," he admitted.

"Don't worry," Louie replied, "if you can't make it, I'll carry you." A few moments later, with Louie holding Rolf's hand as if he were a small child, the two of them walked slowly and boldly to the center of the field. When the Chargers fans realized what was going on, they gave Rolf Benirschke a long, loud ovation. In the two decades I owned the team, that was the most heart-wrenching moment I experienced. We all knew Rolf's football career was over. We just wondered if this was the last time we were going to see him alive.

That night we destroyed a fine Pittsburgh team, 35–7. The team was so charged up because of Rolf's pre-game appearance that the Steelers had no chance at all. After the season, because of that game, the league passed a rule prohibiting anyone not playing in a game from being presented to the crowd or making a public appearance. I sat silently at the meeting while the rule was debated and passed. It was a good rule; we really did play with twelve men that night, and no team in football could have beaten us.

Rolf responded so well to his two operations that he wanted to play football again in 1980. At first we were extremely reluctant to let him play because of the external pouch he had to wear, but finally we agreed, provided he did not try to block or tackle anyone after kicking off. "You kick the ball and get off the field," Coryell ordered.

Benirschke made twenty-four of thirty-six field-goal attempts that season, including sixteen in a row and one from 53 yards out. The only problem we had with him was that he kept trying to hit people on kickoff returns. Finally, we told him that the next time he tried to tackle a ball carrier, he was going to be released. We meant it too.

No, we probably didn't really mean it.

Having lived through this with Rolf and his teammates, it is impossible to describe the joy I felt, we all felt, when Rolf kicked the field goal in overtime against Miami to win the 1981 AFC western-division championship. That was the kind of thrill that made all the problems of 1973, the losing streak of 1975, the name-calling, the abuse, worthwhile. Seeing a young man overcome adversity to become a hero is the stuff of which sports legends are made.

Eventually, doctors discovered that the original diagnosis had been wrong; Benirschke was actually suffering from ulcerative colitis, and surgeons were able to reverse his colostomy.

Like Charlie Joiner and so many other Chargers players, Benirschke became active in the San Diego community. In 1979, he founded Kicks for Critters, a conservation organization. Rolf announced he was going to donate $50 for each field goal he kicked, then solicited matching donations from businesses and individuals. In five years, Kicks for Critters raised $784,000 to aid in the preservation of endangered species.

Not to be outdone, quarterback Dan Fouts helped start Passes for Porpoises, donating $100 for each touchdown pass he threw and $500 for each touchdown he scored running, to the Hubbs–Sea World Institute, for the study of marine life. Fouts also actively solicited matching donations.

There are five ways in which a team obtains players: drafting them directly out of college, as we did Dan Fouts and Kellen Winslow, claiming them on waivers for a minimal amount of money, as we did Benirschke, trading other players or draft picks for them, as we did Duane Thomas, buying them from another club, as we did Johnny Unitas, or signing them as free agents, as we did Hank Bauer and my waiter from the Triton restaurant.

The NFL holds its draft of college players once each year. Teams pick in inverse order of the way they finished the previous season, worst team first, first team last. The first four, five, ten years I owned the team, this was the only day of the year when we were near the top of anything. After each team has made a selection, the entire process starts again. Supposedly, this system allows the worst teams to get the best college players and thus become competitive. Of course, this assumes that the worst teams can pick out the best players. But if we had been able to recognize talent, we wouldn't have been drafting near the top in the first place.

Once a team selects a player, he belongs to that team. If he wants to play in the NFL, that is the team he is going to play for. There is really no parallel to the draft in the business world, although with the twenty-one major lawsuits the NFL has fought since Rozelle became commissioner, Art Modell once suggested we would probably be better off drafting lawyers.

Each team has two objectives in the draft: to select players who will improve the team, and to make their fans believe they've selected players who will improve the team. Part of the importance of the draft is that it allows teams to convince their fans that this season will be better than last season, and that they should order their season tickets early.

In each draft, there are usually ten or fifteen "blue chippers," college players who every team is sure will become solid pro players. Of these players, three or four won't make it. After that first group has been taken, selecting players becomes educated guesswork. If a team selects a player no one has ever heard of, fans are told he was picked because he plays a certain position and "We were drafting to fill our needs." If a team selects someone who plays a position at which it is already strong, he was picked because he was "the best athlete available." Anyone chosen in the later rounds, fifteenth, eighteenth, twenty-third, is a "sleeper," someone with whom "our scouts have been very impressed, and we feel he has the potential to be a football player." Perhaps it was the shoulder pads and large helmet that gave him away. Most players with potential are like underexposed photographs—they just don't quite develop the way you expect them to.

No team really has much hope that players selected in later rounds are going to help the team, and toward the end of the draft there are always some track stars or basketball stars or movie stars named. One year, for example, the Saints selected John Wayne on their final pick, and on another occasion they picked female track star Wyomia Tyus. Neither one made the team.

No team is ever better than it is the day after the draft, when the general manager, anxious to build fan enthusiasm, reports to the media that it had been a good draft, that he had been able to fill some big holes, that there had been some players available in later rounds he didn't expect to be able to get, and that he is confident the new players will make the team competitive.

In fact, when we were winning two, three games a season, the draft was the only day of the year on which we were competitive. On that day, it was just as if we were a real football team. The best thing about the draft was that our mistakes weren't so obvious. During games, anyone could see we didn't know what we were doing. After drafting a player it would take three or four years before anyone could be sure we didn't know what we were doing.

Every team in pro football maintains its own scouting department, in addition to belonging to scouting combines, which are organizations that scout for many teams. We kept records on every player in college with pro-football potential, we scouted these people for three or four college seasons, we had reports from the combines, we heard gossip about how other teams rated players, and then, too often, when it came down to finally having to make a choice, we'd sit there and say, "Who knows, let's just take a gamble."

The most important lesson I learned about drafting was taught to me by Sid Gillman. We'd received the fourth pick of the 1968 draft in a trade with Denver, an opportunity to get the fourth-best college player in America, a real blue chipper. Although our offense was reasonably solid, we were desperate for help on defense. There was a linebacker who everyone agreed could start for us immediately and strengthen our defense. Gillman and I had dinner the night before the draft, sitting together till 3 A.M. reviewing our choices for the draft. We were just praying that the linebacker wouldn't be taken by one of the three clubs picking before us.

Three hours later, 6 A.M. our time, 9 A.M. in New York where the draft was being held, the selection process began. The team picking first did not take the linebacker. The second team didn't take the linebacker. We held our breath; the third team did not take the linebacker. It was our turn. We were gonna get our man.

Sid Gillman got on the phone and announced loudly, "San Diego selects offensive tackle Russ Washington from the University of Missouri."

I still had a tremendous amount to learn about football, but I knew an offensive tackle wasn't a linebacker. I also knew we already had two outstanding offensive tackles in Ron Mix and Ernie Wright. In fact, tackle was probably the one position on the team at which we were strong. "Sid," I asked, "Sid, what happened to the linebacker? Why'd the hell'd you pick another offensive tackle?"

Sid was unflappable. "It's okay," he said, "I'll turn him into a linebacker."

Gillman tried for two seasons to turn Washington into a defensive player. Then he put him back at tackle where he belonged and he became a Pro Bowl player. The lesson I learned from Gillman was simple: Even the experts often have no idea what they're doing.

Because Gillman was supposedly a football expert, I allowed him to make all our draft selections. As a mistake, that doesn't rank with not buying the Beatles, but it did hurt us for several years. Besides drafting Washington in 1968, for example, he used our other first-round pick to select defensive back Jim Hill, who eventually became an outstanding television sports reporter. He played three seasons with the Chargers, not a long time for a first-round draft choice.

In 1969, Gillman used our first-round pick to grab Marty Domres, a quarterback from that great college-football power Columbia University, even though we already had an outstanding quarterback in John Hadl. In the second round that year we picked Ron Sayers, undoubtedly the finest brother of Bears superstar Gale Sayers ever to play for the Chargers, even if he did play only one season.

In 1970, we selected a fine wide receiver, Walker Gillette, in the first round. And except for the fact that we already had two outstanding wide receivers, Lance Alworth and Gary Garrison, it was a good choice. Gillette was with us two years. In the second round that year we drafted defensive tackle Tom Williams, who had a reputation as a "tree man." I assumed that meant he was as strong and sturdy as a tree; it meant he liked to climb trees, he was a hippie. He lasted two seasons.

In 1971 we drafted Leon Burns in the first round. Most players are drafted out of college. Leon Burns came out of prison. He was already twenty-six, twenty-seven years old when we picked him. The thing I remember most about him is that he used to wear a Superman T-shirt under his uniform. After watching him play, I assumed he had gone to jail for false advertising. We would have been better off drafting John Wayne. Burns was with us one season, and eventually played in the World Football League.

Tommy Prothro's great strength was his ability to select young players. Tommy's mathematical mind, his experience as a college coach, and his ability to predict how rapidly a player would develop made him a tremendous judge of talent. While most people were very intense during the draft, yelling, screaming, trying to make trades, Tommy was always relaxed. He knew that a good draft was a combination of good preparation and good luck. We'd work all year putting together our list of desirable players. Then Tommy would take the thirty players we considered the best in the country and bet anyone that some of those players were going to be available after the fourth round. That meant that the other twenty-seven teams, using basically the same data we had, didn't rate these players among the top hundred in the country. Invariably, he was correct.

Tommy also had the assistance of Johnny Sanders. John McKay, who coached USC to a national championship and the Tampa Bay Buccaneers to last place, once said of Sanders, "He can look at a little baby in a crib and tell you what size he'll grow to and how fast he'll run forty yards in a football suit when he's eighteen years old."

When we won the first of our three consecutive division championships in 1979, twenty-nine of the fifty-one players on our active and reserve roster, including fifteen starters, had been selected in the draft, most of them by Prothro and Sanders.

They were the architects of our 1975 draft, perhaps the best draft in pro-football history. We drafted six players who would be starters on that championship team: Fred Dean, Mike Williams, Mike Fuller, Billy Shields, Louie Kelcher, and Gary Johnson, plus a key reserve, Ralph Perretta, and running back Rickey

Young, who we traded to Minnesota for all-pro guard Ed White. Dean, Johnson, and Kelcher eventually became all-pro players.

A tremendous amount of preparation went into making those selections. We would spend as much as $1 million in hopes of getting three or four players who could help us. Our scouting department began by compiling information on as many as 1,500 college players, beginning with measurable statistics; age, height, weight, and speed for the 40-yard dash. Those are about the only objective figures they got; everything else was subjective; character, stamina, mental alertness, medical history, agility, balance, competitiveness, strength, and explosion—the ability to get into action quickly and deliver decisive hits. Then each player was rated on the specific skills required of his position, from passing ability in quarterbacks to pursuit agility in defensive backs. Everything was rated on a 1-to-9 scale, 9 being the highest. Scouts collected this information by attending every possible college practice or game and every all-star game, by looking at thousands of hours of films, and by talking to coaches. Those players we considered live prospects were invited to our training camp, where we measured them, tried to determine how much muscle they could add to their frames, saw how fast they were, and discovered as much as we could about their character. If we were considering making a player a high-round draft pick, we did an in-depth investigation of his background. As it turned out, we couldn't measure the most important thing of all—heart. How will a player react the first time he's hit so hard his ancestors get shaken up? Does he have the courage to catch and hold the football when he hears the PATTER of eight huge feet bearing down on him? Will he play in the final minutes of the fourth quarter when the temperature on the field is 101 degrees? A lot of college players look good in the lobby; they're great in practice but just don't perform during games. Heart was the intangible that turned a player with third-round abilities like Dan Fouts into a superstar. Heart was what allowed the very last player chosen in the 1971 draft, Don Nottingham, to become a fine fullback with the Baltimore Colts. It's probably the most important facet of all, and it can't be measured.

We were always trying to discover additional means of judging players. The Cowboys, the Rams, and the 49ers were the first teams to experiment with computers. We were in the next group. In the first major experiment, all pertinent data on hundreds of players was fed into a main-frame system to determine the best possible selection. The computer picked a player no scout rated in the top two hundred players. Computer technology has improved tremendously since then, but while computers can measure, compare, and isolate whatever data is fed into them, no computer can measure heart or courage. The conclusions reached by a computer are based on the subjective information it is given, making the computer no better than a team's scouts.

One season we experimented with handwriting analysis. A San Diego psychologist claimed he could determine players' abilities based on a handwriting sample. Of course, part of the sample consisted of writing down their size and speed, which is sort of like determining if an individual has money by analyzing his signature on a check. Obviously, picking players based on a handwriting sample was an absurd idea, but spending a million dollars in hopes of finding three or four useful players isn't particularly logical either. So we sent questionnaires to several hundred prospects and handed over their responses to this psychologist, deleting the players' names and colleges.

He carefully analyzed the results, then gave us his list of selections. We compared it to the actual draft. The first player he named was not among the first three hundred players picked, ending our experiment with handwriting analysis.

Although we were willing to try anything that might help us evaluate a player, we made out our final list of the two hundred players we were interested in the old-fashioned way, screaming at each other.

Our scouts and coaches and front-office personnel would sit in a room and argue. The defensive coaches were desperate for defensive players; the wide-receiver coach demanded that we use a high pick to get a receiver; the linebacker coach wouldn't take responsibility for what was going to happen next season if we didn't get him a quality linebacker. No team is ever worse than it is in these meetings held to determine which players to draft. Each assistant coach pleads for help for his squad. Everything bad about the team comes out in those meetings; the offensive line is in shambles, the defensive line is aging rapidly, two defensive backs have bad knees and might not be able to survive another season, the wide receivers got away lucky the past year. I'd sit there listening to these coaches confessing how bad their squads were and I'd think, geez, I didn't realize we were this bad. How are we going to win any games at all next season?

Eventually, we would hammer out a list of our top two hundred prospects. Although I don't know for sure, I would guess that our list exactly matched most other teams' for at least one, perhaps two players. Every team rated almost every player differently. Once we had compiled our list of two hundred, which we were continually changing, we had to decide which of those players would fill our greatest needs. And then the arguing began again.

After firing Gillman I took an active role in compiling our "dream list," the list of players we really wanted to get in the draft. The final decision on whom we would take eventually came down to the general manager and me.

Those seasons when we didn't make the playoffs, draft day was the most exciting day of the year. It was like opening a pack of bubble-gum cards to see which players you'd gotten. We would really promote the draft in San Diego. Our local radio station would broadcast live from our offices. We'd serve breakfast to any fans who wanted to come out to the stadium. We'd put up a big board and write in the names of each draft pick. When we selected a player, a coach would come down and announce it, and we'd show films of the player in action if we had them.

The fans certainly took it seriously. One year, I remember, I was living in the small town of Carlsbad. About 4:30 A.M. on the day of the draft, I was awakened by a loud crash in the living room. Someone had thrown a rock with a note attached to through a large picture window. "Klein," the note read, "You goddam better draft some goddam good players today." Or else what, he was going to throw a rock through my picture window?

I immediately called the Carlsbad police department and asked the switchboard operator to send someone over. "We'll be glad to," the operator replied, "as soon as he gets back."

He? *The* policeman? The entire Carlsbad police force arrived about an hour later. He looked to be about nineteen years old. He took one look at the scene of the crime and surmised, "Someone threw a rock through your picture window, huh?" The perpetrator of the crime was never apprehended.

After the hundreds of hours spent evaluating prospects, after the million or so dollars spent compiling our dream list, on draft day we rarely got the players we wanted. The real problem was that other teams were also allowed to select players. So no matter how intense our own arguments had been, we'd sit in our office and see other teams take the players we wanted, and have to adjust our list once again.

Every year some players we expected to be available in the third or fourth rounds were taken in the first or second rounds, while other players that we had projected as certain first- or second-round picks weren't taken in the first four rounds. What happens in that situation is that you begin second-guessing yourself. One year there was a player we believed was a marginal first-round, sure second-round choice, but as our turn came in the fourth round he was still available. Why? Why hadn't another team picked him? Maybe they had information we didn't. Maybe he wasn't as good as we thought he was. Geez, I thought, Dallas could have taken him and look who they took instead, a player we had barely ranked. And Dallas always drafted well. We talked ourselves out of this player.

There was absolutely no way to figure out how other teams were going to pick after the first few rounds of the draft. One year, for example, the Dolphins, drafting twenty-seventh, found quarterback Dan Marino still available. After they'd taken him, Miami coach Don Shula was asked if he knew why twenty-six teams had passed on Marino. Shula had as good an explanation as any, explaining, "Why do you think I go to mass every day?"

Sometimes, after spending three or four years gathering information on a prospect, we'd ignore that information and take a gamble. When our turn came in the third round of the 1973 draft, for example, quarterbacks Dan Fouts and Don Strock were still available. We liked them both, although our reports on Fouts questioned his ability to withstand the punishment he'd have to take. Harland and I finally decided to ignore our scouts and take Fouts.

Some weeks later Svare, Oscar Dystel, of Bantam Books, and I were vacationing on a boat off the coast of New England. We were watching television, switching between tapes of John Dean testifying in the Watergate hearings on one channel and a college all-star game from Lubbock, Texas, on another channel. Fouts was at quarterback for one squad, and this was our first opportunity to see him in action. On the second or third play, Fouts faded back to pass, his protection collapsed, and he was buried under a wave of tacklers. After they peeled the linemen off Fouts, he started walking off the field. It was obvious he'd been hurt—either that or he'd been born with three collarbones.

Harland and I glanced at each other. We'd ignored the warnings of our scouts and drafted him. After a moment of silence, Harland suggested, "Why don't we see what John Dean has to say?" Our scouts had been right: Fouts was injury-prone. He'd broken his collarbone. And just ten years later he was hurt again. But during those ten years he became the leading passer in pro football.

In 1975, most teams believed defensive tackle Louie Kelcher was too slow to be a successful pro player. Even our scouts had him timed in the 40-yard dash as slightly slower than a cloud on a windless day. "If I have to run forty yards to catch somebody," Kelcher admitted, "I ain't gonna catch him nohow." But he had overpowering strength, great size, fine blocking technique, and the instinct to be where the play was taking place. He was so strong, according to a college legend, that once, when his car had had a flat tire and he couldn't find a lug wrench, he'd simply ripped the tire off the car. Four years after we'd ignored the scouts' recommendations and taken him, he was an all-pro.

In fact, we ignored our scouts and played hunches many times. We got Fouts, Kelcher. . . . Kelcher, Fouts. . . . Fouts. Kelcher. Certainly there were times when it didn't work out; unfortunately, I can't recall any of them.

First-, second-, and third-round draft choices should be able to help the team immediately, but lower draft choices need time to develop, and there is no way of knowing if and how much a young player is going to develop. So in the lower rounds we were more likely to take a gamble. In the fourth round in 1979 we drafted a player with a broken arm, believing that if his arm hadn't been broken he would have been drafted much higher. Of course, his arm *was* broken. We figured if we let him sit out one season his arm would heal and he would help us the following season. We were half right. His arm did heal, but he never helped us.

Another year there was a player we liked in an early round who had a speech impediment. Our head scout convinced us that this problem affected his football, so we didn't take him. But in a later round, this same scout wanted us to take a player who stuttered. I asked him how he could recommend this player when he'd talked us out of drafting a better player who had a similar problem. "Oh, it's different," the scout explained, "this player is so dumb that his stutter doesn't bother him."

On draft day our offices resembled a war room. We had the names of the two hundred players we liked posted on one board, on another board we listed every selection as it was made, and we had numerous telephones. We were continually making adjustments in our strategy based on other teams' choices. For example, one year we intended to take a running back with our first pick. Detroit, picking well ahead of us, took a linebacker that we figured the Giants were going to take. The Giants then had to take a player Houston wanted. And Houston, picking just ahead of us, took our running back. We proceeded to select a lineman the Redskins really wanted.

In that room we not only debated among ourselves, but we were constantly on the phone with other teams, talking about trading draft picks. In 1979, we rated tight end Kellen Winslow of Missouri one of the top three college players in the country. We wanted him badly, but we had twentieth pick and no real hope that he would still be available by the time we took our turn. Even if Winslow was not among the first selections, the Bears were drafting eighteenth, two spots ahead of us, and we knew he was their top choice too. But as the draft progressed through the ninth, tenth, and eleventh spots, Winslow had not been taken. His name was just hanging there on the board, taunting us. With each pick the tension built. The closer our turn came, the more difficult it was to accept the fact that we weren't going to get him.

When he wasn't the number twelve selection, we decided to try to make a deal with the Cleveland Browns, picking thirteenth. The Browns were set at tight end, so we knew they weren't interested in Winslow. I got on the phone with Tommy Prothro, who was picking for the Browns. No one knew our personnel better than Tommy, so he knew how much we wanted Winslow. "Who you gonna take?" I asked him.

He named two defensive linemen. "We like either one of them."

"Look," I said, "There're only seven spots between you and us and chances are pretty good that one of those linemen is still gonna be available in our spot. So why don't we trade picks?"

No one figured the odds better than he did. "What'll you give us to switch?"

"What'll you take?"

After a pause to think it over, Tommy said, "Tell you what, you give me your first and your second and . . ." he named a player, ". . . we got a deal."

"Too much, Tommy," I said. "How about our first and second picks?"

In the background, one of my scouts moaned, "Not our second pick too?"

"Not enough," Tommy decided. A team is permitted fifteen minutes before having to make a selection. The clock was ticking. Meanwhile, on another phone, Johnny Sanders was trying to make a deal with the Jets, who were picking fourteenth, and whoever was picking fifteenth. Undoubtedly, the Bears knew what we were doing, and were trying to counter it by moving up themselves. I suspect the Browns were speaking to the Bears on another phone. This scenario was probably being repeated a hundred times that day. And all of it being done over players who might not be pro players anyway.

Tommy and I went back and forth until the Browns had less than a minute left to make their selection. Tommy made a last suggestion. It was still too much. "Go ahead and take your lineman," I conceded. "Let me see if the Jets want to make a move."

Tommy is one of the best poker players I've ever known, and I didn't know if he was bluffing, trying to raise the ante, or if he really didn't want to make a deal. Of course, he didn't know if I was bluffing either. The clock was running out.

Finally, with less than twenty seconds left, he folded. "Ah shucks, let's just do it."

We immediately called the league office and reported the deal, then selected Kellen Winslow. A few of my scouts were very upset. "How can you give up our second?" they wanted to know, reminding me that the next selection we had was the seventy-third pick overall, pretty deep into the talent pool to find any real help. If Winslow wasn't an impact player, we would have a bust-out draft, a draft in which we hadn't gotten any useful players.

"Deal's done," I said, "you guys have no vote." Fortunately, Winslow was as good as we hoped he would be, being selected an all-pro four of his first five seasons.

Unfortunately, by the time the Browns picked in our spot, both linemen Prothro wanted had been taken. Sometimes the odds don't work out. Prothro took a wide receiver who never really made it. He used the second pick we'd traded to him to take offensive lineman Sam Claphan. The Browns eventually cut Claphan, we claimed him, and he became a starter for us.

Sometimes, if you are a very good person and you try to treat people well, and contribute to charities, and try not to say anything bad about anyone except Al Davis, sometimes, if you do all that, and you're very lucky, everything works out just the way you want it to.

And sometimes you get Duane Thomas.

How valuable is a draft pick? If you don't have the pick you need, very valuable. One year when Hank Stram was with New Orleans, he called Tommy Prothro and offered to buy our first-round selection for $500,000. Five hundred thousand dollars? For one draft pick? I hadn't realized a selection was worth that much money, and if it was worth that much money, I certainly wasn't going to sell it.

Some picks, however, are worth a lot less. One year when we were still a bad ball club we'd made some trades and ended up with the twenty-eighth or twenty-ninth pick in the first round, much too late to get a player who could really help us. At a party in Los Angeles before the Super Bowl, I had one drink more than I should have had, and was driven home by the owner of the team picking directly after us. His team was as bad as the Chargers, and his pick wasn't going to make them much better. As we drove home, I had a wonderful idea. "Listen," I said, "neither one of us is going to get anything worthwhile in the draft. Why don't we flip a coin, with the winner getting both picks and the loser won't have any." I've often flipped a coin to close a stubborn deal, but this was the first time I did it to make a trade.

"Yeah," the other owner agreed, "that's a good idea. That way at least one of us might get a little help."

We went into the lobby of the Beverly Hills Hotel. This owner flipped a coin. "Tails," I called.

"Tails it is," he said. "You got two first-round picks."

A few days later he called me up. "You gotta help me, Gene," he said. "When I told my coach what happened, he went through the roof. He just exploded. If the writers find out I flipped a coin for our first-round pick, they'll just tear me apart. I want to live up to my agreement, but if you can mitigate it some way . . . I mean, I've got no excuse for giving away our first-round pick." He paused. "Would you take one of my seconds instead?"

In the corporate world I'd been known as a tough businessman, believing that a deal was a deal and stayed a deal. Perhaps this was the moment when it became clear to me that football was simply an association of owners trying to muddle through, and some muddlers were better at it than others. This owner and I weren't discussing a life or a company, it was simply the right to make another mistake. It could have been one of the best deals of my life—we were getting something for nothing. But the way we were drafting, I knew that by the time we agreed to a contract, we would have ended up with nothing for something. "All right," I agreed, "we'll take the second." At least it gave us the opportunity to make a less expensive mistake.

7

In the NFL's annual draft of college football players, each team is allotted one selection in every round. There are actually two ways in which a team can convert that right to make a selection into a player: use it in the draft to pick a college player, or trade it to another team in exchange for a veteran player. The Redskins' George Allen was the acknowledged "past master," trading almost all of his draft choices for veterans many football people believed were past their prime. To George, a draft choice was like a bad cold—it wasn't exactly fatal, just something mildly unpleasant you try to get rid of as quickly as possible. The Redskins were humorously referred to as "The Washington Football Team and Retirement Home," but George Allen's famed "Over the Hill Gang" eventually made it into the Super Bowl.

George Allen was able to get more use out of a draft choice than anyone else in football—sometimes twice as much use, in fact. In 1971, for example, Sid Gillman traded cornerback Speedy Duncan to the Redskins in exchange for a fifth-round pick in the 1973 draft that Washington had acquired from the Detroit Lions. But just prior to the 1973 draft we received a league memo listing the order of selection. Apparently Allen had gotten maximum use out of the Lions' fifth-round choice, trading it to another club, the Rams I believe, as well as to us. When I complained to the commissioner's office, Allen contended that he had given us his fifth-round pick in the *1974* draft in exchange for Duncan. Rozelle invited everyone to New York for a hearing.

I've made big mistakes and small mistakes in my career. I've bought failing companies, I've dialed wrong numbers. Every time I start thinking I might be infallible, I listen to a Beatles album. But in this situation, I knew I was right. After the deal had been completed, Allen and Gillman happened to be together on an airplane and Allen had written out the details of the transaction. It's nice to know you are right, but it's much more important to be able to prove it.

George Allen, however, had Edward Bennett Williams, the Redskins co-owner and a brilliant trial lawyer, with him.

The Redskins were well prepared for the meeting. George had put together a large board listing every Redskins draft choice over the next five years and what he had done with each of them. He made an elaborate presentation, explaining that he had carefully kept track of the disposition of every pick, so it was not possible that he'd made a mistake.

If I hadn't had that note in my pocket, even I might have believed him. When George was finished, I asked politely, "Now, George, you're sure about this?"

"Positive," he said emphatically.

"There's no possibility you've made a mistake?" I asked. I felt just as Perry Mason must have when he was the only one who knew that the fingerprints on the champagne glass matched those on the murder weapon.

"Gene," George said sincerely, "I'm sure about this."

"Well, then," I said, producing the damning evidence, "what about this?"

Had there been any spectators, they would have gasped. George and Ed Williams examined the document, then George pursed his lips and shook his head. "I'm not sure that's my signature," he decided.

A plot twist? The counterfeit-document ploy? Commissioner Rozelle interrupted, asking George, "Are you saying somebody else signed your name?"

George frowned. "No," he admitted, "I'm not." The commissioner eventually awarded us an extra draft pick. Once again, justice triumphed.

Most coaches and scouts were firmly against trading a draft choice for a player, insisting that it was unwise to trade your future for another team's past. If a player was any good, they argued, he wouldn't be available for an eighth-round draft choice.

I'd learned in business that it didn't matter why someone wanted to sell. I never cared why something was for sale; my only concern was how it fit into my plans. Would it help me accomplish my objective? If I were investigating a company, I wanted to know if it would help my bottom line. If it were a player, I wanted to know if he could fill a hole we needed filled. When coaches complained about trading a draft choice for a player, I'd ask, "If Chuck Muncie (a great running back we'd gotten for a second-round pick) were on the board in the second round, would you take him?"

"Of course."

"Then why wouldn't you trade him for a second?"

"Because you can't trade away the future."

Players, conversely, hated losing a teammate in exchange for a draft pick. The day after we'd gotten popular tight end Pat Curran from the Rams in exchange for a third-round pick, Rams coaches went out to practice and found a hand-lettered sign in the tight-end position reading, THIRD ROUND DRAFT PICK.

When Harland and I took over from Gillman in 1972, we decided to try an instant fix. We saw how successful George Allen had been in Washington in a similar situation and believed we could be just as successful in San Diego. Of course, we were missing a key element—George Allen. The main difference between what we did and what Allen did was that he got talented veteran players for his draft choices while we simply got veteran players. For example, we traded one of our two first-round picks in the 1973 draft to the Eagles for Tim Rossovich. Rossovich only lasted parts of two seasons. Our second 1973 pick and one of our two third choices went to the Rams for Deacon Jones, Greg Wojcik, and Lee White. Jones and Wojcik were with us two years, White, one year. One of our two fourth-round choices and our eighth 1973 pick went to the Colts for defensive tackle George Wright. Six weeks after obtaining Wright, we traded him to Cleveland for their fifth-round choice. So that deal was a fourth *and* an eighth for a fifth, and we used that fifth to select a linebacker who didn't make the team. We traded one of the three fifth-round choices we owned in the 1973 draft to Buffalo for defensive end Cal Snowden. Snowden lasted two seasons. Our seventh-round pick in the '73 draft went to the Patriots for Ed Philpott. Ed Philpott didn't make our squad.

We did not limit ourselves to trading away our future; we also traded away our present to obtain other teams' pasts. We easily broke George Allen's record for most trades by completing twenty-one deals in seven months. Besides Rossovich and Duane Thomas and Deacon Jones, besides buying Johnny Unitas, we got nine-year veteran Dave Costa from the Broncos, nine-year veteran Lionel Aldridge from Green Bay, and we signed ten-year veteran John Mackey when the Colts released him. "We've finished in third place six years in a row," Svare told reporters, "and we couldn't get out of that rut with small adjustments."

Costa and Aldridge both lasted two seasons. Mackey didn't survive one season. The result of all our dealing was that we did finally manage to get out of the third-place rut. We finished fourth, and last, the next four seasons. If George Allen's team was known as the Over the Hill Gang, it probably would be accurate to describe the team Harland Svare and I put together as the "Boot Hill Gang."

We had so many players coming and going in 1973 that instead of charging fans admission, it probably would have been more profitable for us to install a turnstile in front of our locker room. The situation got so confusing during training camp that we actually cut the wrong player.

At the end of the first week of training camp Svare was cutting about a dozen rookies. An assistant coach would bring them to the office, Harland would tell them that they did not have the ability to play for the Chargers, then they would leave. It was an unpleasant job, but it had to be done. Kicker Ray Wersching was the fourth or fifth player to be brought into Svare's office. Harland gave him the spiel, then sent him on his way. But after Wersching had left, Harland began thinking, Wait a second, that wasn't the kid I wanted to cut. He'd cut the wrong player. Two assistant coaches had to track down Wersching before he left camp to give him the reprieve. Thirteen seasons later, Wersching was still alive and kicking in the NFL.

I never claimed to be an expert on strategy. In time, I became a fair judge of raw talent. But the two things I could do as well as anyone in football were make a trade and negotiate a contract. Trading was an area in which I could put my business experience to good use. I don't know for sure, but I suspect that while I owned the Chargers we made more deals than any team in football. We were always on the telephone trying to get something going. Our annual phone bill was usually several hundred thousand dollars. We weren't exactly trying to reach out and touch someone. It was more like reaching out to put the touch on someone.

It wasn't always easy. One of the problems I had faced in business was the middle-management syndrome. Over and over I saw employees get promoted to comfortable middle-management positions and, instead of continuing the aggressive style that had enabled them to reach that point, they began making conservative decisions to protect their job. They were the corporate version of the movie star who did everything possible to become famous and, when he finally made it, fought with the photographers trying to take his picture.

I found a similar attitude in pro football. Many executives in positions to make deals were afraid to do so. They knew that making bad trades could cost them their job. But if they made no trades, they certainly couldn't be blamed for a trade not working out. I've never seen a sports-page headline reading, CHARGERS DO NOT TRADE PLAYER TO BEARS.

I was never afraid to make a deal. Never. In football as well as in business, you cannot negotiate if you're afraid to fail. What was going to happen to me if a deal I made didn't work out? I wasn't going to fire myself. My philosophy of trading was exactly the same as my philosophy of corporate acquisitions: Some deals are going to be successful, some deals are going to be disasters, but what counts is the overall balance. It was acceptable to lose $35 million on Minnie Pearl as long as I made $300 million on Great American; it was acceptable to trade two young players for Duane Thomas as long as we also traded two draft picks for the right to select Kellen Winslow.

The object of a trade is to get rid of a player or players you don't need or want in exchange for a player or players you need or want. Of course, it's important not to focus on the fact that the player or players you're getting are also people their team didn't need or want.

We always had a number of players we were willing to move, and we always knew at which positions we needed help. In one of our offices we had listed every player on every team, so we knew which teams had a surplus at which positions. What we would do every day was examine those lists and try to figure out how to use our excess players to get the help we needed.

I've always found that nothing happens unless you make it happen. You can't make the phone ring by wishing. So I always tried to force the action. At National General I would be on the phone with investment bankers six, seven times every day, telling them what I was looking for, listening to what they were pitching. In football, my general manager was constantly canvassing other teams. Every deal must begin with a conversation, and what we were trying to do was get people talking.

I was an advocate of the "Wudyatake" method of negotiating, whether I was buying a company or trading a football player. This method is best illustrated by the classic story in which a young man asks a young woman he's recently met if she will make love with him. "Absolutely not," she replies.

"Would you make love with me if I gave you a million dollars?" he then asks.

She thinks about that, then says, "Oh? Well, for a million dollars, I would."

"Fine. Then would you make love with me for two dollars?"

She slaps his face, "What kind of woman do you think I am?"

"We've already established that," he explains, "now we're just negotiating."

This was the same method we used when trading football players. Harland Svare or Johnny Sanders or Tank Younger were on the phone "wudyataking" every day. They would make a cold call to the general manager of another team and ask if that team's starting right tackle was available. "Absolutely not," the general manager would usually reply. "He's the key to our line. We wouldn't think of trading him."

"Well, would you take two first-round draft choices for him?"

"Oh? Well, for two first-round draft choices, sure we would."

"Fine. Then would you take a fourth-round draft choice? I'll give you a firm offer for a fourth."

Everyone would laugh at that—at least my general manager would laugh at that—but we'd started a discussion. Often that general manager would call back a week later to tell us, "We can't give you that right tackle, but we wouldn't mind moving our back-up wide receiver."

My general manager would report that conversation to me and I'd find out how highly our coaching staff rated that wide receiver. If he was better than the player we had at that position, we began negotiating seriously.

Most of the deals we made were initiated with a cold call. The one thing I stressed to my executives in the insurance business, in the movies, in football, was the importance of communication. That was how I found out Bantam Books was available. And that was how we obtained all-pro offensive guard Ed White from the Vikings. In 1978, White was having well-publicized problems negotiating a new contract with Minnesota, so we called Vikings general manager Jim Finks to ask if he would consider trading White. "Absolutely not," Finks said. "If we don't sign him, he's not going to play football and that's it. We're not going to trade him." In the vernacular of general managers, that meant Finks expected to be able to sign him to a new contract.

We did some "wudyataking," but Finks was adamant. White was going to play for the Vikings or he wasn't going to play football. We called back periodically, just to remind Finks that we were interested in making a deal. Only when it became apparent that White and the Vikings were not going to be able to reach an agreement did our conversations become serious. "You guys need a running back," Johnny Sanders told Finks. "We've got Rickey Young and he's not happy with us. I'm not saying we could do this, but would you take Young for White?" After some dickering, we closed the deal on those terms.

Young was a solid running back and had been our leading rusher in each of his three pro seasons. But Ed White was an all-pro. One of the factors that persuaded the Vikings to make the deal was the fact that White was six years older than Young, and had already played nine seasons of pro football. In fact, many people criticized us for making the deal, but we relied on statistics that showed that a lineman is much more durable than a running back. Ed White played for the Chargers through the 1985 season; Young retired in 1983.

Any team in pro football could have had Ed White. We got him because we were on the phone at the right time.

Very few trades are really big deals. We rarely put a player on waivers, meaning any other team could claim him for $100, before we've tried to get something in return for him. Something? Anything? A few deflated footballs, a sideline marker, anything. After we decided we were going to cut a player, our assistant coaches called every team in the league "wudyataking" and "wudyagiving." If we were lucky, we might get an "if-eighth," which meant that if the player made their team and survived two games, we would get an eighth-round draft choice for him. Usually, though, all we got for our efforts was a larger phone bill.

It was unethical to attempt to fool another team about a player's ability or physical condition. More important, it was almost impossible to get away with it. Every team in football has game films of every other team, so they know what a veteran player is capable of doing. They also have their original scouting reports on younger players, so they have some idea how talented first- and second-year players are. And finally, every trade is conditional on each player involved passing a thorough physical examination.

But it was possible to fool another team about why a player was available, and every team tried to do just that. As long as I was in football, no team ever traded a player because he was a troublemaker, a drug abuser, unable to remember the plays, or simply not good enough. Teams usually claimed that the only reason a certain player was available was that the team had a surplus of good players at his position. In at least one situation I found that difficult to believe—the team was asking for a man who played the same position in return. I tried not to be cynical, but I had learned enough to know that when a team confessed to me that the only reason they were even considering trading a player was that his family lived in Southern California and he was unhappy playing in the cold so far away from home, that that player had a drug problem, a salary problem, or he didn't get along with his teammates. About the only reason a team *wouldn't* trade a player was to make him happy.

I always tried to be honest, and I tried to be even more honest with those teams that were honest with me. One of the best trades we ever made was getting Charlie Joiner from the Bengals for Coy Bacon. Bacon was a character we'd gotten from the Rams for John Hadl. He played three seasons for us, playing well the first year, decently the second year, and poorly the third year. But as time passed, he had become a disruptive force on the team. When Cincinnati's Paul Brown called to ask me about him, I told him truthfully, "He'll be great for you one year, maybe two, then he's going to cause you problems. Believe me, I don't think you want him."

I think Paul Brown suspected that my honesty was actually a clever negotiating ploy. "Oh, that's all right," he told me, "what do you want for him?"

There is a considerable difference between honesty and insanity. I had been honest with Brown. If he still wanted Bacon, I wasn't going to try to talk him out of it. We needed a wide receiver and the Bengals had one of the best wide receivers in football. "Charlie Joiner," I said.

"No, seriously," Brown responded.

"Charlie Joiner," I repeated.

Paul Brown decided to be even more honest than me. "You don't want Joiner," he said. "He's already thirty years old, maybe he's got two seasons left. Why don't you take so-and-so, he's only twenty-four, twenty-five."

"When you say the name Charlie Joiner to me you've got a deal."

We spoke every few weeks during the next four months. I kept telling Paul Brown that he didn't want Bacon, and Brown kept telling me I didn't want Joiner. I felt I had an advantage. I knew I didn't want Bacon and did want Joiner, but Brown didn't know he really didn't want Bacon. Finally, Brown called me again. "You still interested in the deal?" he asked.

"You want Bacon for Joiner?"

"Do you?"

"If you do. But just remember what I told you about Bacon."

"And you remember what I told you about Joiner." We made the deal. Bacon played six more seasons. But ten years after we'd made the deal Joiner was still playing for the Chargers, having caught more passes than any receiver in NFL history.

Most deals of any consequence usually take weeks or months to negotiate, but not all of them. Sometimes you just make the right phone call at the right time. One day in 1980 I walked into the office at 8:30 A.M. and Johnny Sanders caught me in the hallway. "I was just on the phone with New Orleans," Johnny said. "I think we can get Chuck Muncie."

Muncie was an all-pro running back, certainly not the kind of player who becomes available unless there is a problem. When Sanders said, "I think we can get Chuck Muncie," what he really meant was, "New Orleans is trying to get rid of Muncie."

"What'll they take?" I asked.

"I think we can get him for a second-round pick."

An all-pro for a second-round draft choice? It had to be some serious problem. I hoped it was a salary dispute, but I decided it was impolite to pry into the private life of a star running back. If it was anything else, a drug problem for instance, I didn't want to know, the Saints didn't want me to know, Chuck Muncie didn't want me to know, and the NFL Players Association didn't want me to know. "Get on the phone and close the deal," I told Johnny. "Don't even try to negotiate with them, just get him."

"You know there's gotta be a problem," Johnny warned.

"Whatever it is," I said, "we'll take care of it." So we made the deal. For the next four years Chuck Muncie played outstanding football for the Chargers, becoming our second all-time leading rusher. And in 1984, when he publicly admitted that his cocaine habit was out of control, we paid all his expenses at the detoxification center.

One of the most important things to know when negotiating a deal, whether selling a used car or trading a football player, is who you're dealing with. When I was selling cars, I could tell within seconds after an individual walked onto my lot whether he was a live one or a tire-kicker. In football, I learned quickly who liked to deal and who liked to talk about dealing. George Halas was just great fun to negotiate with, but we rarely got anything done. "My boy," he'd say, "don't fight me too hard on this because I'm trying to give you the best football player I have, but you have to help me. I know you're going to take advantage of me, I know it, but just take it easy on me and you can have my best player." I would ask him if a certain player was available and he would respond by moaning, "Oh no, now you really do want to take advantage of me, don't you? I wish I didn't like you so much so I could say no. . . ."

Whenever Bob Irsay, who was actually a pretty good negotiator, got serious, he would say, "If you twist my arm hard enough I'll give you so-and-so for a first-round draft pick. But you've got to twist my arm."

And George Allen? If you asked George Allen what time it was, he'd trade you a draft choice. If you asked him how his family was, he'd trade you a defensive back. And as his record proves, he knew what he was doing. As owner of the Chargers I helped make some deals of which I'm very proud. Kellen Winslow. Charlie Joiner. Ed White. Wes Chandler, an all-pro wide receiver we got from the Saints for a first and third-round draft pick and a rookie receiver. But probably the deal of which I'm most proud, the toughest deal of all, the deal that many people believed was impossible, the only deal I made in football that ranks with the takeover of Great American or, for that matter, the construction of the Great Pyramid, was getting George Allen to actually give us something of value for Duane Thomas.

After it had become obvious that we had to get rid of Thomas, the question became who would take a player so difficult to deal with that even the San Diego Chargers, the worst team in football, no longer wanted him? Who in their right mind would do that?

Some people have unpleasant things to say about George Allen, but I'm not one of them. George Allen, the coach of last resort. The most important thing to know about George Allen is that if anyone should ever ask what the largest object in North America is, the answer is George Allen's ego. So the key to making a deal with George Allen was helping him build up his ego—not that he would have admitted needing help. After Duane Thomas had failed to report to the Chargers in 1972, I started building a case for him with George Allen. Every time I saw George at a meeting, every time I spoke to him on the phone, I'd sigh and say, "You know what I think, George? I think the only man in football capable of handling Duane Thomas is George Allen. Really, I think you're the only guy who can handle him. If Harland wasn't so dead set against it, I'd trade him to you right now. But you know Harland, he thinks he can get Thomas to play. Frankly, I doubt it; I think you're the only one who can. I promise you this, if I can ever talk Harland into trading him, you're the first person I'll call."

George agreed with me completely. "See what you can do," he'd encourage. "Try to talk Harland into it."

"I'll try, but if he doesn't want to, there's nothing I can do about it."

When we decided to get rid of Thomas, I told Harland, "Get on the phone and call George Allen. Say that I've been on your ass and that you really don't want to trade Thomas, but that you've finally got to admit that you can't handle him. Tell him that you know that he's probably the only guy in football who can bring out Thomas's talent—make sure you tell him that. Then tell him you want two first-round draft picks. If I know George, he'll come back and offer you a first and a second. Don't hang up the phone till you've made the deal."

A few hours later I was having dinner at a San Diego restaurant and Harland found me. "You've got to be clairvoyant," he said. "I called Allen, I told him that he was the only guy in football who could handle Thomas. He agreed with me. Then I told him we wanted two firsts. He offered me a first and a second. We went back and forth for a while, I complained, but finally I took it."

We used that 1975 first-round pick to take cornerback Mike Williams. Williams played with us eight years and was a starter on our championship clubs. I believe Allen got about half a season out of Duane Thomas, which was half a season more than anyone else could have gotten.

Obviously, with all the deals we made, some of them were clinkers. Trading a first-round pick to the Eagles for Tim Rossovich is a deal I wish I hadn't made. Deacon Jones. Dave Costa. Trading a fourth and an eighth pick for a fifth was mathematically difficult to defend. And switching first-round picks with Dallas, meaning we drafted twenty-fourth rather than fourteenth, as well as giving the Cowboys a second-round pick for snake-wrestling quarterback Clint Longley has to rank with helping producer Robert Evans get the co-starring role in the National General motion picture *The Getaway* for his wife, Ali MacGraw. MacGraw's co-star was Steve McQueen, for whom she left Evans.

But the important thing to remember was that there was a balance; some trades worked out very well, some did not work out at all, and once we got Duane Thomas.

In the entire time I owned the team I bought only one player for cash, Hall of Fame quarterback Johnny Unitas. Including the cost of the contract I gave Unitas, that deal cost me $600,000 and the only season he played we were 2-11-1. But it still turned out to be one of the better deals I ever made.

Unitas was close to forty years old when I bought him, and it was obvious to everyone he had very little football left. At most, I was hoping to get two seasons from him. I remember when we got Unitas, a reporter asked him what was wrong with his knees. "They're old," he replied, accurately. I was just hoping that his knowledge and his experience would enable him to overcome his physical limitations. As many owners will admit, hope is often the rationale behind giving long-term contracts to veterans.

Even Unitas was reluctant to play any longer. I offered him a two-year guaranteed contract at, I believe, $250,000 a year, and told him that he could decide at any time that he didn't want to play and I would still pay him. When I put this clause down on paper and gave him the contract to sign, he asked me, "Has your lawyer seen this?"

I told him he'd drawn up the contract.

"What'd he say?"

"He said it was a rotten deal for me and I shouldn't give it to you."

"I totally agree with him," Unitas said, "but if you're crazy enough to offer it to me, I'm certainly crazy enough to sign it."

I wanted him to sign it. I needed Johnny Unitas. I had a new stadium and a bad football team. I needed something I could promote. My experience in show business had taught me the value of putting a star's name on the marquee. Sentiment sells. The prospect of watching the greatest quarterback in pro-football history playing for the Chargers really excited San Diego. We'd won only four games in 1972, but we sold 40,341 season tickets for the 1973 season, more than we'd ever sold before, and the most we would sell until 1979. So within a week of signing Unitas, I made back most of what he had cost me in increased season-ticket sales.

In addition, we'd drafted Dan Fouts in the third round that year. We knew Fouts had a tremendous amount of raw ability, but we also knew he had a lot to learn. Unitas turned out to be an invaluable tutor. Day after day Unitas and Fouts would go off by themselves to a corner of the field and practice taking snaps from center, dropping back into the pocket and getting set up to pass quickly. The ability to set up quickly is often the difference between a pro-football quarterback and a former college quarterback now working at an insurance company. Eventually Fouts became a mirror image of Unitas; from a distance it was impossible to tell the two of them apart. Four games into the 1973 season we were trailing the Steelers at halftime, 38–0. Harland took out Unitas and put in Fouts. Fouts completed eleven of twenty-one passes, threw for one touchdown, and led the team to two others. Whoops, I thought as I watched him, looks like we got ourselves some kind of quarterback.

And finally, no matter how tough a businessman I was supposed to be, no matter how much attention I paid to the bottom line, no matter how much of a realist I was, I was also a football fan. And the fan inside me wanted to believe that Johnny Unitas was going to end his career in one last magnificent burst of glory. He was going to lead the San Diego Chargers to the Super Bowl.

Besides, it was a great thrill for me to be able to go to practice every day and see Johnny Unitas playing for my team.

The only problem was that Unitas couldn't play anymore. His legs were gone and he had no lateral movement. With our offensive line even a young, mobile quarterback would have had difficulty convincing a life-insurance company to write him a policy. Unitas was just a standing target. He was a tough competitor, though, and dragged himself through the 1973 season.

When Unitas reported to training camp in 1974, Tommy Prothro was put in an uncomfortable situation. He knew Unitas was through, but he didn't want to be the coach who cut a legend. So Tommy invited Unitas into his office and asked him bluntly, "Do you think you can still play in the NFL?"

"No, coach," Unitas admitted, "I can't."

"Well, then, why don't you retire?"

"I can't," Unitas told Prothro. "I wouldn't feel right about just walking out and taking the money. You're gonna have to cut me."

Tommy had no choice: He cut Johnny Unitas. He told me afterward that it had not been as hard to do as he thought it would be, because Unitas had had the chance to fulfill his dreams. The toughest cuts, Tommy said, are the rookies who are never going to get the chance to make their dreams come true.

Unitas had been one of the rare free agents to become a star in pro football. Free agents are players who are not drafted, meaning not one team thought they were among the best three hundred or four hundred college players, or players who had been cut by the team that had drafted them, traded for them, or originally signed them as a free agent. One team's free agent is every other team's mistake. But discovering a free agent who can actually help the team is about as easy as getting Howard Cosell to admit he's wrong.

A free agent needs to be lucky to make the team. The Chargers signed a number of free agents while I owned the team, among them running back Don Woods. Woods had been the Packers' sixth-round draft choice in 1974, but was cut in training camp. Any team could have picked him up for $100. We signed him only because his college coach had become our defensive-line coach. Woods became the NFL's Rookie of the Year in 1974 and played seven seasons for us, finishing his career as the third-leading ground gainer in team history.

The biggest obstacle a free agent has to overcome to make the team is a lack of playing time. Coaches believe that if a player had real ability other coaches would have recognized it, so they tend not to give free agents the same opportunities that draft choices get. Running back Hank Bauer, for example, signed with the Cowboys as a free agent in 1976 after a great small-college career, but failed to make their squad. The following summer he came to camp with us. Tommy Prothro didn't play him at all in our first two preseason games, and it looked like he didn't intend to use him in the third game either. A player who didn't get into the game didn't appear in the game films, and coaches relied heavily on game films when cutting the team. So Bauer's pro-football future was about as secure as a man dangling over the Grand Canyon on a length of spider's web.

During a game, when Prothro wanted to send in a player, he'd shout out that player's name, assistants would notify the player, who would report to Tommy for instructions and then go into the game. In the second half of that third preseason game, Tommy needed a running back. Pat Curran, who had become friendly with Bauer, happened to be standing behind Prothro when Tommy began scanning the sidelines for a running back. "Bauer," Curran whispered loudly, "put in Bauer."

"Bauer!" Prothro screamed, although he probably didn't even know who Bauer was. Bauer! Bauer! Bauer! The message was relayed. Bauer went into the game and impressed the coaching staff with his blocking ability. Gradually, Prothro learned who Hank Bauer was, and started using him intentionally. Bauer made the team and played six seasons, starring on special teams. After retiring in 1982, he became a member of the Chargers' coaching staff.

We spent almost a million dollars a year scouting potential draft choices. We spent hundreds of thousands of dollars a year in telephone bills trying to make trades. We had coaches for every conceivable area of the game. We had a podiatrist, we had a psychiatrist, we had a team dietitian. We had computers. We even had employees clipping stories out of newspapers. We did everything possible to put together a winning football team. Pat Curran happened to be standing behind the coach during a preseason game and we discovered a valuable football player.

If I wasn't so smart, every once in a while, I'd think there was an element of luck involved here somewhere. And I never could figure out how to buy luck.

For every Don Woods and Hank Bauer, though, there is a waiter at a seafood restaurant. As the six-foot-five-inch owner of the Chargers, I was one of the more easily recognizable people in San Diego. I was constantly being approached by people who believed they, or someone they knew, had the ability to play or coach in the NFL. The fact that they hadn't been able to play on their college teams, or had no coaching experience, did not intrude on the fantasy. Usually I just put these people in touch with our scouting staff. Usually. Only once did I actually get involved. Joyce and I have a favorite restaurant in San Diego, a little fish place on the beach named the Triton. We ate there about once a week and thus became friendly with some of the young people working there. One of them was a fine waiter named Paul, and after we'd gotten to know him, he told me that he was actually a terrific punter. The better we got to know him, the better his punting became. Finally, one July about two weeks before we opened training camp, he served us halibut and said, "Mr. Klein, I know you don't believe me, but I really can punt. You think I could get a tryout with the Chargers?"

I knew he couldn't really be very good; good waiters do not punters make. But the possibilities intrigued me. What if he could kick? What a wonderful story it would make—local waiter makes the pro-football team. It was so outlandish that it appealed to me. The more I thought about it, the more I liked the idea. So I set up a tryout for him. We had him sign a standard player's contract, gave him a complete physical, and issued him a uniform. We did not give him a signing bonus. I barely gave him a tip.

I went down to the field before practice one day to watch him try out. I made sure Coryell was watching. My waiter took the ball, made a good approach into it, and boomed the ball, really boomed it, maybe 20, 25 yards. It wasn't even a good kick for a waiter. I didn't say anything. Anyone can blow a punt, I thought, particularly under all this pressure. I knew he couldn't really be that bad; after all, he was my waiter.

He tried again. This time he got his foot into it. It went about 35 yards. Coryell started walking away, muttering, "Where'd that guy come from?"

I didn't answer. What was I going to say, the Triton restaurant?

Soon after that fiasco Joyce and I saw Paul at the restaurant. He told us he was very disappointed he hadn't done better, but appreciated the chance he'd been given. And that was the end of it for an entire year. The following July, Joyce and I were at the Triton again and, as Paul served us a platter of clams, he said, "You know, Mr. Klein, my kicking has really improved since last season and . . ."

"Do you have any more red sauce?" I asked quickly, thereby ending his professional football career.

Only once did we actively search for a free agent. In 1973, we were desperate for a placekicker. It seemed as if every team in pro football, except the Chargers, had been able to sign a Europ-ean-style placekicker, a former soccer-playing "sidewinder." So we decided to go to Europe and find the best soccer player we could, then convert him into an American football player.

The search committee consisted of myself, Harland Svare, and former NFL star Charlie Conerly. We packed a bag of footballs and went to England, Denmark, Norway, Italy, Turkey, Greece, Austria, and France in search of a placekicker. Owning a pro-football team isn't all drug problems and Duane Thomas.

The agent representing the Dallas Cowboys' Austrian kicker, Toni Fritsch, had gone before us and arranged for us to try out three, four, or five of the best kickers in each country. Few of the soccer players we met had ever seen an American football before, so all we were looking for was someone with a strong kicking leg and the ability to lift the ball into the air quickly. Most soccer players punch line drives, we needed someone who could lift the ball over charging linemen. We also told the agent we wanted athletes who had played in front of large crowds. We didn't want a kicker who would get in front of sixty-two thousand screaming fans and freeze.

Tryout conditions varied in each country. In Athens, we held our tryout in a narrow alley. In Oslo, we had to bulldoze a foot of snow off a parking lot before we could begin. In Istanbul, we worked out in the mud.

Some of the players we met were unforgettable. In Rome, a young soccer player told us somberly that he was trying out for the Chargers because he hoped to get "football asylum" in America. An English kicker blamed his poor showing on atmospheric conditions, meaning he couldn't kick in the rain. And in Istanbul, the ex-mayor of the city served as our guide and interpreter. Except for the fact that he barely spoke English, he did a fine job. The ex-mayor told us that he himself had once played American football and knew all about the game. He had personally arranged for the very best kicker in all of Turkey to try out. When this young player arrived we walked over to an empty, muddy field, and the ex-mayor announced he would be honored to serve as holder for this kicker. We explained that we would rather have Charlie Conerly do it, but the ex-mayor insisted it was an honor he deserved.

So the ex-mayor and the young kicker went to one end of the field. The ex-mayor got down on one knee in the mud and held the ball in kicking position. The kicker got set, made his approach, pulled back his leg and, just as he started swinging his leg forward, the ex-mayor let go of the ball. He just dropped it. It rolled away and the kicker missed it completely, ripping a hamstring muscle. He screamed in pain, and started hobbling around. I looked at Svare and said, "Do you realize we're going to have the first international grievance made to the Players Association?"

The kicker couldn't walk back to the hotel, so we got an old station wagon from somewhere and helped him climb into the rear so he could keep his leg stretched out. We drove into the city and when we reached an intersection, the ex-mayor told us to stop. The kicker wanted to get out there. So I went around and lifted up the back door. As the kicker climbed gingerly out of the wagon, that big old back door came down and hit him on the head. That poor guy was staggering around the street in the middle of Istanbul, not knowing which part of his body to grab first. He had one hand on his head, his other hand on his leg, and he was hobbling in a circle, wailing loudly. "You know," Harland said casually as we watched, "if this had happened in America, you'd be paying this guy for the next thirty years."

We finally found our kicker in Austria. His ability to lift the ball quickly made him stand out. After his tryout, we met with him in the lobby of the Ritz hotel in Vienna and invited him to come to America to play football for the Chargers.

He was thrilled. "Vonderful," he repeated over and over, "vonderful." Then he asked us when he had to report to our training camp.

"Practice begins in ten days," Svare explained. "We'll need you there then."

The kicker's shoulders dropped as if someone had let the air out of them. "But I cannot," he explained, "I'm to be getting married in three weeks. I come to America in three weeks and one day."

Who was I to come between young lovers? The owner of a professional football team, that's who. What was more important, being ready to play when the season began or the rest of his life? "I'm sorry," I told him, "but we can't wait that long. You've got a lot to learn and not much time. If you can't be there in ten days,

I'm afraid we're just going to have to try to find someone else."
And some people thought I took football too seriously.

He thought about my warning for a moment, then smiled
broadly. "Is okay now," he decided, "wedding just canceled."

He worked extremely hard in practice, his form was excellent,
and he had a strong, accurate leg. We were all anxious to see him
perform under pressure.

At the very beginning of a football game, before a team runs
onto the field, the players gather outside their locker room and
wait until the public-address announcer introduces them. Before
our first exhibition game, we were all standing there, waiting,
shifting around, and suddenly, toward the back of the squad, I
saw the kicker's head popping up, then disappearing. He was
leaping straight up and down, sort of like a piston. I wondered if
that might be something soccer players did before a game to
loosen up their leg muscles, but I didn't give it too much thought.
It was difficult to ignore though, the way he kept bobbing up and
down.

We lost the coin toss and he had to kick off. His form was
perfect as he approached the ball. And he kicked it almost 30
yards, most of it straight up in the air. He blooped it.

He can always learn how to kick off, I thought; kicking off is
relatively easy. We needed him to kick field goals. That was the
most important thing. In the middle of the second quarter he
attempted his first field goal. It was then that the flaw in our plan
became obvious. When we went to Europe we'd taken with us
about a dozen footballs and Charlie Conerly to act as holder. We
forgot to bring one very important thing—another team.

Without another team on the field this kicker had real ability,
but he couldn't concentrate when eleven incredibly large men
were trying to rip him to pieces. He just couldn't kick during a
game, severely limiting the opportunities we had to use him.

After he missed his first few attempts, the fans began booing
every time he went onto the field. The harder he tried, the worse
he performed, the more the fans booed. It became obvious that
he wasn't going to make the team, and I wanted to cut him.
Harland hesitated, though, because as long as the fans were
booing the kicker, they couldn't boo him.

We cut the Austrian placekicker before the beginning of the

season, but everything worked out rather well for him. He stayed in Southern California and went into real estate, and is currently a successful contractor in La Jolla.

Once we'd drafted, traded for, purchased, claimed, or discovered a player, we had to sign him to a contract. Usually my general manager handled negotiations, but if he reached a stalemate with a player or his agent, or the numbers got very high, I got personally involved.

At no point is the difference between professional sports and business more clearly delineated than in the area of compensation. When I bought the team I intended to run it as I ran my corporation, paying people what they were worth, basing my salary structure on the profit-and-loss statement of the organization. I didn't expect to have any real difficulty negotiating contracts with my players because I had always believed in paying an employee according to his value to the corporation. When I bought Bantam Books, for example, I realized that I couldn't afford to lose Oscar Dystel, so I gave him a ten-year contract at a salary larger than mine, as well as stock options that eventually became worth millions of dollars. I believed in paying full value, and I assumed that that attitude would enable me to keep my players happy.

I learned differently. Oh, did I learn differently. When a young athlete is growing up, he claims that he would give anything for the chance to play professional football. But when he finally gets that opportunity, he realizes that what he really meant to say is that he would *take* anything for the chance to play professional football, provided the first year is guaranteed.

I think I began to realize salaries had gotten out of control during the Iranian oil cutoff. One of our running backs, Johnny Rodgers, had reportedly gotten so upset because he had to wait in line for gasoline for his Rolls-Royce that he bought a San Diego service station. "But I bought it for my friends' convenience too," Johnny said kindly.

Once upon a time negotiating contracts with football players had been quite simple. Negotiations consisted of the owner making an offer and the player accepting it. On occasion, a player would hold out for more money, but rarely would a player fail to sign his contract long before the season began. In those days there were no such things as agents, multiyear contracts, signing bonuses, reporting bonuses, performance bonuses, deferred payments, low-interest and no-interest loans, renegotiations and re-renegotiations. Of course, those were also the days of the $4,000 Cadillac.

Harland Svare told me how he used to negotiate his own contract when he was starring for the New York Giants. "I'd go into the office to see Wellington Mara," he remembered, "and before he even mentioned a figure he'd start telling me, 'Geez, it's been a tough year. I just built a new house and I had a lot of unexpected expenses. . . .' By the time I left Mara's office I'd be feeling sorry for him. I'd sign for whatever figure he put in front of me.

"One year I decided to hold out. He called me up and asked me what I thought I was doing. He was very angry. I told him I thought I was entitled to more money and that I wasn't going to report until I got it.

"'Don't be silly,' he told me, 'just get the hell in here now.'

"'Oh okay,' I said, 'if you put it that way.' That was the way we negotiated in those days."

Tank Younger was one of the greatest players ever to play pro football, but in his entire NFL career he received only two raises. He signed his first contract with the Los Angeles Rams in 1949 for $6,000. He was still earning $6,000 in 1951, when he played both offense and defense, making all-pro as a linebacker and second- or third-team all-pro as a fullback. Before the 1952 season he tried to negotiate a new contract with Rams owner Dan Reeves. Tank carefully recited his season's statistics and told Reeves he wanted a 100 percent raise—a $12,000 salary.

Reeves just leaned back in his chair and said, "You know, Tank, we don't reward mediocre performances here. If I gave you twelve thousand dollars, my children would have to eat hamburgers for the rest of the year."

In those days a player could go to training camp unsigned. Tank reported and played all the preseason games without a contract. In the locker room just before the opening game of the 1952 season, the general manager offered Tank a raise to $10,000, and promised that at the end of the season, if the head coach decided he had had a good year, he would receive a $1,000 bonus. Tank agreed.

After the first game they fired the head coach. Now that was tough negotiating. Eventually, however, Tank did get his bonus.

With the experiences that Tank and Harland had had while playing, I felt secure knowing that they were negotiating for the Chargers.

I knew I could negotiate. Besides having sold encyclopedias and used cars, and having bought and sold companies, I had served with my friend Gene Wyman as co-chairman of Hubert Humphrey's western fund-raising committee in the 1968 presidential election. Hubert Humphrey was a great man, but he was also one of the few people I've ever known who was capable of delivering a ten-minute speech in an hour. The man could talk. Gene Wyman and I were constantly trying to convince him to limit his basic campaign speech to twenty minutes. Trying to convince Hubert Humphrey to stop talking was almost as hopeless as trying to teach a statue to dance. But we kept trying. Hubert finally agreed with us, and we decided that the next time he spoke, Gene Wyman and I would sit in the back of the room, and after twenty minutes we would raise our arms to remind him to conclude his speech.

He started talking, and after twenty minutes we raised our arms. Also after thirty minutes. After forty minutes both of us were standing up and waving both arms. Eventually, Hubert paused, then said, "You know, folks, there are two gentlemen in the back of the room waving their arms to remind me that I've been speaking too long. So I'd like to ask them to put down their arms because if they keep waving until I'm finished, they're going to get very tired." Then he spoke for another twenty minutes.

So after selling encyclopedias and used cars, and trying to convince Hubert Humphrey to stop talking, I was not about to be intimidated by an agent.

Actually, I appreciated the value of a good agent. I'd spent decades negotiating with some of the shrewdest businessmen in the world, so it would be about as fair for me to expect a young football player just out of college to be able to deal directly with me as it would be for the Racing Association to require my horses to race wearing snowshoes.

Most football players are not qualified to negotiate their own contracts. Recently, for example, an all-pro player attempted to renegotiate his own contract. The owner of the team for which he played offered him a reasonable amount of money, but instead of giving the player a signing bonus, he suggested that the player become a one-third partner with the owner and head coach in a cattle-raising combine. The only stipulation was that any two of the three partners could cancel the deal. "You're gonna make a lot of money from this operation," the owner promised the player. "I've got one just like it with my kids and they've made a bundle from it."

"I'm gonna make a lot of money?" the player asked.

"You're gonna make a lot of money," the owner replied.

The player accepted the offer. Shortly thereafter the owner and the head coach canceled the deal, leaving the player with nothing except his salary. The player filed a grievance with the Players Association, which had no choice but to dismiss it.

I wanted my players to be fairly represented. There are many agents who are determined, honest negotiators who do an excellent job. They get their clients the money that they are worth, making them good for the player and good for the team. Unfortunately, they seem to be in the minority. The only thing an individual needs to become an agent is a client. Some agents would do anything to induce a college football player to sign an agreement with them. We saw many instances in which an agent apparently gave college players money or cars, or supplied women and drugs to get these players' signatures on a representation agreement.

Eventually, the players outsmarted the agents. They accepted everything that was offered to them and signed with every agent who offered something worthwhile. We drafted one player and had six different agents contact us to negotiate his contract. He'd signed with each of them. None of the agents had any legal recourse because their actions had been illegal. We told the player to designate one agent as his representative and sign with him.

Some agents convinced players to sign with them by guaranteeing that they could get them a certain amount of money. The player would believe the agent, and when we were unwilling to pay the amount of money the agent had promised, the player blamed us rather than the agent.

There were agents who used tactics that would have embarrassed an owner. Teams usually signed high draft choices to a series of one-year contracts, guaranteeing only the first year. So if these players failed to make the team in their second or third or fourth year, they would not be paid. But the agent who negotiated the contract would take his commission on the entire package up front. For example, we might give a player five one-year contracts at $100,000 a year, guaranteeing only the first $100,000. The agent who negotiated the contract would be entitled to a commission, perhaps 5 percent, or $5,000 each year. But some agents took their entire $25,000 commission out of the first $100,000. If the player failed to make the team, the agent still had his commission.

In addition to taking a commission for negotiating a contract, a few agents set up companies to invest their clients' money, and took an additional commission on that. Other agents didn't even bother setting up a company—they simply invested their clients' money in a deal, then took a commission from their client as well as some form of kickback from the principals in the investment.

This is not to imply that every agent is a thief or is incompetent. Of course that's not true. A few years ago, however, the NFL Players Association required every agent to register with them. Currently there are more registered agents than there are players in the NFL. Among that rather large group there are certainly going to be some incompetent or unscrupulous people.

Many of them seemed to end up negotiating with the Chargers. The most elementary negotiating strategy, for example, is to start with a figure high or low enough to allow some maneuvering room. One day Harland met with an agent representing a high second-round draft choice. Harland began negotiations by "lowballing" him, saying, "We know what your client is capable of doing and we're prepared to pay him fifteen thousand dollars his first season."

"Oh, shit," the agent responded, "I was gonna ask for a hundred thousand." That was his entire negotiating strategy. Eventually we raised our offer, just to make sure the player was fairly compensated.

When we drafted Fred Dean, his agent showed us a signed agreement guaranteeing him 10 percent of everything Dean earned "in the world and in the universe."

Another agent representing an eighth- or ninth-round pick called Harland about a week after the draft. This agent began negotiations by telling Harland what a great player his client was going to be, assuring him that we'd gotten a real "sleeper." But some of the things he said made no sense, so Harland interrupted him and asked, "Have you ever met your client?"

The agent was silent for a moment. "Well, not personally," he admitted, "but we've spoken on the phone a few times."

Once Johnny Sanders and I met with an agent representing a third-year player who was asking for an unusually large salary. He argued that the amount of money he was asking for was what was being paid to third-year players who made the all-pro squad. Johnny pointed out that his client had not made the all-pro team. "You're absolutely right," the agent admitted, "but that's only because the people who picked the team didn't know what they were doing."

An agent representing one of our star players once tried to break a negotiating stalemate by asking me, "Don't you want the people playing for you to be happy?"

"Of course I do," I responded, "but don't you want your client playing for a happy owner?"

Occasionally, lower-round draft choices would try to represent themselves. Players drafted in the tenth round and lower really had little negotiating power, and generally had to take whatever was offered. But one year we drafted a player from the San Diego area who tried to get more than we were offering by arguing, "Have you ever considered what my drawing power is here in San Diego?" Besides his parents? we wondered.

Among the most memorable salary discussions I ever had was one with a star player who was dissatisfied with the contract he'd signed a year earlier that guaranteed him $300,000 a season. Although I never renegotiated a contract, in certain situations I was willing to compensate a player by adding years to his existing contract at a higher salary or by adding performance bonuses. When this player came into my office, he sat with his hands clasped between his legs, his head bowed slightly. This was an intelligent individual and I expected to hear a rational argument for a contract adjustment. "Here's my problem," he said so softly I had to turn up my hearing aid, "I've got to have more money."

I waited. I expected him tell me that he had had an excellent season; I expected him to point out that players who had not equaled his performance were earning more money. But he didn't say another word—he just looked at me and waited for me to respond. "What?" I finally asked.

"I just can't make it on three hundred thousand dollars a year. I want more money."

At least he was direct. It was sort of refreshing to hear someone admit that the reason he wanted more money was that he wanted more money. No fancy arguments here. I tried to be polite. "I'm sorry," I said, "but when you signed your contract I told you I wouldn't renegotiate. I told you not to sign if you weren't satisfied."

He didn't respond exactly as I had hoped. Instead he erupted, shouting at me, "Hey! Don't be such a stupid sonofabitch. Don't you understand what I'm telling you? I want more money!"

Here's another negotiating tip to remember: Never shout at a man who has his hearing aid turned up. That was the end of the negotiating session. I immediately invited this player to leave my office, a suggestion I referred to as negative reinforcement.

The longest, toughest negotiating experience I had as owner of the Chargers was with Dan Fouts. It lasted eleven years. Fouts was as tough at the contract talks as he was on the field. We negotiated three contracts, each one more difficult than the last. My negotiations with Fouts and his agent, Howard Slusher, were representative of the myriad problems I had signing football players.

A few months after we'd picked Fouts in the third round of the 1973 draft, and not long after we'd seen him break his collarbone on national television, Harland Svare and I met with Fouts, his father, and Howard Slusher to hammer out the details of his contract. That very first day I realized Dan Fouts was going to be something special. He walked into the room with his arm in a sling. We didn't know when he'd be able to play again, or even if he'd heal completely, but he asked for more money than we intended to give our first-round pick.

Svare explained that although we were confident Fouts would eventually be our starting quarterback, it took at least three or four years to develop an NFL quarterback. He also mentioned that our quarterback that season was going to be Johnny Unitas.

Fouts listened, and when Harland had finished, told him, "That's all fine, but I'm good enough to start right away."

How did I decide how much to pay Fouts? Draft choices were usually paid within a certain range based on the round in which they had been picked and the length of the contract. Veterans were paid based on their previous salary, their value to the club, the success of the club on the field and on the bottom line, the amount of money players with similiar experience on other clubs were making, as well as certain intangibles, how popular the player was with the fans, how cooperative he was, and probably most important, how little we could get away with.

After some haggling, Dan Fouts signed a three-year contract. By the time that contract expired he was our starting quarterback. To his credit, he never asked us to renegotiate. But when we sat down to work out a new deal, Slusher was determined to make us pay big numbers.

Fouts loved Slusher, but I never liked his methods. There are certain agents who are tough negotiators, but know how to make a deal. Slusher is a deal breaker. His philosophy of negotiation was simple: Give me what I demand or my client will not play for you. He often opened negotiations by making an outrageous demand. Eventually he would come down to a ridiculous figure, then complain because the team wouldn't come up to meet him halfway between their offer and his ridiculous figure.

In negotiating Fouts's second contract, Slusher and I disagreed over the length of the deal. I wanted to sign him for one or two years, and Slusher wanted a five-year agreement. I never thought long-term contracts were beneficial to the player or the club. If the player improved, he was going to be underpaid. If he didn't play well, he was going to be overpaid. "If he's that good," I told Slusher, "let's sign him for two years. After that he'll get substantially more than he will now."

Slusher insisted on the security of a five-year deal. Finally I agreed. Then we couldn't get together on the money. I made what I considered a fair and final offer. Slusher rejected it. Slusher and I became locked in a battle of clichés; he thought I was being as stubborn as a mule, and I thought I was showing the courage of my convictions.

Fouts broke the deadlock. He came to see me in Palm Springs

and pleaded his case. "I'm worth more money," he said, then told me why. The fact that he had personally come to see me impressed me more than his arguments. Five minutes after we'd sat down, we shook hands on a five-year deal worth more than $200,000 a year.

Within two or three years salaries had escalated substantially and it was obvious that Fouts was being underpaid. But he never complained, never asked to renegotiate. However, when that contract expired Slusher demanded another long-term deal at about $1 million a year, almost twice as much as the highest-paid player in pro football was being paid.

I met with Slusher. I met with Fouts. I met with Slusher and Fouts. We couldn't make a deal. I believed Fouts was the best quarterback in pro football and expected to pay him a lot of money. But $1 million a year? As the Falcons' Rankin Smith had once said in a similar situation, "If he doesn't sign we lose him. If he does sign, I go broke."

Finally, Fouts, Slusher, and I got together on the telephone. We agreed to a deal that would pay Fouts about $750,000 a year, with bonuses escalating to $1 million if we won the Super Bowl. We announced that we had reached an agreement.

But when Slusher sent me his draft of the contract, the deal fell apart. The salary figures were accurate, but Slusher had included some clauses which I didn't remember agreeing to and which didn't appear in the notes I'd taken. The three of us met in my office to try to iron out our difficulties. Fouts was irate. "Why don't you live up to your agreement?" he screamed at me.

"Because that's not what I agreed to," I screamed right back at him.

"The hell you didn't."

"The hell I did."

Slusher had to pull us apart. Imagine my embarrassment, being saved by an agent. It occurred to me that I had finally come full circle—from fighting with owners Wayne Valley and Al Davis at the first league meeting I'd attended to fighting with my star player. Fouts and Slusher finally stormed out of my office. The deal was off.

After I'd calmed down I began thinking about what had happened. Negotiations that nearly end up in a fistfight between an

owner and a player cannot be considered successful. I knew that
Dan Fouts was an honorable man. If he said he'd heard me agree
to something, he had probably heard me agree to something. And
Slusher? If Dan Fouts said he'd heard me agree to something . . .

Maybe it was my hearing, I thought. Maybe I just didn't hear
Slusher correctly. The disagreement could have been my fault. I
called Fouts and suggested we forget about what had happened
and try to get together. I met with Slusher in Los Angeles and we
reached an agreement that made Fouts one of the highest-paid
players in football.

One of the many things I admired about Dan Fouts was that
when he was clearly being underpaid, he never asked to renegotiate his contract. The only real difficulty we had was in 1977, if
you consider Fouts sitting out most of the season without being
paid a difficulty. When the Chargers got Rams quarterback James
Harris in exchange for a fourth-round draft choice, Fouts felt that
we had lost confidence in his ability and threatened to retire if we
didn't trade him. This was not a negotiating ploy; Fouts never
asked for a penny more. He just wanted to play and be appreciated. I refused to trade him. Whether Fouts refused to play or
forced us to trade him, the result would be the same for the
Chargers: no Dan Fouts.

We couldn't even find him. He went up to Oregon and shut off
his telephone.

During this time I learned that it is quite possible to be absolutely right and still be very unpopular, which is an important
thing to remember when you're very unpopular. It was not difficult for Chargers fans to choose sides. On one side was the young,
popular, cocky quarterback Dan Fouts. On the other side was the
sixty-year-old multimillionaire owner of the team. In the movie
version, Fouts would have been played by Tom Cruise; I would
have been portrayed by the actor who played Freddie, the title
character in *Nightmare on Elm Street*.

The situation probably would have been mitigated had James
Harris been effective, but we were only 4-4 when Harris was injured and lost for the remainder of the season.

What's popular? Being able to go to a restaurant without someone asking me why Dan Fouts wasn't playing? Stopping at a traffic light without someone blaming me for alienating the best

quarterback the team ever had? My friends casually staying three or four steps away from me when we were walking together?

I remained adamant: Fouts was going to play with the Chargers or not play at all. This was not general-manager talk—this was owner talk. I'd never let an employee tell me how to run a business before, and I did not intend to start at this point. There is a league rule that prohibits activating a player who has not reported after a certain number of games have been played. The week before Fouts would have been required to sit out the remainder of the season, Slusher went to the league office and got him reinstated. The day Fouts reported to the team I went into the locker room and told him how happy I was to have him back. I was very happy, in fact. Not only were we a stronger team, it was a lot easier for me to go out to dinner.

Perhaps if I had traded Fouts, Slusher would have tried to renegotiate his contract with his new team, but he did not even suggest that to me. Slusher knew that I did not believe in renegotiating contracts. Each owner had to make and live with his own policy on renegotiation. My policy was that I didn't do it. I believed that a contract was a voluntary agreement between parties that required each party to perform certain actions. My job was to pay the player, and his job was to play.

There were situations in which it was obvious that a player was being underpaid. In some of those situations I extended a contract at a higher salary or added performance bonus clauses. When Kellen Winslow was being underpaid, for instance, I added bonus clauses one season, then guaranteed them the following season. But I absolutely, unequivocally, refused to renegotiate a contract. If a player had had a bad year, or had been injured and couldn't play, I still paid him exactly what I had agreed to pay him, so I saw no reason to pay a player extra for having an outstanding year.

We had players holding out, refusing to play, practically every season. I never objected to a player holding out when negotiating a new contract. Withholding services is a legitimate negotiating technique. It was certainly a means of establishing a player's value to the organization. But I would not deal with a player who had a valid contract and refused to play. If a player refused to live up to a valid contract, what guarantee did I have that he would fulfill a new contract? I also knew that if I agreed to renegotiate one player's contract, I'd have half the team lined up outside my office the next day demanding that I renegotiate their contracts.

As a fan, I wanted my players to be satisfied. As a fiscally responsible executive, I believed in the sanctity of a contract. The ideal situation was to have players who were satisfied with their contracts. Sometimes, though, that wasn't possible. I became involved in some extremely difficult contractual situations while I owned the team. My resolve not to renegotiate cost me the services of several outstanding players. But I still believe that given the circumstances, I acted correctly.

Wide receiver John Jefferson was our first draft pick in 1978. He signed nine one-year contracts paying him $100,000 the first seven years, $200,000 the eighth year, and $220,000 the final year, a $100,000 bonus, and a $75,000 interest-free loan. At Jefferson's agent's request some of the initial payments were deferred, so he actually received $40,000 in 1978 and $50,000 in 1979. I tried to convince Jefferson to accept a contract of shorter duration, giving him the usual warning—if he performed as well as everyone anticipated, at some point he was going to be underpaid. But he insisted on nine years.

When Jefferson signed the contract, I repeated my warning. "If you're satisfied," I said, "go ahead and sign it. But if you do, I don't expect to see you in my office until this contract expires."

"You'll never have any trouble from me," Jefferson said flatly.

I wanted to believe him. I wanted to believe every football player who told me that. I even wanted to believe them when they came back a year or two later and asked to renegotiate, promising me that if I gave them a new contract, I would *really* never have any trouble from them.

Jefferson turned out to be an all-pro. He was a perfect part in Coryell's passing machine, teaming with Dan Fouts to lead us to the 1979 western-division championship. At the end of that season, Jefferson's agent asked me to renegotiate the original contract.

Compared to what other wide receivers were earning, Jefferson was being underpaid. I refused to renegotiate, but I did add some performance bonuses to the contract and agreed to pay him some of the money that originally had been deferred.

Jefferson again told me, "You'll never have any more trouble from me."

Jefferson earned every incentive bonus in his contract in 1980, collecting $200,000 for the year as we won our second consecutive championship.

Before the 1981 season, Jefferson signed with a new agent, a gentleman named Howard Slusher. The first thing Slusher did was demand that the performance clauses in Jefferson's contract be guaranteed, meaning that he would receive those bonuses whether he earned them or not. As usual, Slusher warned that his client would not play if the contract was not adjusted. Slusher should have learned when Fouts demanded to be traded in 1977 that I didn't respond well to threats.

Jefferson was only in his fourth season and was asking for his original contract to be re-renegotiated. It was getting harder and harder to believe that one more contract would satisfy him. So I refused. I told Slusher that I wanted to be the first person to wish Mr. Jefferson well in his new career.

At the same time, Fred Dean was also demanding that his contract be renegotiated, once again threatening to retire from football if I refused.

Perhaps I should have suggested Dean go into business with Jefferson; instead, I also wished him well in his future endeavors.

It was a very unpleasant situation. Both players had voluntarily signed contracts. Both of them had been represented by agents of their choice. Both of them were threatening to sit out the season if I didn't give them what they demanded. Chargers fans and the local press wanted me to renegotiate the contracts. Once again, it was tough for me to go out to dinner. I was called all sorts of names, "that cheap sonofabitch" being among the kindest. In support of Jefferson and Dean, the entire Chargers squad boycotted the annual "Welcome Home" preseason dinner.

They didn't go, and I got blamed. It wasn't as much the money involved as it was the principle. I'm a rich man, the Chargers were making a profit—paying Jefferson and Dean more money wasn't going to affect my life-style at all. And believe me, there was no one in the world, not the most ardent fan, who wanted the Chargers to win more than I did. But how much is enough? I can be pushed only so far, and Jefferson and Dean had pushed me beyond that point.

Owning a sports franchise does not make a man a saint. Contrary to some suggestions made at the time, I'm a human being. I have an ego and a temper. I'm quite capable of getting angry, feeling betrayed, becoming bitter. There are times, just like everyone else, when I want to get even.

One morning I turned on the radio and heard Slusher announce that Jefferson would retire from football before he would agree to play for only $200,000, including bonuses. That was enough for me. Sanders, Younger, and I got on the phone to find out which teams wanted Jefferson and what they were offering. Apparently, many teams did not share my convictions. We had sixteen offers for Jefferson.

I traded him to the Green Bay Packers for a number-one draft pick, two number-twos, and wide receiver Aundra Thompson. The deal was contingent on Green Bay's being able to sign Jefferson within five days. Two or three days after we'd made the deal Slusher called Sanders and said that he didn't have to reach an agreement with Green Bay, that Jefferson could stay with the Chargers.

I didn't care if the Packers signed Jefferson within five days or five years, he was not going to play for the Chargers again. We had to give Green Bay two extensions of the deadline before they were finally able to reach an agreement with Slusher.

Soon after that we traded two draft picks and Thompson to New Orleans for wide receiver Wes Chandler. Chandler turned out to be an even better receiver than Jefferson. He helped us win our third consecutive championship in 1981, then became an all-pro in 1982 and 1983. We used the first round pick we'd gotten from the Packers in 1983 to pick running back Gary Anderson. Anderson played two seasons in the USFL, then joined the Chargers in 1985 and made the NFL's all-rookie team.

Jefferson did not fit into the Packers' offense as well as he had in San Diego. After a strong beginning, he faded quickly and was eventually traded. He was cut by Houston at the beginning of the 1986 season. Maybe Slusher did a good job for him; he certainly got more money to play in Green Bay than he would have gotten in San Diego. Of course, in San Diego, he might still be be playing.

Was I pleased by the way the deal worked out? I'm the man who put more salt on movie-theater popcorn. I was extremely pleased.

Soon after getting rid of Jefferson, I traded Dean to the San Francisco 49ers for a first-round draft pick. Dean had two great seasons for the 49ers, helping them get into two Super Bowls. But he sat out most of the 1984 season because the 49ers refused to renegotiate his contract. What a surprise. He was injured in 1985 and released in 1986. We used the draft pick we got from San Francisco, the fifth in the entire draft, to select linebacker Billy Ray Smith. Smith became the captain and leader of the Chargers' defense.

Football teams are built through good drafts, careful trading, and just enough luck to sign the right free agents. There is no formula for success. Sometimes a team gets forced into a trade and ends up with Wes Chandler. Sometimes a player like Dan Fouts decides to sit out a season. And sometimes you trade for Duane Thomas.

If you expect to win, however, don't trade for Duane Thomas too often.

8

Apparently, one of the things that fans in San Diego were very interested in learning was what the owner of a professional football team actually did. They must have been, because for almost twenty years I heard people asking, "Just what the hell is Klein doing with that team, anyway?"

Owners are never the most popular sports figures in a city. When a team loses consistently, the owner is the person the fans blame; when the team wins, the owner is the person the fans want to get out of the way so that the announcers can interview the coach and star players. There is a reason that no owner has ever been pictured on a football card.

What does the owner of a football team actually do? Like the five hundred-pound dictator, anything he wants to. For me, after moving to San Diego in 1973, running the Chargers became my full-time job. If the fish does stink from the head, I was the head of the fish. As a job, it didn't pay particularly well, the hours were awful, the perks were limited, and I was subjected to tremendous abuse. It was about the best job anyone could have.

For football players, the week is highly structured. On Monday morning, those players who had been injured in the game the day before reported for treatment. On Monday afternoon, the team had an extremely light workout, mostly to determine who was still breathing.

Tuesday morning, the team watched the films of the previous Sunday's game. They practiced lightly Tuesday afternoon. Players were free to meet with the press after every practice. On some evenings there were team meetings.

Wednesday morning, the game films of our next opponent were shown and our game plan was introduced. The rest of the week was spent recuperating from the last game and "rehearsing" plays and defenses for the next game. It was a full schedule that left the players very little free time.

My week was less formally structured, but no less busy. During the season, I was at the stadium early Monday morning. Anyone walking into the office of a pro-football team on a Monday morning can immediately determine how that team has done the day before. If the team has won, everybody is really up. Even the telephone operators answer the phone proudly. But if the team has lost, the office is as cheerful as a morgue.

The first thing I did Monday morning was look at the game films with the general manager. Reel by reel, offense, defense, special teams. We reran each play several times. If it hadn't worked, we tried to figure out what had broken down, which player had missed his assignment. When a play had worked, when we'd had a long run from scrimmage or had completed a long pass, we'd run that sucker over and over twenty-five or thirty times, ostensibly to try to understand why it had been successful, but in fact we were so pleased that something had gone right we just wanted to enjoy it. Sometimes it was our only proof that we knew what we were doing.

I always thought the best part of watching films was running the projector backward. Watching players leap off the ground as if yanked upward by a string, dash backward into a formation, then drop back into a huddle, was often even funnier than watching our plays run forward. Besides, doing something as silly as running the game films backward made us feel youthfully naughty.

Sid Gillman taught me the value of films in football. Gillman's father had run a theater in Minneapolis, and I'd run the second-largest theater chain in the country; the Chargers were the MGM of pro football. We filmed every game and every practice. We had a four-man photography staff, six expensive movie cameras, eight still cameras, and processing and printing facilities at both the stadium and our training site. We shot 150,000 feet of black-and-white film a season. An hour after a game or practice ended, we could be looking at the films. So we knew exactly what had gone wrong. Every week, every practice, we knew exactly what had gone wrong.

Films are an extremely important coaching tool. After looking at a play five or ten times, we began to understand it. Each time we looked at it we would concentrate on a different aspect—the overall design of the play, the way our opponent defensed it, the way our players executed it, perhaps whether a player tipped off our opponent with some movement or positioning. It was a completely different ball game on the films than it had been on the field. I'll never forget the day after we'd lost to the Broncos, 27–14, in 1978, and Tommy Prothro decided, "After looking at the movies, I don't think we played as poorly as I did after the game." On the films, we'd won that game.

The quality of officiating also becomes obvious on the game films. Officiating is an extremely difficult job. It is much easier to officiate a game on television, on films, or from my private box than it is on the field. And so I did. On Monday morning, I was a tremendous official. The majority of the time officials do an exemplary job, but they're almost human, so they do make mistakes, mistakes that become obvious on the films. When I was looking at the films with the coaching staff and we saw an official make a questionable call against us, or miss an obvious infraction committed by the other team, the coaches would get livid. Their jobs were at stake, their children's food, so they would scream at the film. Naturally, being a little older and a little more mature, I was able to control myself better. I called the league office and screamed.

Sometimes it seemed that part of my normal Monday routine was calling New York to complain about the officiating. Obviously, the game I remember most is the Holy Roller game in which the Raiders threw, kicked, and rolled the ball into the end zone for the illegal game-winning touchdown. Watching it over and over on our films was even worse than seeing it actually happen, because by Monday morning the shock was starting to wear off and we were able to believe what we were seeing. Talk about horror films. The league did apologize for the call but did not change the result, making us one of the few teams to finish a season with a record of 9-7 and 1 apology.

We certainly got to know the idiosyncrasies of the various officials. We knew which men were going to make the gutsy call against the home team in the fourth quarter and which ones were going to turn their heads. We believed that certain officials favored certain teams—never us, of course—and when we were playing those teams we specifically asked the league to assign other officials to our game. Although, officially, that was never done, those requests were usually honored.

One official we didn't like at all just couldn't take any criticism. If a player or coach dared challenge him, he'd destroy them. He'd drop so many penalty flags on them it looked like closing time at the United Nations.

It also became obvious that officials called fewer important penalties during the playoffs than they did during the regular season. Statistics may show that penalty yardage is approximately the same during the playoffs as it is during the regular season, but the timing of penalties is probably more important than total yardage. I've never sat in on an officiating meeting, but I'm quite certain that officials are told before the playoffs that they are not to take the game away from the players. The players are aware of this, and take full advantage of it.

I sympathize with football officials. Of course, I sympathize with them more now than I did before I sold the team.

After watching the game films for four or five hours, and getting a list from the trainer of players who probably would not be ready to go the following Sunday, we knew at which positions we needed help. Two or three people would get on the phones and begin "Wudyataking." We'd also consult our list of free agents and decide who we wanted to sign. Locating these players was not always easy, however. We kept voluminous records of every player who'd been cut by us or by any other team in the league. Theoretically, we should have been able to get in contact with them. But we found that many teams were hiding, or "stashing" these players in case they needed them at some point during the season. With the player limit at forty-five, the forty-sixth or forty-eighth or fiftieth players were about as good as the fortieth or forty-second men on the roster. Many teams told these players to get a private telephone number and give it to no one, promising them that they would be contacted and activated during the season. This was illegal, so we never did it, except when it became absolutely necessary.

Some teams, not us, would pay these players for not playing with another team, installing them in a local hotel or residence so they would be readily available. These extra players comprised the "taxi squad." A taxi squad is similar to the military's Stealth bombers; neither of them exists, but both of them cost a lot of money to keep not existing.

Our list of players who would not be physically ready to play the following Sunday had to be telexed to the league on Tuesday. Supposedly, this "questionable list" existed for the benefit of the team we were playing next, but actually it was for the oddsmakers and bettors. This list was about as honest as far as a nearsighted man could see. We put players on this list who had blisters, hangnails, bruised egos, and contusions. I don't know a contusion from an abrasion, but I think we led the league in contusions. Since we always had scouts at our next opponent's game, we had some idea of the accuracy of their injury list. We never believed that players they listed as questionable weren't going to play against us, but we still cheated on our own list as if our opponents were going to believe us. If anyone took our questionable list seriously, and then compared it to the people who had miraculously recovered enough to play the following Sunday, we would have had more pilgrims coming to San Diego than went to Lourdes.

We did have injuries—we certainly did have injuries. In two decades I saw some terrible damage done to the human body. Football players are monsters in armor and they are taught to try to destroy their opponents. The surprising thing is not that so many players are injured, but that so few players are seriously injured. Probably the first thing anyone who spends any time with a football team learns is that the knee is supposed to bend only one way.

It's impossible to describe adequately the violence that takes place on the football field, and the pain with which these men play. I remember the first time I saw a Charger player get seriously injured. It was the fifth game of my first season, and until then everything had been perfect—we'd won four straight games and suffered no serious injuries, just a few contusions. We lost our fifth game, to the Jets, 17–16, and in the fourth quarter our defensive captain, middle linebacker Chuck Allen, broke his leg.

In the locker room after the game I asked for a round of applause for Allen. There was complete silence. Have you ever felt really dumb? I mean, really dumb, as if you'd mistakenly shown up at a formal party wearing your Halloween costume? That was how I felt. I realized later that the other players were ignoring Allen because they didn't want to acknowledge the existence of a serious injury. Injuries had no place in their world. Injuries were the thing that football players feared most, because injuries were the one thing about which they could do nothing. A single misstep in practice could mean the end of their careers just as easily as being crunched by two defensive backs.

As a fan, I'd chuckle when I heard a broadcaster say something ridiculous like, "Jack Player suffered two broken arms, a severed leg, and severe contusions, and is expected to be out two weeks." But I stopped laughing when I saw how hard players worked to rehabilitate themselves. We had a running back named Dickie Post who had major knee surgery, not arthroscopic surgery—they actually opened up his knee—and five weeks after the operation he was playing professional football again. Five weeks. I've had colds that lasted longer than that. Doug Wilkerson had knee surgery, and he missed four weeks. Four weeks! It made me wonder what was wrong with Dickie Post. I remember seeing a receiver leap for a pass in the end zone and land off balance. The tendon that held his kneecap in place ripped, and his kneecap floated freely up his leg. It was the most grotesque injury I've ever seen. The team doctor told me it wasn't as serious as it looked; and for the doctor, I'm sure it wasn't. But for the player . . .

The team practiced every day, and I was at practice every day. Each head coach has his own theory about how long and how tough a practice session should be, but midweek scrimmages usually lasted two or three hours. The one thing that every head coach emphasized on the field was aggressiveness. No matter how complex the strategy became, no matter how intricate the offense was, the object was simply to beat up the man playing across the line. Coaches stressed that if a player could physically conquer his opponent, intimidate him, that man would be unable to perform.

The only way to learn how to do that is to do that. In practice sessions the offense worked against the defense, and although these players were teammates, and friends, they still went out there and tried to kill each other. Every day, every play, these people were fighting for their jobs. As a player once told me, "It's either a hundred and seventy-five thousand dollars a year or tending bar." So even in practice, they'd use their elbows, they'd kick, they'd knee their best friend, if necessary. In a sense, it was like a marriage. They would fight as hard as possible with each other, but the result would be to make the team stronger.

On Tuesday morning we looked at the game films sent to us by our next opponent, reviewed our scouting reports on that team, and drew up our offensive and defensive game plans. Assuming, that is, that our opponent's game films had arrived. I never realized how slow the mail service was until I had to wait for those films. It had to be the mail service, of course, because the other teams would always claim they'd sent the films on time. Sometimes the films didn't arrive until Wednesday or Thursday, and on one occasion a team sent us two-year-old films by mistake. Obviously, it had to have been by mistake, because no team in the NFL would intentionally try to gain advantage by sending old films.

The game plan is the battle strategy. The object is to identify your opponent's weakness and design a means to exploit it, assuming your opponent has a weakness and you have the troops to exploit it. A team rarely loses in the game plan. Quite often, though, we would go through all the motions, we would do everything correctly, and it would make no difference. For example, a scouting report might read, "Pressure the quarterback and he's likely to throw the football up for grabs," but that implied we had players capable of putting pressure on the quarterback. When we opened the 1975 season against the Steelers, Tommy Prothro had constructed a fine game plan. Realistically, we had no chance to win, but we had a fine game plan. If we had really been honest with ourselves, our game plan would have read: "Try not to suffer any serious injuries."

The one thing that makes a game plan most effective is having the better team. Only occasionally does a brilliant game plan result in an inferior team winning. Basically, all game plans are simply variations of, "Control the football and score more points."

For a player, football is a game of winning and personal performance. For an owner, football is a game of winning and selling tickets. A player measures his success through individual statistics; the owner looks at the attendance figures. When we were winning, I would start getting ticket requests from friends by Tuesday morning at the very latest. When we were losing, they would call the morning of the game. Because the visiting team shares in ticket-sales revenue, the home team is permitted to distribute only a thousand complimentary tickets per game. Additional complimentary tickets may be distributed only with the consent of the visiting team.

Visiting teams are allotted five hundred tickets a game, and most of them are used by players, coaches, and media. These tickets often cause problems, because the people who use them generally assume they are free, which they are not. These tickets have to be paid for. One of our coaches often ordered tickets to away games for his family, but was too embarrassed to ask his mother and father to pay for them. This is not to say he didn't want them to pay for them; he was simply too embarrassed to ask them to fork over the cash. So he asked our business manager, Pat Curran, to collect for him. Pat had to track down this coach's parents and demand payment. When these people complained to their son, he then blamed it on Pat.

For home games, I always held fifty tickets until just before game time, because invariably, at the last minute, I would get an emergency phone call from some politician, celebrity, local businessman, radio advertiser, or friends who had decided to go to the game. Only once did I ever have a problem supplying tickets for a V.I.P.

One Friday afternoon I received a call from an aide to President Richard Nixon, informing me that the President had decided to attend the game in San Diego that Sunday. I suggested that the President and his guests join me in the comfort of my private box, but was told that the President wanted to sit in the open stands with the fans. "Fine," I said, knowing I held my final fifty, "we're sold out, but I'm sure I can get you some tickets. How many will the President need?"

"Sixty."

"Sixty?" Sixty tickets at the last minute? Where was I supposed to get sixty tickets to a sold-out football game?

"The President will be arriving approximately forty-five minutes before the game."

My fifty tickets were scattered around the stadium, and some of them were not very good. I had a day and a half to find a bloc of sixty tickets. Since I did not believe that the right of eminent domain extended to football tickets, I got on the phone and started calling season-ticket holders. When they answered I told them as firmly as possible, "Your President has confiscated your tickets. Congratulations."

"No way," many of them said, "get the tickets from someone else." After I had appealed to their patriotism, and their pocketbook, and offered them other seats to the game from my cache of fifty, they asked, "Why me?"

"Because you're fortunate enough to have the best seats in the stadium," I said. "Consider that you're giving up your seats for the country. I'll send somebody right over to pick up your tickets."

I managed to collect the last of the sixty tickets I needed Sunday morning. Nixon's helicopter landed on time and we walked to our seats together. "Great seats," the President said as we sat down.

"Think so?" I asked casually.

The price of tickets to Chargers games was determined much the same way I priced movie-theater tickets or softcover books. I compared our expenses and revenues. I was aware of how much other teams in the NFL were charging. Then I looked up in the sky and picked a number. There were no league rules, no regulations, no guidelines to follow—every team set its own ticket price. It was my team, and I could charge anything I wanted to charge. I simply charged as much as I felt traffic would bear.

There really was no other way to do it. I certainly wasn't going to take a survey. Imagine the results of a questionnaire that asked fans, "Do you think the price of tickets to Chargers games should be raised?"

I had to raise ticket prices every few years. The only substantial revenues the Chargers received were from the league television contract and our gate receipts. Since we were playing in one of the smallest stadiums in the NFL, I had to maximize ticket revenues. I tried to raise prices two years out of every three, and I never raised them more than $2 a game. As in the movie or book business, if people wanted to buy my product, they would pay my price. If they weren't interested, they wouldn't have come to the game if I charged them 50 cents less.

Surprisingly, fans rarely wrote to complain when I raised prices. They wrote to complain that their tickets were in the sun or in the shade, they wrote to complain that the people in front of them used profanity, they wrote because they'd gotten divorced and their ex-spouse had kept their other ticket, they wrote to complain that our players weren't on the field when the national anthem was played, but they never wrote to complain when I raised the price of their tickets. A $2-per-game raise over an entire season was only $20 or $24, and that just didn't seem to make any difference.

Besides, I might be the only owner in the history of professional sports to have actually lowered ticket prices. When we moved from decrepit Balboa Stadium into the much larger San Diego Stadium, I lowered prices a few dollars. Many people were surprised, but no one was more surprised than I was. As far as I can remember, that was the only time in my entire career that I lowered the price of the product I was selling. But I had a lot of additional seats to fill in the new stadium.

Sometimes raising prices proved to be a mistake. In 1973, for example, we had the largest season-ticket sale in our history, 40,341. But even with Johnny Unitas at quarterback we won only two games and became involved in the drug scandal. True to the Chargers' motto, the best defense is a good offense; at the end of the season I raised ticket prices $2, bringing the cost to $13.50, $8.50, or $7.00 a seat. The response was underwhelming. We immediately sold 10,000 fewer season tickets, causing our revenue to drop by more than $1 million.

Two years later we were dead last in attendance, so I couldn't really raise ticket prices again. But because my expenses were continuing to rise I had to generate more income. Until that time we had been one of the few teams in the NFL that did not include our preseason games in our season-ticket package. Fans had the option of purchasing tickets to those games. So, I wrote to our dwindling list of season-ticket holders, telling them that "Instead of resorting to a rise in ticket prices," I had included tickets to our three preseason games in the package. We had usually played four preseason home games, but that year we were only playing three. If a fan had previously bought tickets to all preseason and regular-season games, we were actually *lowering* ticket prices. It was explanations like that that made me believe I could have gone into politics. Attendance dropped another seven thousand.

The salient thing I learned about pricing tickets for pro-football games was that price is simply not a significant factor in selling tickets. When we started winning football games in 1977, ticket sales started rising. We sold 11,000 more season tickets in 1978 than we had the year before. At the end of the 1978 season, I raised ticket prices again, yet we sold 11,000 more tickets in 1979 than we had in 1978. By 1980, we actually had to cut off ticket sales at 49,675 so that we would have a few thousand tickets to sell on the day of the game to people who couldn't afford the whole package.

I could have put almost any price I wanted on tickets to our playoff games and still sold every seat in the stadium. When we won our division in 1979, it was the first time we'd been in a playoff game since before the NFL-AFL merger, and San Diego reacted accordingly. Season-ticket holders were permitted to purchase one playoff ticket for each season ticket they held, but we still had a few thousand tickets to sell. The night before those tickets went on sale, three thousand people camped overnight in near-freezing temperatures. We imposed a limit of four tickets per person, but still sold out within ninety minutes. When we made the playoffs again in 1980, we dropped that limit to two tickets per person, and four thousand people camped in our parking lot, some for as long as three days.

For the first time since I'd bought the team, people were actually scalping tickets. Ticket agencies in town had to hire professional line-standers to get tickets for them. The local newspaper, the *San Diego Union*, profited from our success because its classified section was filled with ads from people trying to buy or sell tickets. Tickets that had originally sold for $10 and $17 were being offered for as much as $500, although the actual sale price averaged about $50. Some people were offering or accepting material goods instead of cash: televisions, stereos, clothing, restaurant dinners, even garage parking downtown. One fan told a reporter, "I got myself a lithograph by Salvador Dali for two seats in the end zone. I don't know if it's real or not, but my wife liked it."

We even had to deal with ticket counterfeiters. A few years earlier charities had suggested other charities when we tried to give away tickets to our games, and suddenly people were actually counterfeiting them. We had to hire additional security guards for those games because people who had bought counterfeit tickets objected loudly to being refused admission to the stadium.

So, with all that going on, did it really matter if I charged $22 rather than $20 a ticket?

The one ticket we never got to distribute to Chargers fans was for the Super Bowl. That was certainly the biggest disappointment I had in my career. *I* did get tickets to the Super Bowl each year, however, and that created Superheadaches. Each NFL team receives 1 percent of the tickets available for a Super Bowl. If the game was being played in New Orleans, for example, which holds about seventy-five thousand people, the Chargers were entitled to purchase 750 tickets. Our tickets were distributed among our executives, coaches, players, scouts, staff members, office personnel, the San Diego media, the radio station that carried our games, local college coaches, my family and friends—we even had a drawing to enable a few of our season-ticket holders to go to the game—there was no shortage of people who wanted Super Bowl tickets, particularly when it was being played in Los Angeles. I always kept the last few tickets in my pocket, just in case the telephone rang as I walked out of my hotel room. It never rang, so even with the incredible demand, I found myself at the ballpark with tickets I didn't need. I always managed to find a friend or reporter who could use them.

As the value of Super Bowl tickets increased, they became a serious problem for the league. Super Bowl tickets have become the most valuable tickets to any sports event in America, and accusations have been made that some owners have scalped large blocs of tickets. Recently, for example, Dominic Frontiere has been indicted for failing to pay taxes on money he made selling Super Bowl tickets. And there was a strong rumor that Carroll Rosenbloom made a fortune selling thousands of tickets to the game when it was played at the Los Angeles Coliseum. Once, in fact, while giving a deposition in a lawsuit against Al Davis, I was asked, "Do you know whether any NFL owner or NFL organization is selling Super Bowl tickets or has sold Super Bowl tickets in blocs?"

My answer, under oath, was "I do not." Was Carroll Rosenbloom capable of scalping Super Bowl tickets? Of course he was. Did he do so? I have no knowledge that he did. Do I believe it happened? I know that when a caterpillar crawls into a cocoon it has legs, and when it emerges a few months later it has wings, so anything is possible.

Among the many unpleasant things Al Davis has done is accuse Commissioner Rozelle of profiting greatly by scalping Super Bowl tickets. It's extremely difficult to prove someone hasn't done something—you can't take photographs of him not doing it, for instance—but I've never known Pete Rozelle to utter a dishonest word. When he says, "There is not a shred of truth to that suggestion," I believe him absolutely.

Also, I've known Al Davis so long now that if he told me he *wasn't* telling the truth about something, I wouldn't believe him about that. Ironically, Davis did testify under oath that he had sold between seventy-five and one hundred of his tickets to Las Vegas hotelmen each year. Las Vegas, of course, is best known as the location of Jerry Lewis's annual muscular dystrophy telethon. And although Davis claimed he sold his tickets at face value, he also admitted that he and his employees received free rooms, free meals, and additional benefits from the people who bought his tickets.

Probably the one thing that made me happiest about selling the club, besides the $80 million I got for it, was that I would never again have to hear another person say, "Geez, Gene, I'm sorry to call you five minutes before kickoff, but I was just wondering if you had twenty-five tickets I could get my hands on?"

Raising ticket prices was not a whimsical act. It was a cold, hard business decision. I had no choice. I tried to operate the Chargers as I had National General: I wanted to put more money in my pocket than I took out. That got to be more and more difficult every season. Expenses were constantly rising. When I bought the team, our player payroll was approximately $800,000 a year; when I sold the team the player payroll was over $8 million annually. In addition to players, we had thirty to forty full-time employees on the payroll, ranging from our head coach to the receptionist. The price of transportation probably rose faster than salaries, and after the second oil shock of the 1970s it would cost us as much as $80,000 just to fly the team to New York and back home. Equipment costs were substantial; our annual bill for elastic bandages and adhesive tape alone was close to $40,000. Insurance premiums killed us; in 1966 and 1967 we paid less than $50,000 a year in workman's compensation insurance, but by 1983 we were paying $500,000 and considered that to be a bargain. One of the reasons for that substantial increase in insurance rates is the recent discovery of something known as cumulative trauma, or hidden trauma. That means that seven or eight years after a player has ended his career he may be entitled to compensation for the deterioration of his body due to the pounding he took while playing. It was difficult for me to believe that it took a player seven years to find out he had been hurt, but some of those players really weren't very bright. I suppose that they might have been in shock from having to get a job and go to work every morning. Anyway, the player would get whatever he could get, and the insurance company raised our premium to pay for it. I always thought some insurance company could have made a fortune by offering insurance insurance, a policy that would guarantee insurance rates over a period of time.

So, with everything from equipment to salaries, our expenses were running $22 million to $24 million a year. I knew what we were paying for everything, although I never actually wrote the checks. The bills were paid by the head of the department that incurred the expense. At the beginning of the season we would make out our operating budget, just as if we were running a real business, allocating funds to each department. Unless there was a large variation in a department's operating expenses that needed to be explained, I never got involved in our monthly expenses.

I spent much of my time searching for ways to increase our revenues. In addition to our share of the league television contract and our gate receipts, we were also able to generate income from other sources. For example, we shared revenues from concession sales and parking fees with the San Diego Stadium Authority, from whom we rented the stadium. We sold broadcasting rights to our games to a local radio station. And we derived substantial income from our private boxes, which we rented for as much as $50,000 a box per season.

Originally, the stadium authority had refused to pay for the construction of these boxes because it didn't believe we could rent them, so I agreed to build them myself and give the authority 10 percent of my revenues. I put up twenty of them, which cost me almost $1 million, and I had absolutely no problem renting them. I offered my customers the option of a fixed price for five years if they paid the first and last year's rent in advance, or a one-year rental that was subject to a 10 percent increase each year. Eventually the stadium authority agreed to add another fifty-three boxes, for which they received one third of the revenue.

Once I built those first private boxes, I understood why other owners had built enclosed boxes inside indoor stadiums. The only revenue from those boxes that the home team had to split with the visiting team was the price of the seats in the box, not the rental cost of the box itself. The home team got to keep that. If, for example, there were twenty seats in a box, each priced at $1,000 a season, we had to include $20,000 in our general receipts fund. But since we were charging $50,000 for the box, we were generating a $30,000 profit. This is what is known in the vernacular of the accounting profession as "a great deal."

Somehow, our revenues were usually slightly higher than our expenses. This difference was our profit. Most astute businessmen, however, would have called the percentage of return I received on the value of the investment a joke.

Actually, it didn't really matter how much money we took in—it was always going to be just enough. The maxim by which pro football seemed to be run was: Expenses will rise to meet income. The most creative thing many of my coaches ever did was figure out how to spend every penny we were taking in. We were fortunate—we usually made a small profit—but many pro-football teams are barely breaking even or are losing money, and in the future more teams are going to lose more money. Operating expenses are going to continue to rise; salaries are not going to come down substantially, air fares are not going to get cheaper, bandages aren't going on sale, while revenues are already being stretched. Even I realized, me, Mr. add-more-salt-to-the-popcorn, that there is a limit to how much people will pay to see something at the ballpark that they can see as well, or better, at home. When operating expenses exceed revenues, the result is known as a loss. There is a common misconception that when a professional football team loses money there is really no money involved, that it is just a "paper loss," and that the owners can write off their losses on their taxes.

Dollar bills are printed on paper—that's what a real paper loss is. If you lose money, you lose it. The key to having a viable write-off is to have some profits against which the losses can be deducted, and many owners have no other profit-making businesses. They live on their football income.

Buying a pro-football team does not require taking a poverty vow, and I don't think fans care if owners make money or not. But those losses do affect the fans. Revenue has to come from somewhere. Pro football still hasn't tapped into the potentially lucrative pay-cable TV and closed-circuit markets. How many movie-theater seats, at $20 or more a ticket, could the NFL fill for the Super Bowl? Millions, certainly. Would the NFL be willing to take its showcase event off free television? When a caterpillar crawls into a cocoon . . . The revenue has to come from somewhere.

The real bottom line is that owning a professional football team is a bad business investment. An NFL team is worth a minimum of $50 million and annually returns, with luck, $2.5 million. That's a terrible earnings ratio, and an intelligent investor could do considerably better by just leaving his money in a well-run money-market account. So why do people buy pro-football teams? Why did I buy the Chargers? Why did Alex Spanos pay me $80 million for the Chargers? As a game, it's a bad business; but as a business, it's a wonderful game. I had a passionate love for the game of football, I didn't own a college, so I couldn't own a college football team; that left pro football. It was very difficult to feel passionate about a used-car lot in the San Fernando Valley or a jellied-fruit company or a movie-distribution chain, but I loved the Chargers. And like any deep love, in return for my devotion the Chargers gave me moments of ecstasy and moments of despair. I can't honestly claim that every day was wonderful, but I certainly enjoyed a lot of them. I did it for fun, and profit. So it really made little difference to me if we made $50 or $2.5 million.

As long as we didn't lose money; I didn't think losing money was fun.

I spent several mornings each week in meetings, some of them personal, but most of them involving the team. For example, once every two or three weeks I met with representatives of the stadium authority. The San Diego Stadium Authority is a politically appointed board consisting of nine nonpaid members. Its function is to generate as much income from the stadium for the community as possible. My relationship with the board was just like every tenant-landlord relationship in which the tenant believes he is overpaying and the landlord believes the tenant isn't paying enough.

When I bought the Chargers they were still playing in ancient Balboa Stadium. When Balboa Stadium was built it was one of the finest ballparks in the country. In 1915, however, there weren't many ballparks in the country. It was an old and depressing stadium, the seating consisted of concrete slabs, and even after a major expansion there were only thirty-four thousand seats. There were only four restrooms, few concession stands, and no parking facilities. The lights were dim, the plumbing rusted, and the offices small and dingy. Nothing worked. For example, one of the four restrooms continually needed repair and finally, during a game against Buffalo, the plumbers got the water running so well they couldn't get it stopped. The bathroom overflowed and water cascaded gently down the concrete steps, creating an artificial waterfall and soaking fans, row by row by row.

San Diego Stadium, which was eventually renamed San Diego Jack Murphy Stadium, in honor of the respected sports columnist and editor, opened in 1967. It cost more than $27 million to build, had seventy-four bathrooms, forty-four concession stands, parking for more than seventeen thousand cars, and a seating capacity of about fifty thousand. And one small restroom that overflowed. I don't think that had anything to do with tradition.

Unfortunately, that restroom was in my private box. I re-member the day it overflowed very well, September 10, 1978, the Holy Roller game against the Raiders. Among the guests in my box that day was former president of the United States Jerry Ford. We were so totally engrossed in the game that we didn't even realize the plumbing had broken until one of Ford's Secret Service guards, who had been sitting on the steps, stood up. His pants were soaking wet. Eventually, about two inches of water covered the entire floor of my box. We all took off our shoes and watched the game in wet socks, wading around in the water. I'd heard of lame duck presidents, but this was something entirely different. I was incredibly embarrassed. Exactly what do you say to a former president when the toilet overflows?

We played our first game in San Diego Stadium in 1967. By 1968, I was refusing to pay my rent. A clause in my contract with the stadium authority stated that if the city entered into an agree-ment with a baseball team that was better than my deal, I would have the right to modify my lease. In 1968, baseball's National League expanded, creating the San Diego Padres. We were pay-ing 10 percent of our receipts, and they were paying 8 percent. That was acceptable; what was not acceptable was that the Padres were also being paid $306,000 a year for seven years to manage the stadium. That was clearly a subterfuge to give the Padres a good deal. I screamed and hollered and threatened to move the Chargers out of San Diego. When I said it, I meant it. Eventu-ally, though, I calmed down, the stadium authority calmed down, they made some concessions, I calmed down some more—I had a long way to calm—and we settled. But that was only the begin-ning of our problems.

We seemed to be fighting constantly. I wanted to put in luxury boxes; they didn't want to put in luxury boxes. I wanted to deter-mine the feasibility of installing an artificial surface; they did not want to determine the feasibility of installing an artificial surface. I wanted the field to be in playable condition for our home games; they wanted to generate as much income as possible by renting the stadium to anyone who was willing to pay for it. The rock concerts were bad enough, but once, two days before we were to play there, the authority actually rented the stadium to a rodeo. A real rodeo, with horses and calves and bulls. A fact: Where there once were horses and calves and bulls, there will always be horse-stuff and calfstuff and bullstuff. How would you like to have your face pressed into the turf two days after a rodeo has left town?

On another occasion, I walked into the stadium one lovely Friday afternoon and saw about fifty cars driving around the field. As I discovered, the stadium authority had rented the ballpark to an automobile manufacturer to film a commercial. The cars were ripping up the turf, leaving deep tread marks across the field. "How much did they pay you?" I demanded angrily.

"Two hundred dollars."

Two hundred dollars? How could I be angry? They had gotten a whole two hundred dollars for the ballpark. If they had told me that in the first place, I would have understood. "Uh, listen," I said, "next time I'll give you five hundred dollars not to rent it to them."

I don't want to be unkind, but they couldn't even grow grass in the stadium. San Diego is blessed with the finest climate in the United States. If someone throws a candy wrapper on the ground in San Diego, a candy tree will sprout. But they couldn't grow grass in our outdoor stadium. There were times when we were scheduled to play on national television and we had to spray-paint the ground green to make it look as if it were grass. It was only a few years before I sold the team that they finally figured out how to grow grass in San Diego.

Although as owner I had the ultimate responsibility for our players' behavior and welfare, I tried not to get involved in their personal problems. I wanted our players to understand that the coaching staff had absolute authority, so I didn't want them constantly appealing to me for help.

The team did get involved when there was a serious problem, however. We did help those players who admitted to having drug problems and asked for help. We did help those players who asked us to examine financial deals they had been offered. And we did help the player who needed two seats for a playoff game that were far enough apart to ensure that his wife and his girlfriend would not meet.

I had owned the team only a few months the first time a player came to me with a problem. I was sitting in my office in Los Angeles when one of the team's superstars called. The superstar calling me? I was flattered—it made me feel as if the team were accepting me. I picked up the phone and heard this player crying hysterically. "What's the matter?" I asked with concern.

Between sobs, he said, "I can't play Sunday."

This was serious. He was the key to our offense. "What's wrong?"

"Coach won't let me."

"What?" This was professional football; this was the big time. If Sid Gillman wouldn't let him play, he must have committed a serious offense.

"He says I missed practice so I can't play in the game."

The big time? Perhaps there was something going on I didn't understand. "Let me find out about it," I said.

I called Gillman. "He didn't come to practice so he can't play." He was adamant.

The big time? Sounded like Little League to me. "Listen," I said, "he's your best player, you know he's going to play."

"Yeah," Gillman admitted, "he can play."

And that was how I solved my first major crisis in football.

An important part of the owner's job is helping create a positive image for the team, and one way I tried to do that was by encouraging good relations with the print and broadcast media. We held an informal press conference after practice every day, and tried to make our coaches and players available to the media almost anytime they weren't on the field. Believe me, any man from the Bronx, New York, who dresses up in a cowboy outfit and claims his used cars are cheaper by the pound than hamburger knows the value of free publicity. A symbiotic relationship existed between the Chargers and the media; we needed the media to help us sell our product, they needed football stories to help them sell their newspapers and influence people to watch or listen to their stations. Some reporters spent more time with the team than I did. They were at practice every day, they traveled on the team plane, ate meals with the team, socialized with the players, and were even in the locker room before and after games. They certainly, and secretly, rooted for the team, I certainly tried to influence their perceptions; yet they insisted they were independent and I insisted I was objective.

Generally, I believe the media were fair to me and the

Chargers. They criticized us every time we deserved to be criticized; they complimented us some of the time we deserved to be complimented.

Actually, I've always felt that covering sports was an almost impossible job. Based on everything I've read, a sports reporter has to know more about who should be playing than the coaches, more about negotiating salaries than the general manager, more about operating the team profitably than the owner, more about settling strikes than a labor mediator, and more about dealing with professional football players than a psychiatrist.

I rarely minded when a reporter expressed a negative opinion; I'd spent almost two years testifying in front of a hostile congressional committee after National General took over Great American—I can take criticism. I did object, however, when a journalist reported his opinion as if it were fact.

I always tried to be honest with reporters. I always tried, but I didn't always succeed. There were problems with players that I felt should be private. There were times when my temper or my disappointment made it impossible for me to be cooperative. When I realized I had to fire my friend Harland Svare, for example, I just didn't feel like discussing it with reporters. When the drug scandal erupted, I just didn't feel like discussing it with reporters. When the legitimate needs of the press conflicted with my personal needs, whose side was I going to be on?

I certainly had my share of problems with the media. Probably every owner of every professional sports team has fought with the press at some point. It's as much a part of the job of owner as being stomped in the head, kneed in the groin, and slammed against the ring post is part of the job of professional wrestler. But it's probably more painful. I never minded a good fight, particularly when I thought I had been wronged. When I was having that rent dispute with the stadium authority, for example, Jack Murphy wrote a column that I thought was unfair and unnecessarily nasty. In other words, he agreed with the stadium authority. For a while, our relationship was very cool, but time passed, as it always does, and eventually we became good friends. After his death, I helped rename the stadium in his memory.

The most bitter disagreement I had with a reporter occurred the week before we were to play the Raiders in the 1981 AFC championship game. Mel Durslag, a *Los Angeles Herald Examiner* reporter, wrote a column about my feud with Davis, then implied that the Raiders were being cheated by NFL officials because Davis had dared challenge the league by attempting to move to Los Angeles. "Considering what happened to them in Cleveland [the previous week]," Durslag wrote, "the Raiders should begin the championship round by asking for a change of venue, arguing that they can't get acceptable officiating within the confines of the 50 states . . .

"When the pass was intercepted, you looked immediately for a flag because this was a day on which a team suing the league for $160 million and rocking the boat with ticket scalping charges wasn't going to get the better of anything.

"At extremely critical junctures, it got the worst of ball-spotting. It also got nailed for a marginal interference call that, strangely, wasn't shown to the folks at home on the replay.

"Coming in the closing stages, this call brought Cleveland back from the dead . . .

"A model of comportment, Cleveland played the entire game without a single holding call, without a single interference call, without a single major penalty of any kind. Now that's what you call restraint.

"Certainly no proof exists that the officials were groping for a way to beat the Raiders.

"But, to be on the safe side, Oakland should ask for a change of venue Sunday, and, failing, should request an officiating crew from Canada."

Oh, I don't know, perhaps I was feeling a bit oversensitive because of our upcoming game, but it seemed to me that Durslag was accusing the officials of doing everything except changing the numbers on the scoreboard to ensure that the Raiders were beaten. And apparently NBC was in on it too, because they didn't show a replay of "a marginal interference call." At a press conference the morning after this column appeared, I told reporters, "I think it is an insidious attempt to intimidate the officials in this game Sunday, and casts aspersions on the integrity of the National Football League from top to bottom." I also charged that Durslag was "a Raider mouthpiece . . . who continues to write huge lies and incredible accusations. Where does that so-called information come from? It couldn't be that he got a call from someone in Oakland asking him to write this? That couldn't happen, could it?"

For some reason, Durslag was upset at these comments. "Mr. Klein is a deliciously scurrilous individual who takes the position that if you are not on his side you must be crooked," he replied. "As for his remarks on my column . . . his piety is touching. When Oakland rolled the ball 20 yards to beat him on a phony fumble a while back, Gene, of course, was a model of sporting comportment. With a benign smile, he jumped the net and shook everyone's hand. We all know Gene would never knock officiating . . ." Another reporter quoted Durslag as suggesting that my real reason for criticizing his column was "an attempt to equalize this business on officiating. This way the officials won't go out of their way to be nice to Oakland because they're going to be watched."

In other words, Durslag thought that I thought that his column was going to persuade the officials to be fair to the Raiders, so by criticizing him, I was trying to convince the officials to favor the Chargers to prove to me that they hadn't been intimidated by Durslag's column in which he claimed they had been unfair to the Raiders. It was clear to me.

In fact, I had no deep feelings about Mel Durslag. I'm sure he's a decent, hardworking, community-minded individual doing the best job he can. I simply felt that he was being manipulated by Al Davis. Davis had a few sportswriters in each NFL city with whom he tried to cultivate a favorable relationship by giving them stories. The same week that Durslag's column appeared, for example, *Chicago Tribune* columnist David Israel reported this conversation with Davis: "'I've got a big story for you,' Davis said.

"'Tell me,' I said.

"'I don't know if you've got the guts to write it,' Davis said.

"'Try me,' I said.

"'It's big,' Al Davis said, 'It's biggah than flippin' Watahgate.'

"'Please tell me,' I said.

"'Latah,' Al Davis said.

"He must have discovered the secret of life. I can't wait until he tells me what it is."

I had absolutely no knowledge that Davis called Durslag to discuss the officiating in the Browns game with him, but in 1974, I proved to my own satisfaction that Davis was capable of making such a phone call. At that time we were still speaking, and he would call me occasionally just to chat. I had mixed feelings about his sincerity, because on occasion things I had mentioned to him appeared in print a few weeks later. So I decided to see just how circumspect he was. I told him, in confidence, that I was considering selling the Chargers, provided I could obtain the new NFL franchise in Seattle. I had to tell him in confidence, because it wasn't true. I had made up the story and told it to no one except Al Davis.

The following morning Jack Murphy wrote, "From a trusted source one hears that Klein would surrender his interest in the Chargers, but with one major stipulation. He wants to remain in the National Football League and the team of his choice is the new expansion franchise in Seattle."

When a Seattle sportswriter questioned Murphy about his column, Murphy told him, "First of all, it was a damn good source which told me, a damn good one. I didn't even call Klein for comment, because I knew he would deny the story."

Of course I would have denied the story—I always denied stories that weren't true. I didn't blame Jack Murphy for doing his job, although perhaps he should have called me to confirm his information. But that was just about the last time I had contact with Al Davis without a lawyer making money.

The two most significant differences between newspapermen and television sports reporters is that sportscasters rarely do more than read the scores and headlines, and that you don't get newsprint all over your hands when you watch TV. In some cases the primary qualification of a TV sports reporter was his good complexion. Some TV sports reporters did not have the in-depth knowledge of newspaper people, but since they only had two minutes a day, or less, to report the sports news, they really didn't need to know much more.

The television broadcasters who did have to know the game were the men who announced them, the play-by-play man and his color-commentating sidekick. Individual teams had no participation in the selection of announcers. They were hired by the networks and they worked for the networks. There were many fine broadcasters on television, among them Frank Gifford, Al

Michaels, Merlin Olsen, Bob Trumpy, John Madden, Dick Enberg, and Brent Musburger. These were people who did their homework; when they were broadcasting a Chargers game they would come to our practices, they would take time to talk to our players and coaches, they would watch our game films. As a result, they were able to bring insight to the viewer. They complemented the game.

And then there was Howard Cosell. He complimented himself. Without question, Howard Cosell has been the dominant figure in sports broadcasting over the past quarter-century. Howard would be the first to confirm that, and since he acknowledges the fact that he is an expert on just about everything, that would make it official.

On television, Cosell comes across as an opinionated, egotistical, intelligent, knowledgeable broadcaster. In real life, Cosell is opinionated, egotistical, intelligent, and not quite so knowledgeable about the game of football.

Without doubt, Howard Cosell had a tremendous amount to do with the initial success of *Monday Night Football*. His approach to football was fresh, even outrageous; people either liked him or hated him, but most important, they watched him. He attracted viewers. At some point, though, his ego got out of control. No one or nothing was good enough for him. For example, he was constantly complaining that jocks, former athletes, did not belong in the broadcast booth. "Who does?" I'd ask him. "Former lawyers like you?"

Cosell became so bombastic, in real life as well as on television, that he alienated many people who had once respected him. Boxing publicist Irving Rudd, for instance, once heard someone claim that Howard Cosell was his own worst enemy. "Not while I'm alive," Rudd told him. And after *Monday Night Football* games, Cosell's broadcast partners, Gifford and Don Meredith, would leave the booth separately and meet for dinner afterward, just to avoid having to eat dinner with Cosell.

I don't blame them; I've often eaten with him. One Sunday night, I remember, he was in San Diego for a Monday night game and we met for dinner. Howard had his share of vodka, and his wife, Emmy's share, and my wife's share, and my share, and began singing the entire score of *My Fair Lady*. Loudly. Off-key. I

asked him to stop. When he finally did, he started criticizing everyone he could think of. Loudly. I almost asked him to start
singing again.

At the end of the evening we walked him to the car. On the
way, he tripped and sprained his ankle. During the game the next
night the phone in my private booth rang. It was Cosell, telling
me he was in great pain and asking if he could borrow my plane
to fly him back to New York.

Howard loved private planes. After the drug scandal broke
wide open, the commissioner asked Svare, my attorney Frank
Rothman, and me to come to New York for a hearing. As we were
checking into our hotel we ran into Cosell. The first thing
Howard asked me was if he and Emmy could fly back to Palm
Springs with us in my plane. "I'd love to have you, Howard," I
told him, "but it's only a small plane. We've only got a limited
supply of oxygen and I doubt we have enough to sustain you all
the way back to California."

Unfortunately, Cosell's legendary ego prevented him from fully
developing his talent. Since he believed he knew it all, he wasn't
interested in learning more. Howard was the perfect sports-
caster—he had two minutes of knowledge about everything. His
wit, his intelligence, his exaggerated manner, made it easy to
overlook the fact that he often didn't know what he was talking
about. Unlike some of those ex-jocks whom he ridiculed, Howard
just didn't like getting down into the trenches and doing the dirty
work. At the 1985 Preakness, for example, my horse, Tank's Prospect, was an 8-to-1 shot. When I saw Howard, he immediately
began asking me about the race. Now, I was relatively new to the
sport. I knew a little, but I was certainly not an expert. Who did I
think was going to win the race? My horse, of course. Otherwise I
probably would not have entered him.

"No," Howard said firmly, "he didn't do anything in the Kentucky Derby."

I repeated what I had been told by my trainer, Wayne Lukas.
"But he did win the Arkansas Derby and track conditions there
were similar to what they are here. . . ."

Soon afterward, I heard Cosell pick Tank's Prospect to win the
race. I'd convinced the expert. And when Tank did win the race,

Howard was not shy about reminding everyone that he had picked the longshot winner.

The great tragedy of Howard Cosell is that at some point, for some reason, he became a hater. He became embittered. Perhaps the saddest moments of his once-brilliant career took place during the NFL-USFL antitrust trial. Obviously, in that case I was biased. I knew that the NFL owners had done nothing to destroy the USFL. I knew that because I'd sat in owners' meetings for almost two decades, and I knew that even if they had wanted to, they never would have been able to agree on a plan.

At the trial Howard testified that network executives had told him the NFL was putting pressure on them to ignore the USFL. I certainly wasn't there when they supposedly told him that—it's possible they did. But the network executives denied it. I knew those people. I'd spent a lot of time negotiating with them; they were tough, and they were not about to be intimidated by the NFL. They knew the league needed them as much as they needed the league. And I knew these people were not going to confide in Howard Cosell. In fact, I'd often heard them poke fun at his pompous attitude. But maybe I am wrong, maybe they did confide in him; I wasn't there.

Howard was on the witness stand for several hours. Evidently it was a vintage Cosell performance. He was screaming, yelling, he was extremely insulting to NFL attorney Frank Rothman. After the trial, one juror told a reporter, "Howard Cosell was very entertaining. He certainly likes to draw attention to himself, doesn't he?" Even the judge thanked him for being so entertaining. Not necessarily effective, but entertaining. Rothman told me afterward that Cosell had been so abusive on the stand he had destroyed his own credibility. He had made a fool of himself. "The only thing I was afraid of," Rothman said, "was that he would fall down as he got off the stand, because I didn't want the jury to feel sorry for him."

At one time, Cosell was the most important sports reporter in broadcasting. Why, at this point, he felt it was necessary to demean his colleagues, to insult his friends, to turn on those people who had supported him, no one really knows. Perhaps Frank Rothman suggested an answer during his summation in the trial.

"With respect to Mr. Cosell," Rothman began, "I thought long and hard about how to fairly respond to Mr. Cosell, and perhaps the thing I ought to say is, one, you saw him. You saw his performance. You heard his testimony.

"There was a great movie once made called *Twelve Angry Men*, where twelve jurors go into a jury room to deliberate and one of the jurors is an elderly gentleman, and you finally find out what his problem is when he says: 'Nobody listens to me anymore.'

"And I think that's Mr. Cosell. I don't think anybody really listens to him anymore and it's bothering him. I don't want to demean him any further than I am doing now. He is unfortunate and his performance in this case was unfortunate. From time to time it reminded me of the *Caine Mutiny*, where the captain was rolling the three balls in his hand in a state of paranoia. Perhaps what I ought to say to you is, you judge Mr. Cosell, and let's leave it at that."

The jury found that the NFL had created a natural monopoly, as opposed to an intentional monopoly, and awarded the USFL $1 in damages. Under antitrust laws, those damages were trebled to $3.

Howard Cosell was capable of incredibly silly behavior on television, as during one Winter Olympics, when he concluded an interview with Cuban premier Fidel Castro so ABC could show a speed-skating race by telling Castro, "I'm sure your country will be very strong in speed skating too." But at times he was innovative and brave, and certainly made an indelible mark on sports reporting. Perhaps what I ought to say is, let history judge Mr. Cosell, and let's leave it at that.

One of the most important things I learned in the corporate world was the importance of promoting my product. Promotion takes many forms, from slapping a meaningless slogan on the back of every car to improving the lighting of the concession stands, but the best promotion of all is a satisfied customer. If I hadn't promoted my used cars, all I really would have had was a large parking lot. So if I was going to make people pay, I was determined that they would get full value for their money. Promotion is the fine art of getting the customer in the door, then making him want to come back.

When I bought the Chargers, there were a number of things I intended to do to make attending a football game more enjoyable for my customer. I wanted to install a children's movie theater in the new stadium, a real Mickey Mouse operation, staffed with nurses, so fans could leave their kids there while they enjoyed the game or had dinner at one of the stadium restaurants. I also wanted to put closed-circuit television sets in the restrooms, bars, restaurants, and at the concession stands, so my customer could spend his money without missing any of the action. I wanted to install radio outlets near each seat, enabling fans to plug in a set of headphones and listen to a broadcast of the game. I also wanted to provide courtesy tram service from the parking lot to the ballpark, so my customers wouldn't have to walk half a mile to get into the place. I also wanted to have a winning team.

I didn't get everything I wanted. In fact, I didn't get anything I wanted. Because we were the only tenant in the new stadium at the time, the funds just didn't exist to do these things. Today, however, many stadiums have closed-circuit TVs at their concession stands and in their bars and restaurants. Portable radios and pocket television sets have eliminated the need for a plug-in radio system. Insurance problems have made a children's game-care center impossible. If you want tram service, go to Disney World.

I was always trying to do things to make Chargers games more enjoyable. After the success of the Dallas Cowgirls cheerleading squad, we decided that the Chargers should have cheerleaders. Pretty girls in short skirts go with football like Mercedeses go with agents. So in 1977, we created the San Diego Chargerettes. I really had very little to do with it, at least until one of our cheerleaders, a former Miss Nude California, appeared in a *Playboy* layout. Additionally, the cheerleaders began making paid public appearances in uniform without our permission. Image is extremely important in selling a product, and I didn't want anyone over whom I had no control representing the Chargers. So we had the Chargerettes turn in their uniforms.

We did many of the same promotional things that other teams did; we let fans in to watch our preseason training sessions, we served breakfast at the stadium the morning of the draft, we had a speakers bureau that provided players free of charge for civic events, we had a Chargers Jr. club and let members into the stadium at reduced admission, we distributed our team highlights and 1975 team lowlights films to groups, we had various giveaway days on which we handed out bumper stickers, pompons, and team pictures, we had dozens of items for sale, ranging from T-shirts to caps that had a rubber lightning-bolt shooting out of them. During games we'd shoot off a large cannon every time we scored. We even had our very own team song.

Houston, I believe, was the first NFL team with its own song, which was played in the Astrodome every time the Oilers scored. That damn song drove me crazy, so naturally I wanted one of my own. In 1979, I commissioned my son, Michael, to get the team a song. Michael contacted some friends in the music business, helped write the lyrics, and two weeks later we recorded it. I wanted a song with a raucous rolling beat, a loud song, a better song than Houston had, and I wanted a song with meaningful lyrics. The result was the "San Diego Super Chargers":

San Diego Super Chargers
San Diego Chargers,
San Diego Super Chargers,
San Diego Chargers,
Charge!
We're coming your way,
We're going to dazzle you with our play,
The time has come,
You know we're shooting for No. 1:
With thunderbolts and lightning we'll light up the sky,
We'll give it all we've got, and more,
With a Super Charger try.

It probably doesn't read as good as it sounded. Actually, it didn't sound that wonderful either. But it was loud, and it had a lively, catchy beat, and the fans loved it. If my customers loved it, I loved it; it became very popular in San Diego and enhanced the festive atmosphere we were trying to create at the ballpark.

We never had a mascot. What would it have been, a giant charge card?

It very quickly became obvious to me that the only promotion that made a significant difference in attendance was a winning football team. You can't promote a dead horse, unless, of course, you're selling flies. Once we started our seven-year losing streak, I did everything I could think of that might help turn the team around. I hired and fired head coaches, at one point I seriously considered installing a system with two head coaches. I signed marquee-value players like Unitas and Jones and Thomas, as much to help us sell tickets as win football games. I joined the scouting combines. I put in a computer system. I installed a WATS telephone line. I spent a fortune filming every practice and game. When Gillman wanted someone to instruct players on conditioning and development, we hired the first strength coach in the NFL. When I learned that football players had problems with their feet, we became the first team to hire a staff podiatrist. And when I really got to know football players, we became the first team to hire a psychiatrist.

Actually, two psychiatrists. In 1967, I hired a local doctor to work primarily with the wives of our players to help them adjust to pro football. That didn't seem to make any difference at all. Five years later the team was falling apart. One week we would be competitive and the next week we would be blown away. In business, when one of my companies was failing, I hadn't been satisfied simply trying to improve on those things we were already doing. All our failure proved was that those things weren't working. Instead, I examined the situation, tried to identify our problems, then took specific actions to correct them. With the Chargers, I realized, I hadn't identified the problems. I had just continued to add more coaches, more scouts, and better equipment, as if spending more money were the solution. But we were still drafting the wrong players, making bad trades, and playing inconsistently. Other than that, we were doing fine.

I wanted to know why our players could beat Denver, 45–17, then lose to Houston the following Sunday 49–33. I wanted to know why our players did not consistently perform to the level we knew they were capable of reaching. I certainly didn't know the answer, so I decided to find someone who did. I found a psychiatrist.

This was a brand new type of head coach. His name was Dr. Arnold J. Mandell, and he was co-chairman of the Department of Psychiatry at the University of California at San Diego Medical School, as well as a respected researcher in brain chemistry and the effect of drugs on behavior. Mandell knew nothing about football, but he was intrigued by the opportunity to work with professional athletes. He warned me that he didn't know if he could accomplish anything, but he was willing to try.

I thought this was a tremendous idea. For the first time in history, we were going to actively apply psychological tools to the playing field. Even if Mandell wasn't successful, I figured, he certainly couldn't do any harm. What could possibly go wrong? I wondered. The answer, as it turned out, was absolutely everything.

Initially, Mandell seemed to be making progress. The players liked him and he developed some fascinating concepts. For example, he identified those personality traits best suited to each position on the field. His theory was that certain personality types performed certain tasks more efficiently, and therefore it might be possible to maximize performance by playing a certain personality type at the position for which he was best suited. This knowledge would also, theoretically, allow coaches to better motivate players. The best offensive linemen, for instance, are solid, stubborn, slower to react emotionally. They are highly organized individuals, the type of people whose rooms are always clean, whose desks are neat, and who always remember to take out the garbage the night before it is to be collected. That made sense, because on the field offensive linemen had to follow very specific plans. Creativity was not necessary—it was not even desirable. An offensive lineman has a specific assignment to fulfill on each play.

Defensive linemen, on the other hand, are pretty much of a mess. The best defensive linemen are volatile, angry, rebellious, distrustful—they react badly to neatness. They're the kind of people who throw their underwear in a pile on the floor and just leave it there. For months. The kind of people who throw the garbage out of the window even when it is not supposed to be collected. They tend to ignore the rules of acceptable public behavior—they just like to go out and kick ass. That made sense too, because on the field defensive linemen must get the man with the football, wherever he goes, whatever he does. They have to create situations for themselves.

Wide receivers, according to Mandell's theory, crave attention, even unfriendly attention.

And quarterbacks, to be successful, have to be either extremely arrogant or very religious. I agreed with that. To stay in the pocket when four or five defensive linemen are breaking their necks to get at you, a man either has to believe that those linemen can't hurt him, or that there is an afterlife.

The more I examined Mandell's theory, the more accurate it seemed. Our best offensive linemen were neat. Their lockers were always tidy. And our defensive linemen were slobs. And our two quarterbacks, Unitas and Fouts, were delightfully arrogant.

So it seemed like Mandell was making progress. Having identified these traits, he was working on motivational techniques. In fact, the experiment was going so well, the only thing I couldn't figure out was why our players weren't performing any better. There was still no consistency, no predictability. Well, I thought, even if "El Shrinko," as I called Mandell, hasn't improved the team, he certainly hasn't done any harm.

In retrospect, I would have to admit I was wrong there, given the book that he wrote and the drug scandal. I didn't know that when Mandell joined the staff he had decided to write a book about his experiences. The book, *The Nightmare Season*, was published in 1976. It was, I felt, an inexcusable violation of the privacy of our coaches and players. Mandell revealed information that he had learned because the coaches and players trusted him, things that embarrassed and hurt people.

Even if *The Nightmare Season* had been the extent of the damage he inflicted, it would have been too much. But as we later discovered, Mandell had spent much of the season writing prescriptions for amphetamines—speed—for the players. When finally confronted, Mandell claimed he'd written the prescriptions because the players had previously been buying their pills on the street, and that by supplying the pills to them he knew that what they were taking was safe and he knew how much they were taking. Thus he could begin to stabilize their drug usage and begin weaning them. He really had no choice, he said. "It's hard to persuade veterans who have not known any other way of playing that there is another way. 'Doc,' they'd say, 'I'm not about to go out there one-on-one against a guy who's grunting and drooling and comin' at me with dilated pupils unless I'm in the same condition.'"

The National Football League conducted an investigation that resulted in the first major drug scandal to erupt in professional sports. After that, the deluge. The commissioner's office fined eight players between $1,000 and $3,000 each and placed them on probation. Svare was fined $5,000 and placed on probation for failing to properly supervise the situation. The commissioner offered me the choice of firing Svare, or paying a $20,000 fine for lax supervision. I paid the man his money.

Al Davis was just as outraged about the $20,000 fine as I was. "What's twenty thousand dollars to a guy like Klein?" he said later. "I think Klein should be thrown out of football." I was pleased to have his support. Almost a decade later he blamed the NFL's drug problems on Rozelle's failure to act decisively in the Mandell case.

Obviously, the drug problem in professional sports had little to do with Dr. Mandell, whom I'm sure believed he was doing the correct thing. The problem existed before him, and it continued after he left the Chargers; he was just caught in the middle. So, other than the embarrassment suffered by my coaches and players from his book, the stain on the Chargers' image, and the $40,000 in fines, hiring Mandell had been a good idea. At least I came out of it with the knowledge that, based on his personality profiles, I would have made an outstanding defensive lineman.

Whatever business I was conducting during the week, whatever deals we were negotiating, whatever problems I was trying to solve, everything stopped on the weekend. The weekend was for the game. The game was the reason behind everything we did, the game was what we spent all of our time building toward; in football, the game was the bottom line.

Preparations for home games and for away games were obviously very different. Traveling to an away game was like being part of a military troop movement. Our traveling party usually numbered about 110 people, including 45 players, the coaching staff, the medical staff, supervisory personnel, assistants, coaches' wives, the security people we began bringing with us after our drug problems emerged, reporters, and our invited guests. Everyone checked in at the stadium and was assigned to one of the four chartered buses. There was always at least one person who was missing, so invariably we ended up sitting on the buses waiting for him. Finally, we went to the airport.

Everyone had an assigned seat on our chartered airplane. As each person boarded the plane, his or her name was checked off. Although it would seem impossible to get lost between the bus and the airplane, we occasionally ended up sitting on the airplane waiting for someone.

Our flights were often exciting. Because football players are so strong, it's easy to forget that they suffer from the same fears and phobias as everyone else. A lot of football players are terrified of needles, for example, and practically have to be dragged to the medical office to get their flu shots or blood tests. In camp one year we had a rookie who actually tried to cheat on his blood test, paying someone else to give blood for him. But their fear of needles was nothing compared to their fear of flying. When we encountered bad weather these huge men would be shaking, moaning, some of them would cover their heads with blankets. Naturally, their teammates would be sympathetic, screaming things like, "Oh my God, what was that?" or "Can you believe how close that lightning came?" or, simply, but effectively, "Watch out!"

We did have to make several unscheduled landings, although we were never in danger. The worst flight we ever had was a return trip from Washington, D.C., to San Diego. We flew into a terrible storm and our 727 was slipping and sliding across the sky. I'd done a lot of flying in a lot less reliable crates, but that night even I was nervous. I remember one player in particular, sitting way in the back, shrieking, promising, "I'll never do it again, Lord, I swear, you get me out of this and I'll never do it again." When we landed in San Diego some of the people on board got down on their knees and kissed the ground. That was fine—there hadn't been a rodeo at the airport.

When we arrived in the city in which we were playing, everyone climbed off the airplane and climbed onto waiting buses that took us to our hotel. A football team checks into a hotel with about the same degree of calm and order as, say, the landing force at Normandy. Our advance people had gotten there a few days earlier, collected the keys, and made room assignments. When the buses arrived the advance people handed out the keys. Then, approximately 110 people, some of them weighing as much as three hundred pounds, all tried to get into two elevators at the same time. If anyone liked watching the circus, they would have loved this act.

A half hour to an hour after we'd checked in, everyone came down on the elevators, climbed back onto the buses, and we went to the stadium for a light workout. This enabled the players to loosen up after the plane flight and get the feel of the turf. Then we climbed back onto the buses and went back to the hotel for meals and meetings.

Some coaches wanted the team to eat as a group, while others believed the players should have some time on their own. We gave each player $25 a day in cash for meals. Once, though, our business manager, Pat Curran, forgot to bring cash with him. He solved that problem by allowing the players to charge their meals to room service. In the vernacular of business managers, that was known as "the most expensive meal in pro-football history." Forty-five pro-football players can work up a sizable room-service bill. In fact, one player can work up a sizable room-service bill.

There was always a team breakfast the morning of the game. Then some players attended religious services, while others went to the ballpark early to get ankles taped or minor injuries taken care of. I tried to get to the park two or three hours before the game, partially to beat the regular crowd, partially because I was too nervous to wait in the hotel. In addition, some owners served a nice brunch for their guests.

The owner of the visiting team was always provided with a private box for himself and his guests. Most teams were very generous, assigning the visiting owner a box with an excellent view and serving food and beverages. Not every team, of course. Once, for example, after we'd played the Giants in New York, I received a bill in the mail for the food we'd eaten. On another occasion, a few days before we played the Rams in Anaheim, I received a menu allowing me to order what I wanted served in my box. After the game they sent me a bill. I did the same thing in both cases: I wrote "opened by mistake" on the front of the envelope and sent it back. Never heard another word about it.

Occasionally, an owner will try to stiff other owners. When the

Colts moved to Indianapolis, Bob Irsay put his fellow owners in a box in the end zone. Great view of the goalposts. That ended when another owner threatened to give Irsay bad seats in the open stands. The only time I wasn't treated very well was in Oakland, California. I can't imagine why. I was given a box far away from the field and was not served any food at all. When the Raiders played in San Diego I put them in a box right next to a public restroom and made sure they didn't have anything to eat. Not surprisingly, the next time we played in Oakland we were treated very well.

I never understood how owners could fail to treat their fellow owners well. What did they think, we were going to forget about it when they came to our city? I've never known an owner to turn the other cheek, unless he was ducking to get out of the way of a punch.

When the game ended, the problem became locating the buses in a strange stadium. Eventually, everyone found them, and then we sat and waited, and waited, and waited some more, until everyone was aboard, and then we raced to the airport. At least we tried to race to the airport. In 1980, after we'd lost to the Cowboys in Dallas, the bus driver got lost in the stadium parking lot. We just kept going around and around the stadium. Now, I knew Texas was big, but I knew it wasn't that big. After circling that ballpark for the third time, we began to suspect that the driver didn't know where he was going. I'd spent a lot of years believing the Chargers were simply going around in circles, but this was the first time I had hard evidence of it. The players began shouting at him, which made him nervous, and the more they shouted, the more flustered he became and the longer we drove around that stadium. It took him forty-five minutes to find an exit.

Usually, though, when we got to the airport we all climbed aboard and got ready to wait. We knew we were going to have to wait, because we always waited. Most often, we were waiting for the equipment truck, but on occasion, we waited for a missing player. Once, we sat on a plane in Houston waiting while mechanics tried to repair a hole in the cockpit windshield. They finally gave up, and we all had to climb off the plane, get back on the buses, go back to the hotel, register, spend the night, get up in the morning, get back on the buses, go back to the airport, climb aboard the plane, and wait again. Finally, after all this, as the engines began warming up, a player stood up and shouted, "Stop the plane! I've been robbed." He'd spent the previous night with a prostitute, he explained, and she'd robbed him.

"Geez," another player said, "it took you long enough to decide that."

Someone else said he should just ask for his money back.

And another player wanted to hear her side of the story.

As it turned out, she'd taken all his cash out of his wallet and stolen his wedding ring. He got off the plane and went to search for her. Two days later he showed up in San Diego.

Winning and losing makes all the difference on the trip home. If we'd won the ball game no one really cared how long it took us to get back to San Diego. If we'd lost, everybody wanted to get there as quickly as possible. It was always very late Sunday night by the time we got back. And even after we landed, we still had to climb back on the buses for the drive to the ballpark to pick up our cars.

The longest trip I ever took was the flight home from Miami after we'd beaten the Dolphins to win the 1981 AFC western-division championship. Passenger aircraft are not permitted to land in San Diego after 11 P.M., and we didn't get back till after 1 A.M., so we landed at the Naval Air Station, which was way out of town. As usual, we got off the plane and onto the buses. My family and friends climbed aboard an old beat-up bus; there were twenty of us, and all our luggage. As soon as we all got on, that bus took off. Everyone was so happy because of our overtime victory, we were singing, laughing, it was the finest day I'd enjoyed as Chargers owner. And then, just as we crossed an old bridge, the bus broke down. It just died. The driver couldn't get it started, so I got out and stood in the middle of the dark deserted road. Perhaps half an hour later the three other buses carrying our players came barreling down the road. I waved to the players and they waved right back. And they kept waving too, until the three buses disappeared into the night.

Another half hour later—it was 2:30 by then—an empty bus arrived. So everybody climbed off the broken bus and climbed onto the new bus, and we transferred all our luggage and we took off again. And once again we were happy—we were singing so loudly that the bus driver turned on his radio to try to drown us out. My son, Michael, asked him to turn it off. This was obviously not the most intelligent bus driver in the world, because instead of turning off the radio, he turned off the ignition. The bus stopped and he couldn't get it started.

It was 3:30 A.M. and once again I was standing in the middle of a dark deserted road. Sometime later, a police car arrived. I asked him to call some cabs. "Are you kidding?" he said. "I watched that game today and you people almost gave me a heart attack." The difference between winning and losing that day was never more important than at that moment, because I didn't try to strangle him. I didn't laugh either. Eventually, cabs arrived. I got home just in time to return to the stadium to begin preparations for our game the following Sunday.

Even that was not our longest road trip—distance-wise, that is. In 1976, we played a preseason game against the St. Louis Cardinals in Tokyo, Japan, the first pro-football game ever played outside North America. Scheduling a game in Japan had absolutely nothing to do with our 2-12 record in 1975. The game was arranged by a California lettuce magnate, Frank Takahashi, in cooperation with the *Mainichi News*. The only problem we had on the trip was best summed up by the Cardinals' five-foot-ten-inch running back, Terry Metcalf, who claimed that the trip enabled him to fulfill a lifelong dream. "Over here," he said, "I'm six foot two."

Everything was smaller there, making our players seem even bigger. The hotel beds were too short, the bus seats were too narrow, the ceiling at Korakuen Stadium was too low. In the locker room there were only thirty-five dressing stalls for fifty players and there was no shower room; it didn't matter: The room was too small for the players to dress in anyway, so they got taped and put on their uniforms in the hotel banquet room.

The game itself was played exactly as it would have been in America. The only obvious differences were that the public-address announcer never said "fourth down" (instead he called it "last down," because, as we discovered, in the Orient the number four signifies death), and that the fans, instead of eating hot dogs and peanuts, ate dried noodles with chopsticks.

Some things are the same wherever you play, though. The Cardinals beat us 20–10.

When we played at home I got to the stadium by 9 A.M. so that I could watch the eastern game on television in my private box. But no matter how early I got there, the fans were already partying in the parking lot. A Chargers game often seemed to be just an excuse for a tailgate party. There was some serious partying done in that parking lot. People would set up elaborate buffets. They would use tablecloths, good china, real silverware. Before a Chicago Bears game in 1978, one couple held a black-tie wedding outside the stadium, the first time I'd ever heard of a catered parking lot. When we played the Buffalo Bills in the 1980 divisional-championship game, one large group roasted a buffalo.

Hours before the game began, I'd start pacing back and forth in my box. I was so nervous, so tense, there was no way I could simply sit down and enjoy the game.

I usually had fifteen or twenty guests in my box for the game, ranging from ex-presidents to business associates to good friends. One game, for some reason, the wife of the owner of the visiting team decided to sit in my box. Unfortunately, she started drinking heavily, and got so inebriated she couldn't even sit up straight. I had to have security people carry her out of my box, and that owner has rarely spoken to me since that day.

One Monday night we were playing the Steelers at home and Howard Cosell asked me if his grandchildren could watch the game from my box. I agreed, and then they showed up waving Steelers pennants that their grandfather had given them. They were welcome to stay, I told them, but they were not allowed to cheer.

Actually, it didn't really matter who my guests were. I was so emotionally involved in the game I was a terrible host. I'm sure that during some games I sweated off more weight than some of the players. I just couldn't help myself—that was my business playing down there.

After the game I'd go into our locker room. If we'd won, I'd congratulate our players; if we'd lost, I'd commiserate with them. Win or lose, they were all tough games. If we had lost, I'd often stop in the visiting team's locker room to offer congratulations. At first that was a difficult thing for me to do, but with practice it became easier.

One thing was always the same whether we'd played at home or on the road—I didn't sleep that night. It didn't matter what time I got home, there was no way I was able to get to sleep. I'd lie there replaying the game over and over, every play, every mistake, every official's call. And I'd wonder, Why do I put myself through this?

Then I'd answer, Because I love it.

And first thing Monday morning, I would begin all over again.

9

By 1984, the single biggest problem facing the owners of pro football's twenty-eight teams was that we were so busy dealing with serious problems that we no longer had time to enjoy pro football. Sometimes it felt as if we were living inside a giant pinball machine, just bouncing from one problem to another. Among the reasons I decided to sell the Chargers was that these difficulties had taken much of the fun out of football for me.

When I bought the team, I believed my primary concern would be obtaining players, keeping them healthy and happy, putting a winning team on the field Sunday afternoons, and making sure there was enough ice in my private box. Instead, I ended up spending a tremendous amount of time trying to prevent drug abuse among my players, upholding the league rules about gambling, trying to coexist with the Players Association, and fighting lawsuits.

The Chargers did not introduce drugs to pro football, although sometimes it did seem that way. Long before I bought the team, the use of amphetamines, which got players up for the game, tranquilizers, which got them down after the game, painkilling analgesics, and strength-building steroids was widely accepted in pro football. These drugs were believed to temporarily improve a player's ability, while drugs like marijuana and cocaine were considered harmful. Who would ever believe we would be nostalgic

for tranquilizers? Even Harland Svare, who was so straight he
made Lawrence Welk seem like a wild and crazy guy, once took
amphetamines before playing in a Giants game. "I was so jacked
up for that game I was flying," he remembers, although he
doesn't remember the game at all. "I was talking so fast no one
could understand me. The thing I do remember is that after the
game I was still jacked up. I couldn't get to sleep for two days. I
spent two full days walking the streets of New York trying to come
down."

The first indication I had that the Chargers had a drug problem
came in 1973, when former defensive lineman Houston Ridge
sued the team, claiming that the muscle relaxants, painkillers,
and amphetamines he'd been given before a game against Miami
in 1969 contributed to a career-ending hip injury. The testimony
given at his trial revealed that these drugs were readily available
to anyone who wanted to take them, not just on the Chargers, but
practically throughout pro football.

One player who admitted taking amphetamines said he gave
them up because they altered his personality. Asked by an attorney if he had stopped using them because he was afraid of
losing his job, he replied, "Oh, no, I was afraid of losing my
wife!"

The insurance company settled with Ridge for $300,000.

At that point, I don't think anyone realized how dangerous
these drugs could be. Amphetamines had always been handed out
in locker rooms like popcorn. Half the non-football-playing population of the United States seemed to be using tranquilizers to
relax and painkillers to deal with minor aches and pains. Olympic
athletes all over the world relied on steroids. In fact, at a league
meeting in 1971, Tommy Prothro, then with the Rams, made a
motion that the NFL begin a random drug-testing program. No
one seconded his motion and it was dropped.

I was conscripted into the war against drugs. Once I became
aware of the fact that the Chargers had a drug problem, I tried to
do something about it. I just didn't know what to do. Before the
1973 season, for example, we instituted a $1,000 fine and threat-
ened to suspend anyone caught using illicit drugs. We hired a
special investigator to look into the problem. And part of Dr.
Mandell's job was supposed to be educating the players about

drug abuse. During the season, when the league informed us that several players were suspected of using drugs, we questioned each of them at length, and every one of them swore he was not using drugs.

After the scandal broke, I took what I considered to be firm steps to finally eradicate the drug-abuse problem on the Chargers and in the league. At first I thought it would be an easy fight. I just sort of assumed that everyone in pro football would be against the use of drugs. I demanded that a random urinalysis sampling be taken after each game, and any player found to have violated the drug rules be immediately suspended. "A pro athlete," I wrote in a statement distributed to every owner, United States senator, and congressman, "because his virtues are greatly magnified, must conversely stand above reproach and suspicion of any kind. To assume that illegal drugs are not prevalent on many pro-football teams would be putting one's head in the sand. . . . It is my hope that an accord can be reached between the National Football League Management and the Players Association. . . . In the event this does not happen, I think it is time for the Congress of the United States to act and pass legislation enforcing these tests."

Ed Garvey, executive director of the Players Association, immediately replied that his union would never permit such an invasion of its members' privacy. Garvey felt that it was a tremendous insult to suggest that players were guilty of abusing drugs before any evidence of guilt had been presented. Of course, without drug testing, it would be almost impossible to get that evidence.

The Players Association was not the only group to be against drug testing. Beginning in 1974, and at several owners' meetings since then, I tried to get a mandatory drug-testing program enacted. I received very little support. When I sold the team in 1984, pro football still did not have a meaningful drug prevention program.

There were many arguments made against mandatory drug testing. Invasion of privacy. Self-incrimination. I often heard people claim that it was unfair to single out athletes for testing, that employees in other industries do not have to take drug tests. Quite simply, people working in other businesses do not have children worshiping them and trying to emulate them. Professional athletes, whether they like it or not, are role models for children. Accountants don't sign autographs.

The thing that surprised me most was how little I could actually do to prevent drug use on the Chargers. When I was running National General, the most serious problem we had among our employees was alcohol abuse. We handled that problem by firing those people who proved incapable of showing up for work and doing their job.

I couldn't do the same thing in pro football. When it became obvious that we were not going to get any sort of viable drug-abuse program from the league, I decided to institute my own. My head coach Tommy Prothro and I each consulted attorneys to find out what we could legally do to stop the use of drugs on the Chargers and what we were prohibited from doing. Basically, we could do anything a player gave us permission to do, and nothing he objected to. The attorneys advised us that if we actually caught someone using drugs, we should wait a few days and then release him specifically because of his poor playing ability. If we cut him because we had caught him using drugs, we were told, we would probably be spending much of the rest of our lives in a courtroom.

Over the next few years we tried everything we could think of to prevent our players from using drugs, short of the only thing that would have worked—mandatory drug testing. Our policy was that we would help anyone who asked for help. If a player asked for assistance in overcoming a drug dependence, we would pay for him to go through a drug-rehabilitation program and pay his salary while he was there. But we also warned our players that if they were apprehended by a law-enforcement agency, they were on their own. We were not going to help them.

To emphasize that point, I asked San Diego's chief of police to lecture the team, suggesting that he specifically look at those players we suspected of using drugs, so that they would know we were aware of their activities. The chief of police gave a tough speech, outlining police procedures, explaining the laws, and warning the players that if they used drugs, the next sound they were liable to hear was the clank of a jail door slamming behind them.

Additionally, we spoke privately to players known to frequent bars in which drug deals were made, requesting that they find another place to hang out. And when we went on road trips, we brought several off-duty police officers with us, stationing them on the players' hotel floors to keep out undesirable visitors.

In 1974, we became the first NFL team to hire a full-time "narc." He referred to himself as our "health coach," explaining, "I try to improve the players' health by keeping them away from drugs."

I was so determined to root out those players using drugs that I brought in a drug-sniffing dog and an experienced border agent to search our locker room during a game. I was fully aware of the legal ramifications, but I was getting desperate. The drugs being used by our players were no longer pep pills and downers—they were marijuana and cocaine. The dog was named Supersleuth, and we brought him into the locker room after the players had gone out onto the field. To demonstrate the dog's ability, the agent put him in the equipment room, then wrapped some marijuana in a towel and hid it on the bottom of a laundry hamper containing about thirty wet, used towels. Then he let Supersleuth out of the equipment room.

Bam—that dog went right to the laundry basket and started barking. I thought Supersleuth was the best thing I'd seen since the creation of the $5 movie ticket. We started taking him around the locker room, stopping first in front of the locker of a player we strongly suspected was using drugs. The dog barked loudly. Then we went to the locker of a second player we believed was using drugs. Again, he barked loudly. Then we went to the locker of a player we thought was drug-free. And again, Supersleuth barked loudly. In fact, he barked loudly in front of almost every locker. He hit on something like thirty-five of our forty-five players. As we discovered, an individual didn't have to be smoking marijuana to have its scent on his clothes or personal belongings. Everyone in a room in which marijuana is smoked, for example, would probably have the scent on his clothes. We couldn't use that information at all.

Policing the team became an incredibly time-consuming job. We were constantly getting memos from the league office identifying "hot spots" in each city, those places in which drug transactions were known to take place, and the players known to frequent them. We often got late-night telephone calls from contacts in the police department, informing us that a player was somewhere he shouldn't be, and warning that if he was still there in an hour they might have to arrest him. I was always being contacted by anonymous people telling me that a player had been seen in Mexico buying a load of marijuana or hashish.

We did our best to investigate every rumor, to prevent the distribution of drugs, to educate our players, to offer help, but after a while I realized that there was really nothing I could do that would make a difference. My mama didn't raise me to be a cop.

The league did have a drug program. It didn't work, but it was a program. It was basically an educational program. Once, for example, Carl Eller, the great Vikings lineman whose life was almost destroyed by cocaine addiction, spoke to the team. On another occasion an ex-FBI agent working in the league office gave a powerful lecture about the physical and legal consequences of drug abuse. Unfortunately, at a cocktail party after the lecture, he got drunk and fell into the salad bar.

I imagine everything helped a little bit. I suppose some players listened to the warnings and stopped using drugs. But if pro football is serious about eliminating drugs, the only thing that will really work is a mandatory drug-testing program.

I just had to learn to live with the problem. Even when we received irrefutable information about drug usage among our players there was nothing we could do about it. For example, four months after our great overtime victory over the Dolphins in the 1981 playoff game, I learned that some of our players had purchased a kilo of cocaine in Miami and had partied for a day and a half upon returning to San Diego. The information came from a Florida law-enforcement agency and a private security firm I'd hired. I spoke to every player named. Every player denied it. What could I do about it?

I did my best, and it wasn't good enough. When we had evidence that a player was using drugs, we got rid of him. We didn't get rid of him because we had evidence he was using drugs—certainly not—but because we didn't feel he was a very good football player. However, if the user was a star, or superstar, we learned to live with his problem.

Was that hypocritical? Of course it was. But we weren't going to be the only team in pro football to strictly enforce drug regulations. The result of that policy probably would have been a drug-free, losing football team. And fans, the people who buy tickets, aren't interested in curing drug addiction; they are simply concerned about the final score.

It's much easier to be idealistic about the drug problem if you don't have fifty thousand seats to fill every Sunday. I became a pragmatist. I never, ever, condoned drug use, but if the Players Association didn't want to help us solve the drug problem, and if most of the other owners didn't want to enforce strict regulations, we weren't going to make a stand. I was running an $80 million business, and I decided to run it by the same rules my partners and competitors were following.

About the only thing we could do without fear of a lawsuit was not acquire players who we believed had drug problems. Before we decided to draft a college player we did a thorough background check on him, and if there was a strong suggestion of drug use we stayed away from him. We also would not trade for a player believed to have a drug problem, unless, of course, we thought he could really help the team. If we thought a player could significantly improve the team, we'd trade for him and try to rehabilitate him. When we traded a second-round draft choice to New Orleans for Chuck Muncie, for example, we heard rumors that Muncie was addicted to cocaine, but we thought we could help him overcome his addiction. Muncie played some outstanding football for the Chargers, and we did send him through a comprehensive rehabilitation program, but, in fact, we couldn't do anything to help him beat his addiction.

My final effort to get a meaningful drug program implemented took place in 1982. In June that year, *Sports Illustrated* printed an article by former NFL defensive lineman Don Reese, in which he detailed extensive drug abuse on the Chargers as well as other teams. "Cocaine can be found in quantity throughout the NFL . . ." he wrote. "Just as it controlled me, it now controls and corrupts the game, because so many players are on it. To turn away from it the way the NFL does—the way the NFL turned its back on me when I cried for help two years ago—is a crime. . . .

"Muncie has to be a superman to do what he does on the field and use coke the way he does off it. . . .

"San Diego is a team that should have won the Super Bowl twice by now, as talented as it is. San Diego has a big drug problem."

My immediate reaction was disbelief. "I suppose drugs made it sixty degrees below zero in Cincinnati last January," I protested, when reporters questioned me, referring to our loss to the Bengals in the AFC championship game. "We're not claiming we're lily white," I continued. "There's no question in my mind that pro athletes are using chemicals, just as other parts of our society are. Our policy has been to help anyone who comes forward, but we can't be their keepers."

Obviously, though, we had to do something. When the team gathered in August to open our preseason camp, I announced a mandatory drug-testing program. We intended to conduct random tests. Players found to be using drugs would be given the opportunity to undergo additional testing and treatment, if necessary, at a private rehabilitation center. Those players who refused to be tested or treated would be subject to severe penalties. "It's a shame that totally innocent people have been touched," I said. "We've got to clear those people that are clean and help those few who are affected. We will do so with total compassion and in secrecy. This will be a family matter, not a media event."

Ed Garvey once again responded that the program I was attempting to institute was "clearly illegal," and said that he would seek an injunction to have it terminated as an unfair labor practice. "In addition to being an illegal invasion of privacy," he went on, "it is an illegal change of working conditions."

Even many of our players were in favor of the program. Doug Wilkerson told reporters that the tests would be beneficial, "and I'm for anything that will help our ball club. Some of the guys I talked to have no qualms."

Kellen Winslow, while acknowledging that testing was prohibited by the union, said, "It's something that has to be done. It should help clear the air."

But before we were able to institute our testing program, the Players Association called a strike when it failed to reach an

agreement with the NFL's Management Council on a new collective-bargaining agreement. The primary area of contention was
that the Players Association was demanding 55 percent of all revenues, and management didn't want to give it to them. In other
words, money. I saw the strike as a perfect opportunity to get the
union to finally agree to a mandatory drug-testing program. In
fact, Chuck Sullivan, head of management's negotiating committee, promised me that we would not agree to a contract that did
not include such a program.

But after fifty-seven days, half the football season, management
and union reached an agreement that did not contain any provi-
sions for drug testing. I thought that was ridiculous. Garvey was
having a difficult time holding his union together. Many players
wanted to report and start playing immediately. Once the money
issue was settled, I didn't believe they would stay on strike over
the inclusion of a drug-testing program. The drug-free players, in
particular, the majority of players in pro football, certainly would
have been in favor of the program. And if I was wrong, if the
players would have stayed on strike over that issue, I was willing
to end the season. That was the time to ram it through, perhaps
the last time for a while.

I signed the agreement because I felt I had no choice. I was in
the minority, and I wasn't going to try to prevent the majority
from ruling.

After the time I've spent in football I know that there is only
one way to rid the game of drugs: mandatory testing. I don't know
how to solve society's drug crisis, but I do know how to solve pro
football's: mandatory testing. Given the power, I would begin
mandatory, random testing. Those players found to be using
drugs would be given the option of going through a rehabilitation
program or being banned from football. If they chose to go
through the program, at their team's expense, they would continue to receive their full salary. After finishing the program they
would be permitted to return to football. But if they failed another test, they would be thrown out of football forever.

That plan, or a variation of it, is in the best interest of the
players as well as the owners. Because if pro football does not
institute some sort of program soon, I guarantee that the league
will be ripped apart by the biggest scandal in sports history.

This probably will not surprise too many people, but there are some individuals who actually make illegal wagers on the outcome of professional football games! In fact, it is estimated that as much as a billion dollars is bet on pro-football games every week. Supposedly, there is more money bet on the Super Bowl each year than on any other single sports event.

Pro football zealously guards its image as an absolutely honest sport. The NFL has a full-time security force that thoroughly investigates every rumor. In addition, each week the league issues an injury list so that gamblers will know which players probably won't be able to play the following Sunday or Monday. When a player is found to be involved in gambling activities, as were Paul Hornung and Alex Karras, he is immediately suspended. The league does everything possible to ensure that the bettor is going to get a fair shot. And drug use affects that. "What you see on the tube on Sunday afternoon is often a lie," Muncie wrote. "When players are messed up, the game is messed up. The outcome of the game is dishonest when playing ability is impaired. You can forget about point spreads or anything else in that kind of atmosphere."

It is not, however, the effect of drugs on players that the NFL fears most—it is what the player might do because of drugs. Pro-football management is petrified that a player will attempt to throw a football game or affect the point spread in return for drugs or to settle a drug debt. "Twice," Muncie confessed, "I looked down the barrel of a loaded gun, held by men who said they would kill me if I didn't pay the debts I owed. Debts for cocaine." Any player dependent on drugs is vulnerable. The more drugs he uses, the more vulnerable he becomes. It would not be difficult for a player to affect the outcome of a game. All a wide receiver has to do is run the wrong pass pattern or drop a pass. An offensive lineman can let a defensive player slip by him to sack the quarterback at a key point in the game. A linebacker can miss a tackle or let a receiver beat him. No one would ever know the difference. On the game films it would simply look like a bad play. It can happen. There have been rumors that it has happened. And as long as drugs are being used by professional football players there is a good chance it will happen. You can bet on that.

But you can't bet on a pro-football game unless you go to Las Vegas. I was always in favor of allowing states to pass legislation legalizing gambling on pro football, the commissioner was always against it. It is no secret that people bet on football games; every newspaper in the country prints the injury list, the point spreads, and their sportswriters' selections, and the television networks provide so-called expert analysts like Jimmy "The Greek" and Pete Axthelm to discuss their picks. Illegal bookmakers currently handle hundreds of millions of dollars in bets every weekend, and all I wanted to do was cut the good guys in on the action. My plan was to permit people to bet on the games and let the government take the "vig," or fee, for handling those bets and put it to some use that would benefit society. Right now that money is going to the bookmakers and organized crime.

Our society has already accepted gambling as a legitimate form of personal entertainment. Is there really a difference between betting on a horse race, a jai alai match or a football game? Is it more of a gamble to spend $10 on lottery tickets where the odds are millions-to-one against you or on a football game? Many European nations have legalized gambling on team sports like soccer and rugby without catastrophic results.

The subject of legalizing gambling was often brought up at owners' meetings. One state, Maryland, I believe, took steps to legalize betting on pro football, but stopped when the commissioner vowed to fight any law their legislature passed. The commissioner and I have argued about this many times over the years. He used to ask me, "Can you imagine what would happen if a placekicker shanked a short field-goal attempt in the last few seconds to affect the spread?"

I replied that whatever was going to happen was already happening.

As an owner, I was extremely conscious of the fact that people around me were betting on Charger games. One of my friends, for instance, was betting as much as $250,000 a game. And I was constantly being asked for inside information, not just by my friends, but by gas-station attendants, store clerks, even waitresses. I would tell them all the same thing; "You're asking the wrong person. The fact that I'm not allowed to bet has saved me a lot of money, because I can't beat the system. You want my suggestion, bet on the team you root for and enjoy the game."

I was serious. I couldn't beat the system. The only information that might affect the outcome of a game would be which players were not going to be able to play, and the NFL has done everything possible to make this information available to anyone who wants it. And even that knowledge probably didn't make that much difference. In 1978, I remember, we were playing the Chicago Bears on a Monday night. Someone asked me how I thought the Chargers were going to do. I told him exactly what had been in the newspapers, that we had four or five key players on the injured list. We were a wounded team. "If you're asking me for advice," I said, "I'll tell you we have some serious problems." We won the ballgame, 40–7.

A year later we were playing Houston in the divisional-playoff game. We'd had a great season, beating the Steelers, the Raiders, we'd destroyed the Rams. We were primed to play that game. The Oilers, on the other hand, had three key offensive players out with injuries. We went into the game as an 11-point favorite. I thought we'd win by two touchdowns. We lost, 17–14.

I heard all the rumors about owners and players betting on games. Certainly some owners were heavy bettors, although they claimed they never bet on pro football. I have absolutely no knowledge that any owner, coach, or player ever bet on a pro-football game. I do know that the league investigated several owners and players and, at the conclusion of those investigations, decided to take no action.

The closest thing I had to a problem while running the team occurred when a bartender in a restaurant owned by a minority stockholder in the Chargers, George Pernicano, was caught booking bets. It was a major bookmaking operation—one telephone behind the bar. Pernicano voluntarily took a lie-detector test and passed, and was cleared of any involvement by the league's security force.

After I sold the team I did place a bet on the Super Bowl, and in doing so, I was breaking the law. To me, the entire situation is absurd. The NFL continues to operate under the fantasy that betting is not an important aspect of pro football's appeal, while at the same time supplying information useful primarily to those people betting on football games. It seems logical to me that if people want to bet on football games, and apparently they do, the government should be willing to take their money.

Eventually, I believe, betting on pro football will be legalized. I think it's inevitable. And when that happens, how will pro football change? Absolutely not at all. It won't make the slightest difference. The game will still be played by two teams of eleven men, be four quarters long, and be won by the team that scores the most points. The only difference will be that the profit from gambling will go to society rather than to bookmakers and organized crime.

Toward the end of his life, George Halas's body failed him, but not his spirit. He would come to the owners' meetings in his wheelchair, and it was obvious he was struggling. At times he had tremendous difficulty making himself understood, which I'm sure was very frustrating to him. Once, though, as Jack Donlan, head of the NFL Management Council, the group that represents the owners in negotiations with the players, walked past him, Halas indicated he had something to say. "What is it, Coach?" Donlan asked.

Mr. Halas mumbled something softly. "Sorry," Donlan said as he leaned over, "I couldn't hear you."

Halas again mumbled something. "Sorry," Donlan said again as he leaned down a little farther, until his ear was only inches from Halas's mouth.

And finally, Halas said loudly and clearly, "F--- the union!"

I certainly agreed with that. In principle, I was not against the Players Association, but in reality, I felt that the union under the direction of Ed Garvey became an extremely destructive force in pro football. I firmly believe that the 1982 players' strike, which was damaging to the players as well as to the owners and fans, was absolutely unnecessary.

Anyone who grew up during the Depression appreciates the importance of unions to the working man. Unions have been responsible for significant improvements in salaries, working conditions, job security, and benefits. But some union leaders seem to have forgotten that it is to the benefit of the employees for the corporation to prosper. When I was at National General, for example, we decided to cut down the number of projectionists in our theaters from two to one. Technological advances had simply made it unnecessary to have two men in the projection booth. The union, though, demanded that we continue to pay two men to do the job of one. When we refused, the union called a strike. I understood that the union was trying to protect the jobs of its members. I also knew that unless management was able to substantially reduce operating costs in our theaters we were going to have to close a lot of them, putting two projectionists in each of those theaters out of work.

It was a bitter strike. To keep our theaters open we hired nonunion projectionists. The union responded by throwing stink bombs in our theaters, cutting up our screens, and threatening our nonunion workers. We hired security people to protect our property and our employees. The strike lasted two or three months. Finally, the union settled for a single projectionist working at a slightly higher salary. Until I bought the Chargers, that had been my sole experience with the American labor movement.

There certainly was a time when pro-football players needed representation. As the game exploded in popularity in the 1960s, the players were entitled to share in that growth. But I had grown up believing that unions represented the working man, and I didn't put football players in that category. To me, carpenters, pipe fitters, factory workers, plumbers, people making an hourly wage and working under potentially abhorrent conditions, had to unite in order to have any power at all. But pro-football players are in an entirely different situation. They work only six months a year. They are paid according to their individual skills as opposed to being paid by job classification. Because their talents are unique, they are not easily replaced. And, unlike members of any other union, they get to negotiate with management twice—individually to determine their salary and through the union to determine their benefits. In fact, benefits are not even considered a part of their compensation package. It seems to me, then, that pro-football players are really independent contractors, and as such should not be entitled to the same legal protection drafted to cover sewing-machine operators and bus drivers.

My first confrontation with the Players Association and Ed Garvey took place in 1974. That year, when management and the

union could not agree on a new contract, Garvey called a preseason strike. The veteran players were instructed to stay out of
training camp. Because we happened to be the first team to open
camp that year, Garvey set up a picket line outside the entrance
to our training facility at U.S. International University to try to
persuade rookies and first-year free agents to leave camp. This
might have been the first time in history that striking workers,
carrying signs demanding FREEDOM AND DIGNITY, drove to the
picket line in Mercedeses, Cadillacs, Lincoln Continentals, and
large recreational vans.

We opened camp on July 1 for anyone who wanted to report.
As soon as we officially started practice, Garvey tried to lead a
group of striking players onto the campus to convince our rookies
to walk out. I grabbed my attorney and some USIU officials and
we stopped them halfway up the driveway. The university officials
informed Garvey he was trespassing on private property and
asked him to leave. Eventually, we compromised; Garvey agreed
to stay off school property and we agreed to remove our guards
and do nothing to prevent him from picketing outside the front
gate.

That peace agreement lasted almost three days. On the Fourth
of July someone came running up to me, screaming that Garvey
was once again leading the strikers up the driveway. So once
again we went running down to meet him. Garvey, a few players,
and a young lady wearing a sash identifying her as MISS CHARGER
1974 were marching toward our camp. "I thought we had an
agreement," I said angrily.

"We did," Garvey said, "but this is Independence Day and we
can do whatever we want!"

Miss Charger 1974 proclaimed, "Our forefathers wanted us to
be free and we're not."

Finally, after Garvey had gotten the publicity he wanted, his
group turned around and walked down the driveway.

It became obvious to me during that strike that the relationship
between pro-football team owners and football players had little
in common with traditional management-employee relationships.
For many owners, football is more of a hobby than a business.
These owners, unlike corporate management, are not dependent
on the revenues they derive from football for survival, and there-

fore are not subject to the same economic pressures as business executives. Additionally, some owners have never been involved with unions, and are simply not used to hearing anyone say no to them about anything. The strike of 1974 came as a shock to many owners.

Players, though, are aware that the owners are wealthy men. So even when management's representatives can prove that certain demands are economically unfeasible, the players expect the owners to reach into their deep pockets and take the needed money from their private funds or other businesses. In other words: Klein's rich; he can afford it.

The 1974 strike failed because Garvey had made a basic mistake. By starting his strike before the season opened, he gave the owners time to find players to fill out their rosters. "We will have football," I told reporters. "We're not going to give up control even if it costs us a great deal of money. If necessary, we'll have a rookie league plus the veterans who come in. . . . We'll be happy to negotiate, but we're not going to let the inmates run the asylum." The strike collapsed before the season began, but even that was too late for some veterans. They lost their jobs to rookies and free agents who had taken advantage of the extra time they had in camp to impress the coaches.

What the union did not win by striking, it won in the courtroom. The "Rozelle Rule," which limited free agency by allowing the commissioner to award compensation to a team losing a free agent, was declared an antitrust violation. Basically, that meant players were completely free to move between teams when their contracts expired. This would enable those teams willing to spend the most money to sign the best players without having to worry about losing other players. At the time, this was the most significant victory ever achieved by a sports union.

But what Garvey had won in the courtroom, he lost at the bargaining table. Without some form of compensation provision, it would have been impossible for the NFL to maintain any kind of competitive balance between teams. So we insisted that some sort of replacement for the Rozelle Rule be part of the new contract. Garvey refused.

Three years later, we were still insisting and Garvey was still refusing. But since no agreement had been signed, the vitally important union-dues-checkoff provision was no longer in effect. Under that provision, teams were required to deduct union dues from their players' paychecks and forward those dues to the union. They stopped doing that. The players, who saw no progress made in three years, and many of whom had not even been in the league in 1974, had also stopped paying dues. So by 1977 the union was in serious financial difficulty. Garvey had to cut a deal to stay in business.

The owners needed a deal because a federal judge had ruled that the college draft, which prevented college players from negotiating freely with every team, was also in violation of the antitrust regulations. The judge added, however, that the draft would be legal if the union decided to include it in the collective-bargaining agreement.

I began to feel as if we were running out of rules. We couldn't draft players, and we couldn't keep them after we hadn't drafted them. It was like falling off a mountain, and then having the mountain fall on top of you.

Finally, in return for a union-security clause, meaning that all NFL players had to pay union dues, making pro football a "closed shop," Garvey accepted a modification of the Rozelle Rule as well as a continuation of the college-player draft.

Garvey seemed to believe that he had to make this deal to strengthen his union. After making the agreement, in fact, he tried to win back total free agency through the arbitration process, but failed to do so. The owners had gotten what we needed, and had given up very little in return. I didn't believe any player would object to paying union dues of less than $1,000 a year.

You know what a headache is? A headache is a pain in the ass trying to think. Just before our final game of the 1981 season, a game we had to win to make the playoffs, the union tried to suspend Dan Fouts for refusing to pay his union dues. Fouts, claiming he didn't agree with the collective-bargaining agreement, said he had not paid his dues since 1977. I just wondered why the union had waited until four days before the most important game of the season before attempting to take action against Fouts.

There were times when I genuinely admired Dan Fouts for standing up for his principles, although those times were usually when he wasn't standing up for them against me. There was a lot of name-calling in the newspapers—mostly I called Garvey names—but eventually Fouts's dues got paid. Fouts didn't pay them. Two fans, one who wanted to remain anonymous and the other a retired butcher, both sent checks for the total amount. Fouts led the Chargers to a victory over the Raiders and a spot in the playoffs.

When the management council is not negotiating a new collective-bargaining agreement, it serves as the owners' representative in resolving grievances. A grievance is a complaint that a provision of the agreement has been violated, and usually between seventy and one hundred have to be resolved each year. Grievances cover every conceivable subject, from the interpretation of contract clauses to whether a player was cut because he had been injured or because other players at his position were better. Grievances that can't be resolved by representatives of management and the union are submitted to an independent arbitrator for a decision. Arbitrators are chosen by agreement between management and the union, and they like to split the baby as often as possible in order to keep their jobs. For example, an arbitrator might decide that the player who had been released probably would have lasted two more weeks before being cut, and thus direct the club to pay him two weeks' salary.

Players often claimed to be hurt just before they knew they were going to be cut in order to stay on the payroll a few more weeks. To prevent this, we filmed every practice and kept extremely detailed medical notes. Sometimes, in fact, if a player appeared to have been injured in practice, we tracked him down at night to see if he had gone partying, just to protect ourselves in case he filed a grievance.

Occasionally, ridiculous grievances are filed. Once, for example, a player went through all the drills the first few days of training camp, but just before the team began contact drills, he asked for permission to go to the bathroom and never came back. He just disappeared. Since it is awfully difficult to play an individual who isn't there, the team cut him. The union then filed a grievance, claiming the player had been improperly terminated since he hadn't been informed he had been cut. The team claimed it couldn't tell him he had been cut because he wasn't there. The union lost that claim.

A member of Jack Donlan's management council once described Ed Garvey to me as a man who didn't know what he wanted and wouldn't be satisfied until he got it. I thought that was an understatement. I believe Garvey started planning for the 1982 strike when he signed the collective-bargaining agreement in 1977. By then it had become obvious that Garvey was an ambitious, shrewd lawyer; he was a litigator, not a negotiator. Rather than trying to find an area of compromise, he looked for confrontation. A lot of owners believed he wanted the players' strike in 1982 to prove that he had the ability to manage a strike, and he got what he wanted. And in getting it, he caused tremendous damage to pro football and his union members.

Generally, during the course of a contract between management and labor, union leaders support the industry they're in. They rarely threaten a strike while a contract is in force. Garvey began threatening to strike in 1978.

The management council began meeting with union representatives to work out a new collective-bargaining agreement in February 1982. Normally, that first meeting is perfunctory; the two sides meet, exchange ridiculous proposals, and gradually get down to serious negotiations. But from the very beginning it appeared that Garvey intended to create a hostile atmosphere. As the six representatives of management sat on one side of a long table, Garvey led a group of twenty-eight players and attorneys into the room to present the union's demands. It took thirty-five minutes just to say hello.

Garvey decided to have a different player read each section of the union's twelve-page proposal. Unfortunately, some of the players couldn't read. Even worse, the player chosen to read the section containing the demand for a dental plan had to take out his teeth before beginning.

Usually, the union makes specific demands. Delete section thirteen of the old agreement, change clause three, add this, give us that. But Garvey's proposal simply reiterated his position that the players had been abused by management. It didn't contain any specific proposals. What the union seemed to want was more of what they already had, in addition to new things.

Our proposal was much more specific. We proposed things like deleting the union-dues checkoff, deleting job security, pretty much deleting the entire union. It was a proposal that gave us a tremendous amount of room to reduce our demands.

The main thing Garvey wanted was 55 percent of the gross revenues of pro football. Certain benefits were to be included in that 55 percent, among them guaranteed base wages, insurance, pension, and per diem. When Garvey was asked to be more specific about what he really wanted, so that management could cost out those benefits and perhaps find a less expensive means of providing them, he was unable to do so. Garvey was capable of developing broad concepts; he just couldn't figure out how to implement them. Would base salaries be paid by position? By longevity? What incentive clauses would be included? Garvey refused to provide any details, claiming he couldn't be more specific until he had an opportunity to examine the owners' books. We reminded him that the players were our employees, not our partners, and that they had no right to see our books.

Just before the season was scheduled to open, the management council submitted a five-year, $1.6 billion package. Garvey responded by calling a strike. What he failed to understand was that the threat of a strike had been a more potent weapon than the strike itself. Once the strike became a reality, he could no longer threaten to strike. This time, at least, he was smart enough to call the strike two games into the season. It lasted fifty-seven days; eight weeks, seven games.

At first, some owners wanted to negotiate immediately, while others became militant. I was a hard-liner from the day the players walked out. After the first few weeks had passed, I wanted to set a deadline, and if the players failed to report by that date, cancel the season and start fresh in 1983. My goal was not to break the union, but end the strike. As the weeks went by, more and more owners agreed with me. I really believe that if the players had stayed out one more week we would have ended the season.

Negotiations remained stalled because Garvey wouldn't make specific demands until he saw our books, and we wouldn't let him see our books. He wanted management to make proposals that he could respond to, and we wouldn't do that either.

Things got very nasty after a while. At one point during a discussion of the terms of a disability clause, management demanded

the right to obtain a second medical opinion. The players objected to that, and one large player leaned across the table and
growled, "I suppose the next thing you'll want is for us to get a
second opinion from a veterinarian!"

"We hadn't thought about that," a member of the management
council replied, "but now that you mention it, *you* can see a gy-
necologist."

One afternoon Vince Lombardi, Jr., who is a small man, was
having an argument with Players Association president Gene Upshaw, a former lineman and a very large man. Garvey shook his
head, then said, "You know, if Vince hits Gene, and Gene ever
finds out about it . . ." The rest of the sentence was lost in laughter.

The longer the strike lasted, the more difficulty each side had
keeping its constituency in line. After each meeting, for example,
Garvey would meet with his staff and tell them that he had just
received information something important was about to happen:
The National Labor Relations Board was going to issue an injunction against management; the owners had decided to fire Donlan;
Ted Turner was going to sponsor an all-star game; some owner
had told some player privately that the owners were ready to
give in.

The management council had trouble keeping the owners
united because the revenue from football was much more important to some than to others. The owners had agreed that no one
would make an independent statement, that we would put up a
united front and speak only through our representatives. Finally,
one owner just couldn't take it anymore. He was furious with
Garvey and decided to appear on *Good Morning America* and say
exactly that. This was precisely what we were trying to avoid, so
Chuck Sullivan, president of the owners' executive committee,
and Donlan met with this owner, trying to talk him out of this
appearance. Sullivan tried every possible argument, but this
owner remained adamant. When it became obvious he could not
be dissuaded, Sullivan left and Donlan sat with him for hours,
making sure he properly articulated management's position. At
about 2:00 A.M. the owner suggested that Donlan meet him in his
hotel room at 6:00 so they could review the issues one more time,
then go over to the ABC studio together.

Donlan was there at 6:00 A.M. and they went over everything the owner was going to say. A limousine was scheduled to pick them up at 7:20, but at 7:00 the phone rang. The owner answered the phone and spoke briefly. After hanging up, he turned to Donlan and said, "That was the lady from *Good Morning America*. They canceled me. Brezhnev died this morning and they're going to devote the whole show to him." The owner paused for a moment, then frowned and said firmly, "I'll betcha that f------ Chuck Sullivan had him killed!"

The sportswriters covering the strike made the situation worse. People who write about sports become accustomed to viewing events in terms of winning and losing. In this case they tended to treat each negotiating session as a boxing match, demanding to know who won, who lost, and if any knockout blows had been struck. But as time went on even they learned that negotiating is not a contact sport.

Labor negotiations proceed best in private, and the job of reporters is to make them public. One day, I remember, Donlan and Garvey had scheduled an off-the-record meeting to be held at a motel in Rye, New York, to try to find some common ground on which to begin making an agreement. Reporters found out the meeting was going to take place, but not where. So when Donlan picked up Garvey and Gene Upshaw, the reporters were waiting. Garvey and Upshaw jumped into Donlan's car and Donlan took off, with a convoy of sportswriters in pursuit. He sped up the Hutchinson River Parkway. Finally, Donlan thought he'd lost the reporters. He got to the motel and checked into a room that had been reserved under a fictitious name.

Moments later the telephone rang. A reporter was calling to find out who was winning. Soon afterward, Donlan stepped out of the room for a moment. A film crew had set up cameras in the hallway.

After fifty-seven days, the union settled for the same $1.6 billion the owners had offered before the strike, although it was to be distributed somewhat differently than originally presented and contained more guarantees than the original offer. But there was nothing in the final settlement that couldn't have been negotiated without a strike.

The strike changed the relationship between the owners and

players. It changed the way I felt about pro football. Admittedly, those first few fall Sundays without football were tough to get through. But once I'd gone through withdrawal, once I realized I could survive on Sunday without football, I got along just fine. I discovered other interests. I discovered I didn't have to be at a stadium sweating, swearing, and complaining. After the strike, football was no longer quite as important as it had been.

The strike also marked the end of Garvey's career as executive director of the Players Association. A lot of players found it difficult to accept the fact that after risking their careers, they hadn't gotten what they wanted. Four years later, though, Ed Garvey was running for the United States Senate from Wisconsin.

The fact that Garvey got to make the run for a Senate seat is somewhat amusing. For almost as long as I've known Howard Cosell, he has been threatening to run for the Senate from New York. In fact, I used to call him "Senator," and I don't remember hearing him object. And Wayne Valley told me that Al Davis had also indicated a desire to run for the Senate, claiming at the time that he would be able to stop the Vietnam War. Supposedly, Ralph Wilson, who was with Valley and Davis at the time, even offered to back Davis financially, telling him, "I've backed a lot of losing candidates in my life; backing another one couldn't hurt."

The only good thing I can say about the strike is that while it was going on I didn't get sued once. Lawsuits are nature's way of reminding someone he has too much money. I've been sued numerous times. When a man has pockets as deep as mine, he becomes a target. In this country, anyone can sue someone else for anything; a man can be sued for failing to cut his grass. And, in fact, I have been sued for failing to cut the grass on some property I own, a failure that supposedly caused an automobile accident.

Lawsuits are as much a part of business as expense-account lunches. Sometimes, it seemed to me as I was building National General, my success could be measured by the number and quality of the people suing me. And on that basis, I was doing very well. I was spending almost as much time in the courtroom as in the boardroom. One of the reasons I bought the Chargers, in fact, was that I needed an enjoyable diversion from the endless and serious litigation in which I was involved. I wanted to be able to escape from the lawyers for at least a few hours every day.

Buying the Chargers for that reason turned out to be the equivalent of moving to Guam in 1938 to escape World War II.

While I owned the Chargers I was automatically party to the approximately twenty-one major lawsuits faced by the NFL, including the antitrust suit filed by Al Davis when the league tried to prevent him from violating our constitution by moving to Los Angeles without permission. In addition, I had a number of lawsuits of my very own: The city of San Diego sued me when I refused to pay the stadium rent. Lineman Houston Ridge sued the Chargers after he'd been injured while playing under the influence of pills given to him by our medical staff. I was sued by my minority partners for control of the team after the 1975 season. I was sued by Al Davis for $160 million for allegedly conspiring with Pete Rozelle and Georgia Frontiere to keep the Raiders out of Los Angeles. And after that suit was dismissed, I sued Davis for a paltry $33 million for malicious prosecution in that case. Then he countersued me for $10 million for abuse of the court process.

The team was also sued by fans who claimed they'd been injured through our negligence. For example, one man sued for injuries suffered when he slipped in a puddle of beer, and someone else sued after he'd been hit by an object thrown from the upper deck.

So while I was in football, I was sued by my partners, fans, a player, and the owner of another team. That record makes me an expert on the subject of lawsuits. Based on my experience, the best advice I could give anyone is, Avoid them. Do anything necessary, but avoid them. When you are sued, there is no such thing as winning. The best thing that can happen is that you don't lose. But if you cannot avoid a lawsuit, the proper way to fight back is to be right, be tough, and be rich enough to afford better lawyers than your opponent. And if you can afford the proper attorneys, you don't even have to worry about the first two.

The main thing to do when sued is not panic. Being sued is not the same as losing a lawsuit. Many lawsuits are filed only because the complainant hopes the defendant will avoid a nuisance by

making a settlement. I suspect the fans who sued the team believed that. My policy was to fight every lawsuit. I was firm about
never renegotiating a contract or settling a lawsuit. As soon as you
do either one, other people will start lining up outside the front
door.

Some lawsuits have little legal merit and are filed only to com-
pel the defendant to take some sort of action desired by the complainant. An individual does not have to have a good case to
sue—he or she only has to be able to pay a lawyer. When my
minority partners sued me in 1975, for example, it was obvious to
anyone who could count that they had no basis for a lawsuit at all.
I owned 63 percent of the team's stock and, until they change the
law of the land, majority rules. But six minority owners, among
them Barron Hilton and John DeLorean, announced they had
fired me because the team's poor performance was hurting their
investment.

I didn't fire me, and since I was the majority stockholder, I
went to my office the next day. I didn't really believe that these
minority partners were concerned about the Chargers. I thought
that their real motive in filing the suit was to force me to buy out
their interests at an inflated price, or agree to sell the team to
people who would buy out their interests at an inflated price, and
perhaps move the team out of San Diego. I didn't really know my
minority partners very well. I knew that Barron Hilton owned
some hotels. George Pernicano had a nice restaurant. The only
one who I thought was somewhat unusual was DeLorean. Every
time I saw him, he seemed to have gotten younger; his hair was
darker, his wrinkles had disappeared, even his jaw got more firm.
Watching him un-age gave me the same feeling of disorientation I
experienced when sitting on a train moving so slowly past a building that it felt as if the train were standing still and the building
was moving.

In response to their lawsuit I filed a $15 million counterclaim.
Eventually, the commissioner prevailed upon both Hilton and me
to drop our lawsuits, which we did. Once again, only the attorneys won.

The most difficult lawsuit in which I was involved while in football began when Al Davis decided to move the Oakland Raiders
to Los Angeles without the permission of the other owners in the

league, a clear violation of the NFL constitution. This case threatened to rip apart the basic fabric of the National Football League.

Although the details were complicated, the facts were not. The Los Angeles Coliseum Commission offered Davis a much better deal than he was getting in Oakland if he agreed to move the Raiders to Los Angeles. He accepted. At a dramatic owners' meeting in March 1980, Rozelle asked Davis only two questions: "Are you planning to move to L.A.?"

"Yes," Davis replied.

"Are you planning to ask for approval?"

"No."

Chuck Sullivan then asked for a vote on whether Davis's move should be approved. Davis objected, claiming he was the only one who could ask for that vote and that he did not need league permission to move. The owners then voted 22–0, with 5 abstentions, to prohibit the move. Davis did not vote. Davis and the coliseum commission then sued the NFL, asserting that the league rule prohibiting one team from moving to within seventy-five miles of another was a violation of the Sherman Antitrust Act, and claiming that the league had conspired to prevent him from moving. Davis also sued me for $160 million, claiming that I had conspired with the commissioner and Georgia Frontiere to keep him out of Los Angeles.

I was outraged. "If he had come before the owners with a convincing story on why he should be allowed to move," I told reporters, "I would have listened with an open mind and I believe the other owners would have listened too.

"It's not a question of the Raiders being allowed to move. It's a question of whether you're going to have rules or not have rules. If we're not, what's going to stop me from going out and signing [college player] Herschel Walker, or dressing ninety players Sunday instead of forty-five, or moving to Japan, or Tucson or Phoenix, when my lease is up?

"We have to have rules. We can't just go out and rob banks. If you destroy the constitution and the by-laws, you've destroyed the NFL, and we're back to barnstorming again."

Certainly my animosity toward Davis colored my feelings, but this action was so disgraceful I would have fought against it no matter which owner was involved. Pro football, any professional sport, is completely dependent on the goodwill of its fans for its economic success. The relationship between a team and its fans is an emotional one, a love affair that I always tried to foster. I believed that the Chargers were as important to the city of San Diego as the civic opera, the art museum, or the zoo. Although I owned the team, as long as the people of San Diego supported it, I felt I had an obligation to them.

I had numerous opportunities to move the team or sell it to buyers in other cities. Some of the inquiries I received were simply letters asking if I was interested in moving the team, but others were serious offers. An NFL franchise is of incalculable value to a city, in economic terms as well as in building civic pride. The offers I received included free rent, the construction of luxury boxes with all income going to the team, and very favorable local tax benefits. A group from Memphis, Tennessee, wanted to buy the team and move it there. I had an offer from Birmingham, Alabama. The city of Phoenix, Arizona, has probably approached every owner in the league in an attempt to get a franchise. At a Friars' Club dinner in Los Angeles one night, long before Davis announced his intention to move, a member of the Los Angeles Coliseum Commission told me, "We can really make it worth your while financially if you would consider moving the Chargers from San Diego to Los Angeles." Without question, I could have made a much greater profit by moving the team than I made in San Diego. And after I'd made that profit, I could move the team again and make another substantial profit. Of course, while I was doing that, the other teams in the league would also be moving, and eventually we would run out of cities and fans.

Only once did I seriously consider moving the team. When I had the rent dispute with the stadium authority in 1968, I threatened to move if they refused to live up to the terms of my lease. When the situation was resolved, I agreed to extend my lease, which still had several years to run, an additional ten years. After that I firmly turned down every invitation to consider moving the team.

For several years the Raiders had sold out every home game, making it impossible for Davis to claim that Oakland had not supported the team. Instead he told us how much money he could make in Los Angeles, and pointed out that other owners, Leon

Hess of the New York Jets, Max Winter in Minnesota, and Carroll Rosenbloom in Los Angeles, had each moved their teams without asking for or receiving permission from the league.

Davis neglected to mention that each of those teams had moved to new stadiums that were easily accessible to their old fans. Davis wanted to move 350 miles from Oakland to Los Angeles. As far as I was concerned, he was going too far.

During the next two years, while the attorneys ran up immense bills preparing for the trial, Davis continually and bitterly attacked Rozelle. He claimed that the commissioner's real motive for opposing Davis's move was that he wanted a Los Angeles franchise for himself when he retired. He accused the commissioner of condoning Super Bowl ticket scalping by other owners. And he suggested that Rozelle was simply persecuting the Raiders. Davis also claimed that I was against his move to Los Angeles because it would mean increased competition in Southern California. I didn't bother to remind him that I was already selling every seat in my stadium and was guaranteed one twenty-eighth of the revenue from the television contract, so the competition couldn't hurt me financially. If anything, in fact, I might make a few bucks extra. The Los Angeles Coliseum had thirty thousand or forty thousand more seats than the Oakland Coliseum, meaning the Raiders would have that much more money to split with the visiting team. Since we often played the Raiders at their stadium, I would get to put more money in my pocket.

The trial began on May 19, 1981, in Los Angeles. This is what is known in legal circles as the home-team advantage. What might happen to a member of a Los Angeles jury who voted to force the Raiders to return to Oakland? Rozelle was the first witness and was on the stand for more than a week. I was the second witness.

I testified for more than four hours. After having been involved in so many cases, I would not describe myself as a "shy" witness. When I was asked a question, I answered it to my own satisfaction, sometimes to the distress of the attorney who had asked it in the first place. When an attorney tried to cut me off, I told him, "You asked me a question, counselor. I am trying to answer it as fully and completely as I can. Please do not interrupt me until I'm finished."

Once, while I was giving a lengthy answer to a question, the attorney who had asked it retreated to his seat and sprawled across the table as if he were settling in for the winter. When I'd finally finished, the judge told that attorney, "Next question."

The attorney looked puzzled. "I forgot what it was, judge."

During my testimony I was shown a number of newspaper clippings in which I had been quoted, and was asked if the quotations were accurate. I couldn't honestly remember saying every word, but the quotes accurately reflected my feelings, so I said they were, then added, "I am asked many questions by the media. I answer them forcefully and truthfully. That is my nature." Then I added, "I am not reluctant to express myself."

To which the attorney responded softly, "Amen."

After the first two hours of testimony the court had briefly recessed. While speaking to a reporter during that break, I said casually, "Boy, these lawyers can kill you."

Actually, I meant figuratively. But two hours later I was almost dead. Toward the end of my testimony I began sweating profusely and the questions were not that difficult. Then I felt some pains in my chest. At first I didn't think it was anything serious, but the pains grew worse and worse. I was just about to ask the judge for another recess when the questioning ended. I sort of staggered off the witness stand to a long table, then I fell into my son's arms. "I'm having a heart attack," I told him.

He helped me lie down. A paramedic rushed in with oxygen. A few minutes later they put me in a wheelchair and hurried me to a waiting ambulance. They couldn't get my feet in the ambulance. "Why didn't you bring one that fits?" I said angrily. Finally, they stuffed me inside and we took off. "Take me to Cedars-Sinai," I ordered, a hospital to which I had made substantial contributions and where I served on the board of trustees. Even in my pain I remembered that when you're in medical trouble, it is always an excellent idea to go to a hospital to which you've contributed— unless they know the hospital is in your will.

"We can't," the paramedic said, explaining that they were taking me to a hospital twenty minutes closer to the courtroom. When we arrived at that hospital they rushed me into the emergency room, only to discover that there was no cardiologist on duty.

It took them two hours to find a cardiologist. As soon as he arrived, he made an incision in my chest and inserted a catheter into my heart. That wound soon became infected and my temperature shot up to 105 degrees. Worse, for me, the cardiologist couldn't get my heart back into its normal rhythm.

The following day my personal physician, Dr. Robert Koblin, came to this hospital and said, "It's dangerous moving you, but it's more dangerous leaving you here." This time they found an ambulance that fit me and raced to Cedars. Over the next few days Dr. Koblin tried seven different medications to get my heart beating properly again, and none of them worked. Since only seven medications were used for this purpose, this was considered a bad sign. Luckily, doctors at UCLA were experimenting with an eighth drug. They rushed it to the hospital and it saved my life.

The jury in Los Angeles voted to allow the Raiders to stay in Los Angeles, and awarded Davis $16.4 million in damages, an award that was trebled to $49.2 million under antitrust regulations. That verdict was reaffirmed on appeal.

Before sending the case to the jury for deliberation, however, the judge had thrown out the conspiracy charge against me, Rozelle, and Frontiere, stating "based on the evidence that has been presented . . . reasonable jurors would not find that the three named individuals conspired or that they interfered."

The most immediate result of the Raiders decision took place one dark night in Baltimore, when Robert Irsay backed moving vans up to the Colts' offices and, without the permission or the knowledge of the NFL, moved to Indianapolis. As I'd feared, the league was becoming a circus, with teams packing up their tents in the middle of the night and sneaking out of town.

A few months after the Raiders trial ended, the day of the college draft, actually, I was taking a leisurely walk near my home. I live in a very secluded area, on a street so quiet that people find it only by accident. Perhaps one car passes my house every three hours. I was about a mile from home when I felt a severe pain in my chest. I sat down on the side and waited, hoping it would go away, hoping it was indigestion. I knew I was too far from home to make it back.

I was having another heart attack. I didn't know what to do. Suddenly, a big car came down the road. I managed to get the driver to stop, then went over to him. The driver had a stethoscope around his neck, so I knew he was either a doctor or a stethoscope salesman. "Are you a physician?" I asked.

"Yes, Mr. Klein." I had hit the medical jackpot. His name was Dr. Michael Lundberg and he was a big Chargers fan. To make it even more incredible, he was making a house call! Instead, he drove me directly to the hospital. That second heart attack was much less severe than the first one.

In 1984, I filed a $33 million suit against Davis for malicious prosecution, abuse of process, and intentional infliction of emotional distress, charging that the pressures created by his baseless $160 million conspiracy suit had caused my heart attack.

I believe that is exactly what happened. When an individual files a lawsuit, he can ask for any amount of damages. The numbers have gotten so ridiculously large that most people are amused by them—until the day *they* are sued for $160 million. Being sued for that much money caused me serious problems. Bankers, I discovered, do not have a sense of humor. Although they all expressed confidence that I was not going to lose the suit, they were not quite as anxious to loan me substantial amounts of money as they had previously been, which certainly inhibited my business activities. I knew I was going to beat Davis too, but it cost me a great deal of time and money to prepare to testify, and the knowledge that a Los Angeles jury could wipe me out financially created tremendous pressure. Davis's suit prevented me from moving forward with my life for two years.

I filed my case in San Diego.

Davis countersued for $10 million, asking the court to throw out my suit about his suit. His suit was thrown out of court. The case was scheduled to be heard during the 1986 football season. I could barely wait for the kickoff.

Certainly the most widely publicized of all cases involving the NFL was the antitrust suit filed by the United States Football League. The USFL claimed that the NFL had created a monopoly that prevented another football league from playing in the fall, and asked for several billion dollars in damages.

Although I was not a party to this suit, I was an extremely interested observer. Testifying for the USFL were Howard Cosell and Al Davis. Heading the NFL's defense team, partially at my strong recommendation, was Frank Rothman.

Basically, if the USFL could prove that the NFL had actively taken steps to keep the new league out of the marketplace, thus protecting the monopoly it enjoyed, the USFL would win its case. Among several claims, the USFL contended that the NFL had put pressure on the networks to prevent them from televising USFL games in the fall, and that the NFL owners had secretly agreed to keep the USFL out of the vitally important New York City market by pretending that the Jets might move back to the city from Giants Stadium in New Jersey.

Cosell was to testify that network executives had told him they were being pressured by the NFL. Davis was to testify that he had attended a secret meeting of the NFL owners at which the so-called New York Conspiracy was formulated.

"When I took the case," Rothman told me after it was over and the NFL had been vindicated, "I couldn't believe what I was hearing about Al Davis. I just couldn't believe he would come back to New York to testify to a set of facts that, in my belief, were not true, and if they had been believed by the jury, would have been devastating to his fellow owners.

"I just didn't believe he was going to testify. But four or five weeks into the trial, I received a call from his lawyer telling me that Davis was going to testify and inviting me to meet with him to find out what he was going to testify to. The meeting was scheduled for one o'clock on the Saturday before he was going to appear, at the Regency hotel.

"As soon as we sat down, Davis started on me. 'I'm gonna bury you,' he said. 'You can try to cross-examine me, but if you do you'll be sorry. This case ought to be settled. The evidence that we know exists is devastating and you're gonna get tagged for a big number.'

"'Wait a second,' I said. 'You invited me over here to tell me what you're going to testify to and here you are beating me up. Now I'm going to ask you a question. What are you going to testify to?'

"'You'll find out when I get on the witness stand.'"

Coincidentally, Rothman also had an appointment with Cosell

that same afternoon. "I was still reeling from my meeting with Davis," he remembers, "and I head over to Cosell's. He takes me up into his study, then *he* starts on me. He's going to bury me. All in all, I had a very bad Saturday afternoon."

Davis and Cosell both testified as they had warned they would. It didn't seem to make any difference, the jury found for the NFL on all major issues.

A week before the trial ended, however, Davis had a letter hand-delivered to Rozelle. "Dear Commissioner," it read, "We have previously recorded our position that the Los Angeles Raiders partnership is not liable for contributions to any judgment or litigation expense . . .

"We are not a defendant in this case. If you again violated the antitrust laws we were not a party to it.

"The NFL faces the verdict of a jury only because a few of our executives and agents are guilty of gross mismanagement and malpractice, exhibiting a reckless disregard for the rights of others and the economic welfare of NFL members. . . .

"Moreover, we request that the NFL explore reasonable settlement negotiations with the USFL to terminate the litigation because in our opinion there is a dangerous probability of a catastrophic judgment that could seriously cripple league operations in the future.

"The NFL has been advised by Judge Leisure to try to settle and, indeed, the judge stated that failure to do so would probably constitute mismanagement.

"Recently, we had good reason to believe that the USFL case could have been settled by granting them four franchises on a staggered basis, for a sales price of $50 million per franchise. The NFL could then form its own spring league with affiliated member club sponsorships to preserve existing jobs and afford the opportunity to develop players, coaches and NFL teams of the future."

Davis then listed a number of "omissions and errors" for which he blamed the commissioner. That list was very fair, although personally I didn't remember Rozelle starting the Chicago fire, sinking the *Titanic*, or causing World War II.

Davis, who had testified against the NFL monopoly, was proposing that the league absorb four USFL teams, then found its own spring football league, thereby assuring an even stronger monopoly. It was reminiscent of his attempt to convince the league to merge with the World Football League. In fact, the only merger that Davis has been against was the one that actually took place between the NFL and AFL.

The day after the jury awarded the USFL $1 in damages, the commissioner acknowledged receipt of Davis's letter.

It turned out to be an extraordinarily bad week for Davis. While he was in New York testifying in the USFL trial, a judge in Los Angeles ruled that the $49.2 million in damages he had been awarded in the Raiders case was excessive, that the additional profits Davis would earn by playing in Los Angeles would compensate for at least part of the damages he suffered. The judge then remanded the award to the proper court for an adjustment downward.

All of the problems I had had to face added up. The drug epidemic, the lawsuits, our labor problems, my health—everything took a chunk out of me. I don't know when I actually began thinking about selling the team. I don't think I really decided to sell as much as I accepted the fact that it was the right thing to do. But the one event that made me feel the timing was right was being able to get a Super Bowl for the city of San Diego.

The Super Bowl was the first major sports event to be rotated among warm-weather sites. Initially, only cities in California, Florida, Texas, and Louisiana were considered. Then, as domed stadiums were constructed, the league awarded the Super Bowl to cities like Minneapolis and Detroit. The only thing that had prevented San Diego from getting a Super Bowl in the past was the size of our stadium. The league demanded a minimum of seventy thousand seats, ten thousand more than we had even after our major expansion was completed in 1984. Otherwise, San Diego was an ideal site—we had a perfect climate, more than enough hotel rooms and restaurants, excellent airline connections, access to thousands of limousines, a city full of taxis, and good public transportation. So when I began seriously considering selling the team, I thought it would be awfully nice if I could cap my career by bringing the greatest single event in sports to our city.

I met with San Diego's mayor, Roger Hedgecock, and a

number of influential businessmen, among them Herb Klein of the Copley newspaper chain and Leon Parma, head of the city's Sports Association. Everyone was immediately enthusiastic. Working with local architects, we figured out how to cram an additional thirteen thousand seats into the ballpark to enable us to qualify.

At the owners' meeting held in Washington, D.C., in May 1984, the league was to decide where the Super Bowl would be played in 1987 and 1988. A Super Bowl is estimated to generate as much as $150 million in revenues for the host city, making it one of the most desirable conventions. Fourteen cities made extensive presentations, ranging from previous hosts, like Pasadena, California, to those that didn't even have NFL teams, like Phoenix, Arizona.

I lobbied as hard as I could for two or three days. I sold San Diego the way I used to sell used cars, reminding the owners that San Diego had supported the NFL through both good teams and bad teams. I called in whatever markers I'd acquired over the past few years, and I thought we had a reasonably good chance of getting the 1987 game.

Pasadena offered the Rose Bowl with its one hundred thousand seats; we offered seventy-three thousand seats. That meant that each owner would receive at least 270 more tickets if the game were played in Pasadena than they would if it were played in San Diego. A fact of life in professional football—you cannot outlobby 270 Super Bowl tickets. Pasadena got the 1987 game.

That put us in a difficult position. It was unlikely the owners would be willing to return to Southern California two years in a row. Miami was also a strong contender for the 1988 game, and eventually the decision came down to Miami or San Diego.

It required 21 votes to make a decision. The first vote was Miami 14, San Diego 14. The second vote was also Miami 14, San Diego 14. The third vote . . . Six hours later the seventh vote was Miami 14, San Diego 14. I couldn't convince a single owner to change his mind. I had about as much chance of getting seven owners to change their minds as I did having Al Davis drop by the house for a barbecue.

"This could go on forever," I said, "and I don't know about the rest of you, but I don't intend to spend the rest of my life here."

For one of the few times in memory, I had made a point on which everyone could agree. We decided to abandon the 21-vote rule and accept a simple majority. Both cities made a final appeal. "We've got two deserving cities here," I began, "even though Miami has already had the game and San Diego hasn't. But whatever we decide, let's do it now. Let's forget all the deals, all the agreements. I'm telling everyone committed to San Diego, vote your conscience. I release you from whatever commitment . . ." I spoke for about fifteen minutes. I spoke from the heart, knowing it was probably going to be the last speech I would ever make at an owners' meeting.

We took another vote. San Diego 16, Miami 12. The 1988 Super Bowl, Super Bowl XXII, was going to be played in San Diego.

That vote certainly helped me finalize my decision to sell the Chargers. Of course, if I had told the owners beforehand that I would sell if San Diego was awarded a Super Bowl I might have saved everyone eight hours of arguing.

I wouldn't have sold the team if I hadn't become involved in horse racing. I've never been a true golfing enthusiast. I didn't enjoy tennis enough to spend the rest of my life playing it. I can only sail and fish for so long. I've been a businessman. I've owned a sports team. I've never enjoyed hunting and, to me, camping out means running out of ice in a hotel suite. But I needed to find an interest that would fill the void created if I sold the team. Fortunately, I discovered the sport of Thoroughbred horse racing, the very expensive sport of Thoroughbred horse racing.

My plunge into racing began as a hobby for my wife, Joyce. Friends of ours had bought some horses and wanted Joyce to invest in them, so one day at 6 A.M. we drove over to the training track to watch one of them work out. "Six o'clock," I complained. "Don't these horses ever sleep?"

"Only the ones I bet on," Joyce said.

As we were watching the workout, Dick Butkus, the former Chicago Bears all-pro linebacker, came over to say hello. I didn't even know there was a Dick Butkus at 6 A.M. "What are you doing here?" I asked.

"I got a racehorse," he said.

"You got a racehorse?" I asked.

"Yeah, I got a racehorse," he repeated. At 6 A.M., this is considered an intelligent conversation. Dick then introduced me to his trainer, a former high school basketball coach named Wayne Lukas.

I liked Lukas immediately. That first day he told me a story about a friend of his, another trainer. A horse trained by this man was running in a race and got squeezed into the inside rail. The horse got bumped so hard that he actually flipped over the rail, landing in a deep puddle of water. The horse drowned. "How would you have liked to have been that trainer?" Lukas asked. "When the horse's owner called him to ask how his horse had done in the race, he had to tell him, 'Not so good, he drowned.'

"Now," Lukas continued, "I may not be the greatest trainer in racing, but not one of my horses has ever drowned."

Eventually, I told Lukas I'd be interested in buying one horse. One. "If you come across a horse that you think has something, give me a call." Famous first words.

A few days later, Wayne called. "I've got this filly who's never run," he said, "and I think she's sitting on a win. You can buy her for such-and-such a price."

"Go ahead," I said, "buy her." How bad a deal could it be? She was cheaper than Johnny Unitas had been and had twice as many legs. We all went to her first race, trying to decide how to pose in the winner's circle. The horse finished fifth.

"It's not that bad," Lukas bid.

Well, I figured, at least she hadn't drowned.

"It's her first race," he explained, "she's green. Wait'll she runs again." She won her next race by four lengths. I was hooked.

After that first victory I told Wayne to call me if he found any other horses worth buying. The phone hasn't stopped ringing yet.

In three years, Wayne Lukas, Joyce, and I have built Del Rayo Racing Stables into one of the most successful operations in the country. In 1985, Del Rayo Stables broke the all-time money-winning record by winning $5.4 million in purses, doubling the old record. At the end of that year Lukas received the Eclipse award as the outstanding trainer, Joyce and I won the Eclipse award as the outstanding owners, and two of our horses won Eclipse awards as the best in their classes. But perhaps best of all,

Tank's Prospect won the Preakness, one of America's three classic races.

Winning a classic event is even tougher than winning a Super Bowl. There are only twenty-eight pro-football teams, and two of them are going to play in the Super Bowl every year. But there are forty to fifty thousand Thoroughbred racehorses born every year, and there are only three classic races. Figure the odds.

In many ways, building a successful stable is similar to building a winning football team, although the only limit to the size of the stable is how much money the owner is willing to spend. The annual horse auctions are racing's version of the player draft. That's when we pick our team. Usually, we'll look at as many as one thousand yearlings that are going to be sold, and based on their bloodlines, their size, their conformation, select the fifty or sixty we'd like to bid on. The price of a horse can range from $70,000, or about what I would have paid a middle-round draft choice, to several million dollars, the price of a starting quarterback over a number of years. The most money I ever bid on a horse, as part of a four-man group, was $13 million.

The horse was a half-brother to the great Seattle Slew. Our little group decided we would go as high as $10 million for him. Ten million dollars, that was our limit. Or at least that was our limit until the bidding went to $10.5 million. When the bidding reached $12 million, or $2 million more than I had paid for the entire Chargers franchise in 1966, I told Lukas, "That's enough, let's stop bidding."

Just then one of my partners, Bob French, passed a note to Wayne telling him, "Go to $15 million."

"Thirteen million," Lukas bid.

Fortunately, that was our last bid. The horse was sold to another syndicate for $13.1 million. Adding interest, insurance, and training fees to that, that horse cost $15 million. A year later the horse had still not run his first race. And for all anyone knows, he may not be very good.

In order to be successful in Thoroughbred racing, though, you can't worry about things like that. Well, of course you can worry about it, but horse racing is a game of averages. Some draft choices are going to become stars, some aren't even going to make the team. Some $13.1 million racehorses aren't going to win any races; some $700,000 horses are going to win a few stakes races and eventually be syndicated for $15 million. I bought Tank's Prospect for $625,000. We syndicated him, or sold rights to breed mares to him, for a total of $16 million. Seattle Slew is worth between $110 million and $120 million. The most valuable football team, the whole team, is probably worth about $100 million.

There are so many things I enjoy about horseracing: I can bet on my own team. The officials rarely penalize my horse. And if we lose a race, I don't have to wait a full week, or a full summer, for the next race. I also like the part about being paid for winning.

Our little one-horse stable has grown into a major horse ranch. In 1985, we opened the most modern training facility in America. We stable over two hundred horses, about a third of them owned by Del Rayo Stables, the rest of them horses trained by Wayne Lukas. The most difficult part of designing the facility was installing a safe track. It would be the first track many young horses ever ran on, so it was vitally important that it be as safe as possible. We decided to copy the track at Belmont Park, popularly believed to be one of the best in the country. We measured the depth and the consistency of Belmont's soil, and we had samples of the dirt analyzed. The only element in that track mix that we couldn't find anywhere was a certain grade of sand. Ironically, after looking everywhere else, we found the sand on our own property.

Overlooking the ranch is a real estate development, the sky-boxes of Del Rayo Stables. Sixty-five houses will eventually be built on magnificent sites commanding a view of much of Southern California. Anyone interested in purchasing a site should contact Byron Culver at 619-756-5891. No salesman will call. (I haven't changed that much. Selling real estate in an autobiography is simply a more sophisticated version of dressing up as a cowboy and selling used cars on television.)

Selling a football team is very different from selling home sites, however. You can't do it through the classifieds.

When I decided to sell the Chargers I set the price the same way I set the price on movie-theater tickets or National General. The price was the highest number I thought I could get.

Very few franchises had changed hands while I was in football, but just around the time I started considering selling the team, other franchises were rumored to be for sale. I remember hearing the Saints' owner, John Mecom, complain, "I wish those rumors would start at the horse's head rather than at the other end."

I didn't even have to advertise. In 1982, Stockton, California, real estate developer Alex Spanos had purchased 10 percent of the stock in the team from the 30 percent held by Barron Hilton for $4 million. With that 10 percent came a right of first refusal for the entire franchise if I ever decided to sell the club. From the day Alex bought that 10 percent, he had let me know that if I wanted to sell he would be interested in buying.

I thought Spanos would be an excellent owner for the team. He could afford it, both in terms of money and time, he certainly loved football, and most important, he was as committed to keeping the Chargers in San Diego as I was.

My son, Michael, wanted me to sell the team to a syndicate he had put together. Deciding that I couldn't do that was one of the most difficult things I've had to do in my life. Michael loved the Chargers as much as I did, maybe more, but I knew that I had to get out, way out. I had to completely detach myself from the team. If we had kept it in the family I would have remained emotionally involved. I probably would have continued to try to run it, and that was precisely what I was trying to avoid.

I called Alex Spanos and told him I was prepared to sell the club. At that time, I held 63 percent of the outstanding stock. I asked him for 63 percent of the value I had arbitrarily assigned to the club, $60 million, or a total of $38 million.

Where did that figure come from? It came from my head. I based it on the prices I'd heard other owners were asking for their teams, on taxes, income, on my experience and intuition. It was the most I thought I could get for it.

Alex offered $50 million for the club, or $31.5 million for my stock.

We haggled, but settled on a price of $55 million, or about $35 million to me, with almost all of it payable up front. We shook hands on it. After sixteen years, I'd sold the Chargers.

Unfortunately, when we attempted to close the deal, Alex told me that he intended to pay $15 million down, and the rest over ten years, without interest. "Thank you very much," I told him, "but I don't think we have a deal."

That turned out to be very fortunate for me. Soon after this happened, Clint Murchison sold the Dallas Cowboys and their stadium for $80 million and Edgar Kaiser sold the Denver Broncos for $70 million. Apparently my head had undervalued the team.

By this time it had become publicly known that I wanted to sell out, and I was approached by Dallas real estate developer Carl Summers, Jr., who had been an unsuccessful bidder on the Cowboys. When Summers gave me his word he would keep the Chargers in San Diego, we got down to big business. He had structured an absolutely brilliant deal, a deal that bothered me because I hadn't thought of it first. He was going to buy the team with borrowed money. His plan was to buy zero coupon bonds, bonds that paid absolutely no interest and could be purchased for 25 percent or 30 percent of their value at maturity, and give those bonds and his personal note to the Bank of America as collateral for the loan he needed to buy the team. The sale price was now $80 million, which meant I would end up with $50 million.

This kind of deal had never been done before, which made me like it a lot. It was the kind of original financing I'd used twenty-five years earlier to take over Great American. Until this time only the U.S. government had used zero coupon bonds as collateral. Merrill Lynch had structured the deal and the Bank of America financed it. That was good enough for me. After seventeen years, I'd sold the Chargers. For the second time.

The only possible problem was that Alex Spanos still had thirty days to exercise his right of first refusal. I didn't think he was going to do so, however. "He had the club bought for substantially less a year ago," I told Summers, "and since then we've taken another year's profits out of it and we have a major judgment against us in the Raiders case. His people haven't even been around to examine the books. I just don't believe he'll do it."

Some people still believe that there never was a real deal between Summers and me for the club, claiming that it was just a way of jacking up the price. I know I had a Bank of America commitment for about $50 million on my desk, so I don't care what anyone thinks.

Twenty-nine days after I had closed the deal with Summers, Alex Spanos exercised his option and bought the San Diego Chargers. I had sold the team for the third time. In all honesty, I was getting a little tired of selling it.

The closing took place in Los Angeles. Was I happy to have finally sold the team? To walk away from eighteen years of my life, eighteen years of riding an incredible rollercoaster of emotions? I left Spanos's office and got into the elevator and started laughing. I have the feeling that inside Spanos's office he was laughing too. We'd both gotten what we wanted.

That same week five of my horses won stakes races at Monmouth Park in New Jersey and Hollywood Park in California. When I was asked by sportswriters if selling the team meant I intended to become more involved in Thoroughbred racing, I said, "I don't know exactly what you mean by that. I'm not going to become a jockey."

Then I found out, once again, that maybe I hadn't sold the team. Al Davis must have missed me terribly, because he announced that he was going to challenge the sale of the club until he was assured that I was going to be able to pay my share of the court judgment against the NFL in the Raiders case, plus applicable court costs and legal fees. "Legal impediments" would make it unlawful for me to sell the team, he claimed.

After all those years of trying to get me out of pro football, Davis now wouldn't let me leave. I laughed for a week. There proved to be no basis for his challenge.

I'm still a pro-football fan, still a Chargers fan. I don't go to their games anymore, but I still see as many of the friends I made in football as possible. A lot of them were in racing before me, and more are getting into racing now. I still have all my wonderful memories, but now, on Sunday afternoons, I can bet $500 on the Chargers game, and if they lose, turn to Joyce and say, "That's too bad. What's on now?"

Would I do it again? Soon after I'd sold the team I bought a jet aircraft from J. William Oldenburg, a Los Angeles real estate developer and the owner of the Los Angeles Express professional football team in the United States Football League. A few weeks after I'd bought the plane Oldenburg called me and offered me the opportunity to buy a share of his pro-football team. I laughed for another week. Once was enough.

As I look back on it, the fights with Gillman, the chaos with Svare, the rebuilding with Prothro, the championships with Coryell, the great players like Fouts and Winslow and Charlie Joiner, the friends I've made like Johnny Sanders and Tank Younger and Art Modell and Leon Hess and Commissioner Rozelle, the enemies I've made like Al Davis and Al Davis, the anticipation of the draft, the excitement of a trade, the exhilaration of a victory, the depression of a defeat, only one thought comes readily to mind:

Thank you, Alex, and I hope you enjoy it as much as I did.